LITERARY TOPICS

ISSN 1526-1549

LITERARY TOPICS

Volume **16**

Alienated-Youth Fiction

Kirk Curnutt
Troy State University, Montgomery

A MANLY, INC. BOOK

GALE GROUP

THOMSON LEARNING

Detroit • New York • San Diego • San Francisco
Boston • New Haven, Conn. • Waterville, Maine
London • Munich

ALIENATED-YOUTH FICTION

Matthew J. Bruccoli and Richard Layman, *Editorial Directors*

ISBN 0-7876-5745-X

ISSN 1526-1549

Printed in the United States of America

10 9 8 7 6 5 4 3 2 1

ADVISORY BOARD

For Kip

TABLE OF CONTENTS

ALIENATED-YOUTH FICTION

A NOTE TO THE READER

Gale Study Guides are designed to be helpful by being informative, by removing tedious and unnecessary obstacles, and by pointing you toward further thought. They are also designed to be responsive to the changed conditions of reading literature which have arisen in the past fifteen or twenty years in schools, colleges, and universities. What are these conditions?

by Denis Donoghue, Henry James Professor of English and American Letters, New York University

They are mainly imposed by Theory. There was a time when students read literature—and were instructed to read it—without a theory of reading or a theory of literature. Even a critic as far-reaching as William Empson seemed to play it by ear and to trust to his hunches. It was assumed that everybody knew what a work of literature was and what reading such a work entailed. Teachers tried to offer a persuasive interpretation of the work, and that was that. One interpretation might be more interesting than another, but both interpretations were in the same field of assumption and reference. These assumptions don't hold any longer. If we say that such-and-such a book is a work of literature, we have to explain what we hold a work of literature to be, why it is such, and how it has become such. No attribute of the book can be taken for granted. Theory asks not, primarily, what the book is or what it means or how it works but what are the conditions under which it has come into being. Those conditions are deemed to be social, political, economic, linguistic, formal—and perhaps most insistently, cultural. A novel, a play, or a poem is said to be a work of cultural production. What does that mean? It means that many diverse forces have come together to produce the book, not just the intention of an author.

One result of this emphasis is that the context of a work of literature is not deemed to be a static "background" or scene. In a celebrated essay called "The Historical Interpretation of Literature" (1941), Edmund Wilson assumed that "history" could be called upon to steady the work of literature, to curb its mobility, and to ground it in some value more ascertainable than the author's intention or the formal properties of the work. History is no longer thought to provide such a ground. If there is a contemporary sense of history, it features rather the conviction—or the fear—that history itself is partly fictive. There are histories, but there is no single or stable History. A history of the French Revolution is not a sequence of characters and actions, transcribed. What or who is the real Julius Caesar? In the second chapter of James Joyce's *Ulysses* Stephen Dedalus asks himself: "Had Pyrrhus not fallen by a beldam's hand in Argos or Julius Caesar not been knifed to death?" and in answer to himself he murmurs: "They are not to be thought away. Time has branded them and fettered they are lodged in the room of the infinite possibilities they have ousted." Yes: in some sense, yes. But it is hard to establish "Julius Caesar" as an entity independent of my sense of him, or your sense of him. Granted that he was knifed to death. But that is not enough to establish him or to remove from the image of him the taint of fictiveness. The philosopher E. M. Cioran asserted, in *Précis de décomposition* (1949), that "history is merely a procession of false Absolutes, a series of temples raised to pretexts, a degradation of the mind before the Improbable." We are not obliged to agree with Cioran, but we can't shrug off his skepticism or assume that we are free to invoke History, as Wilson did, without misgiving. The concept of History is, as we have been schooled to say, problematic. History may be everything that is the case, but the force of fictiveness in constituting it can't be ignored.

So a question arises: is literary history possible? If it is: is it necessary or desirable? Why do we talk about literary movements and schools, if the very concept of History is questionable? Was there ever such a thing, for instance, as Romanticism or Modernism?

There was, but not in any fixed or steady sense. Writers who live at a particular time often feel a certain commonality of purpose. They respond in similar ways to the conditions they face. They share, in some degree, a conviction of the expressive possibilities. The revolutionary writers are those few who intuit or divine, among those possibilities, the ones that clamor to be fulfilled. T. S. Eliot saw the possibility of putting fragments of verse together in a seemingly arbitrary or at least unofficial way which would make a rather esoteric kind of sense: the result was *The Waste Land*, a kind of poetry no other writer thought of writing. It soon began to emerge that *The Waste Land*, Ezra Pound's *Cantos*, W. B. Yeats's *The Tower*, Hart Crane's *The Bridge*, and a few other poems had something in common—a distinctive sense of their time—despite their formal and rhetorical differences. The concept of Modernism seemed to be called for, to note similarities of purpose among such writers: Eliot, Pound, Valéry, Yeats, Rilke, Joyce, Proust. This does not mean that these writers thought of themselves as associates. Pound and Eliot did, but not Eliot and Yeats. The concept of Modernism is a worthy one, provided we deal with it flexibly: it is not a place of residence for the writers it designates. Differences, then, persist and have to be acknowledged; but they are folded within a grand sense of "the modern spirit" or Modernism. So we can still use this word. It is more useful to think of a certain consanguinity of purpose among various writers than to assume that one writer is utterly separate from other writers.

So too with the concept of the author, another once-steady notion that has come into question. Of course Shakespeare or Emily Dickinson or F. Scott Fitzgerald or James Dickey wrote the book, but not in utter freedom or sky-blue autonomy. They had to deal with the exigencies of cultural performance: specifically, with questions of language, communication, ideology, audience, readership, money patronage, publishers, genre, literary form, the social forces issuing in taste. Not that any one of these was absolutely coercive. Pierre Bourdieu has maintained, in *A Theory of Literary Production* (1966), that "a writer never reflects mechanically or rigorously the ideology which he represents, even if his sole intention is to represent it; perhaps because no ideology is sufficiently consistent to survive the test of figuration." Otherwise put: the force of an ideology is not irresistible; it must yield in some degree—bend if not break—to the force of the language, the figures of speech and thought, which are entailed by writing in English, French, Greek, Latin, or another language. Total freedom is not available in the production of literature. Writers may proceed as if such freedom were available. They would be wise not to capitulate to the social, economic, or cultural forces at large. A certain measure of resistance is possible. Kenneth Burke maintained, in *Counter-Statement* (1931), that the motto of the imagination is: "When in Rome, do as the Greeks." But it's not quite as straightforward as that.

It is hoped that these *Gale Study Guides* will help you to negotiate these and other issues. They won't tell you what to think about, say, *The Great Gatsby*, or dictate the limits of your experience in reading that book; but they will open up new possibilities.

ACKNOWLEDGMENTS

This book was produced by Manly, Inc. R. Bland Lawson is the series editor and the in-house editor.

Production manager is Philip B. Dematteis.

Copyediting supervisor is Sally R. Evans. The copyediting staff includes Phyllis A. Avant, Brenda Carol Blanton, Worthy B. Evans, Melissa D. Hinton, William Tobias Mathes, Rebecca Mayo, Nancy E. Smith, and Elizabeth Jo Ann Sumner.

The index was prepared by Alex Snead.

Layout and graphics series team leader is Karla Corley Brown. She was assisted by Zoe R. Cook and Janet E. Hill, graphics supervisor.

Photography supervisor is Paul Talbot. Photography editor is Scott Nemzek. Digital photographic copy work was performed by Joseph M. Bruccoli.

Systems manager is Marie L. Parker.

Typesetting supervisor is Kathleen M. Flanagan. The typesetting staff includes Jaime All, Patricia M. Flanagan, Mark J. McEwan, and Pamela D. Norton.

Following is a list of the copyright holders who have granted us permission to reproduce material in this volume of Gale Study Guides to Great Literature. Every effort has been made to trace copyright, but if omissions have been made, please let us know.

COPYRIGHTED MATERIAL IN *Literary Topics, Vol. 16: Alienated-Youth Fiction*, WAS REPRODUCED FROM THE FOLLOWING SOURCES:

Baumbach, Jonathan. "The Young Man as a Saint: A Reappraisal of *The Catcher in the Rye*." *Modern Language Quarterly*, 25 (December 1964): 461–463.

Fiedler, Leslie A. "Boys Will Be Boys!" *New Leader,* 41 (28 April 1958): 23–26.

Hassan, Ihab. "J. D. Salinger: Rare Quixotic Gesture." In his *Radical Innocence: The Contemporary American Novel.* Princeton: Princeton University Press, 1961.

Lhamon, W. T., Jr. *Deliberate Speed: The Origins of a Cultural Style in the American 1950s.* Washington, D.C.: Smithsonian Institution Press, 1990.

Quirk, Tom. "A Source for 'Where Are You Going, Where Have You Been?'" *Studies in Short Fiction,* 18 (Fall 1981): 413–420.

Scott, James F. "Beat Literature and the American Teen Cult." *American Quarterly,* 14 (Summer 1962): 150–156.

Wagner-Martin, Linda. "Plath's *The Bell Jar* as Female *Bildungsroman.*" *Women's Studies,* 12 (February 1986): 55–56, 66–68.

Weber, Ronald. "Narrative Method in *A Separate Peace,*" *Studies in Short Fiction,* 3 (Fall 1965): 64–67, 68–69, 71–72.

PHOTOGRAPHS AND ILLUSTRATIONS APPEARING IN *Literary Topics, Vol. 16: Alienated-Youth Fiction,* WERE REPRODUCED FROM THE FOLLOWING SOURCES:

Brando, Marlon. Courtesy of Stanley Kramer.

Cormier, Robert. Finkle Photography.

Dadier, Richard, and Vic Morrow. Still from *Blackboard Jungle.* Museum of Modern Art.

Ellison, Ralph. National Archives 61-8989, 306-PS-A.

Fiedler, Leslie A. Photograph by Marc DuPlan Lee.

Goodman, Paul.

Greenberg, Joanne. Photograph by Ron Brown.

Hinton, S. E. *Tulsa Daily World.*

Illustration from J. D. Salinger's "I'm Crazy." *Collier's,* 116 (22 December 1945).

Kerouac, Jack, and Neal Cassady. Carolyn Cassady.

Kerouac, Jack, with Long Island friends. Ed Cuffee Collection.

Knowles, John. Gale International Portrait Gallery.

Plath, Sylvia. Plath Archive, Smith Library, Smith College.

Presley, Elvis. Photograph by Robert Williams.

Salinger, J. D.

Young people wearing "Beat Generation" jackets. Martin Schweig Studio, the Photography Archive, Carpenter Center for the Arts, Harvard University.

BACKGROUNDS OF
YOUTHFUL ALIENATION

OVERVIEW

On 8 December 1980 a young man named Mark David Chapman stepped from the shadows surrounding the exclusive Dakota apartment building in New York to murder former Beatle John Lennon. After firing five .38-caliber bullets into the rock star's back, the twenty-five-year-old Chapman pulled a copy of J. D. Salinger's *The Catcher in the Rye* (1951) from his pocket and began perusing his favorite passages in the novel. Upon arresting the suspect, the police discovered a strange inscription scrawled on the title page of the book: "To Holden Caulfield / From Holden Caulfield. This is my statement." Chapman had written the dedication that morning after purchasing the paperback from a Manhattan stationery shop.[1]

As the Lennon murder case made its way through the legal system, more details of Chapman's strange obsession with Holden Caulfield, the teenage protagonist of Salinger's novel, came to light. Several months before stalking Lennon, Chapman sent a letter to a Salinger scholar in which he described himself as a catcher who, like Holden, believed in protecting the purity of childhood innocence from adult corruption. Authorities learned that the killer passed the days preceding the murder reenacting key events from the novel. Chapman himself was outspoken about the role of *The Catcher in the Rye* in the commission of his crime. In early 1981 he wrote to *The New York Times* claiming that he murdered Lennon to promote the condemnation of adult hypocrisy in the novel. The following August, as he was sentenced to life imprisonment, Chapman read aloud a key paragraph in which Holden describes his life's ambition to his younger sister, Phoebe:

> I keep picturing all these little kids playing some game in this big field of rye and all. Thousands of little kids, and nobody's around—nobody big, I mean—except me. And I'm standing on the edge of some crazy cliff. What I have to do, I have to catch everybody if they start to go over the cliff—I mean if they're running and they don't look where they're going I have to come out from somewhere and *catch* them. That's all I'd do all day. I'd just be the catcher in the rye. . . .[2]

A rare photograph of J. D. Salinger in the early 1950s. Shortly after the publication of *The Catcher in the Rye*, the author refused to pose for any publicity photos.

As Chapman later explained, he hoped that by killing Lennon he would transform himself, an otherwise anonymous loner, into "the catcher in the rye of the present generation": "I would be protecting young people from a phony bastard, who had lied to children, who had used his music to mislead a generation of people who desperately needed to believe in love and a world at war that desperately needed to believe in peace."[3]

That *The Catcher in the Rye,* one of the most enduring novels of the second half of the twentieth century, provided an unwitting script for murder suggests the allure of narratives that may serve as what one observer of the Chapman case has called a "catechism of maladjusted youth."[4] Since the early 1950s, the alienated youth has provided a popular perspective for critiquing American culture and its values. Authors such as Jack Kerouac, Ralph Ellison, John Knowles, Sylvia Plath, and Joyce Carol Oates created Holdenesque heroes to assay the American scene and denounce its conformity, materialism, and spiritual vacuity.

Tales of troubled teens constitute a loosely defined literary form known variously as the coming-of-age story, the initiation novel, the young-adult novel, and youth-culture fiction. (Because this study explores the genre's representation of teenage disaffection, the term *alienated-youth fiction* is used throughout.) The disillusionment with adulthood that such works express raises provocative questions. Why, one might ask, do fictional teens regard growing up as an undesirable initiation into a world in which, as Holden puts it in *The Catcher in the Rye,* "All you do is make a lot of dough and play golf and play bridge and buy cars and drink Martinis and look like a hot-shot" (223)? What does the prevalence of novels similar to Salinger's reveal about the glorification of youth in America? Finally, do these texts provide adolescents with appropriate models for navigating the *paysage moralisé* (moral passage) into maturity? Or does their anti-authoritarianism wrongly devalue the wisdom and insight that accrue with age?

Answering these questions requires analysis of the historical forces that allow for the creation of the alienated youth as a literary figure. As Grace Palladino suggests, the teenager's reputation as a rebel without a cause arises in part from society's fear of the autonomy that it grants adolescents: "Youth's determination to establish separate identities and to demonstrate their independence, one way or another, from their parents' world, often brands teenagers as potential troublemakers in the public mind—we tend to expect them to be hostile, indifferent, or messed up, victims of an increasingly complex world that makes them old before their time."[5] It should be noted that this image is a recent invention. Before 1900 the transitional years

REBELS WITH A CAUSE: PROTECTING DEMOCRACY

"Youth is never satisfied with things as they are. Young people in all countries wish to protest against the injustices they see about them. They are not easily fooled by facades of high-sounding words thrown up to conceal bad deeds. They tend to cut through words to the heart of an issue. . . .

"The restlessness of youth is a precious asset of free societies because it always promises regeneration of new vitality from decade to decade."

Eleanor Roosevelt

From "Restlessness of Youth: An Asset of Free Societies," *Department of State Bulletin* (21 January 1952): 96.

between childhood and maturity were defined in America by what Glenn Wallach calls the "rhetoric of continuity and generational obligation." The goal of growing up, as described in sermons, schoolbooks, and etiquette manuals, was to carry existing morals and traditions into the future. As Wallach observes, "The language of generations was corporate, national, civic. It yoked conservative motivations—follow in the footsteps of glorious founders, stay the course, transmit a heritage unimpaired to those who follow—to an activist vision of responsibility for building a new society."[6] Enabling the transmission of this imperative was the relative lack of age segregation within families and communities. Most young people worked alongside their parents in agricultural or artisanal settings. Neither their schooling nor their extracurricular activities were stratified into grade-specific peer groups. Amid this social organization, it was presumed that the young could adjust to adulthood simply by mimicking their elders and that a rigorous regime of discipline and moral policing could prevent adolescent rebellion. Although outbreaks of disaffection and deviance did occur, they were attributed to a failure of parental or civic oversight, not to any psychological trauma innate to the maturation process.

By the beginning of the twentieth century, however, conceptions of the adolescent experience underwent a decisive transformation. According to an emerging group of social scientists, adolescence was a distinct stage in the life cycle that was inherently fraught with distress and anxiety. Foremost among these theorists was G. Stanley Hall, whose *Adolescence; Its Psychology and Its Relations to Physiology, Anthropology, Sociology, Sex, Crime, Religion and Education* (1904)—a study every bit as voluminous as its title—depicted growing up as a perilous journey: "It is the age of sentiment and of religion, of rapid fluctuation of mood, and the world seems strange and new. Youth awakes to a new world and understands neither it nor himself. The whole future of life depends on how the new powers now given suddenly and in profusion are husbanded and directed."[7] As Hall cautioned, the confusion that accompanied growing up was exacerbated in the modern age by unceasing waves of social change that occasioned heightened exposure to sexual temptation, a scarcity of intellectually invigorating job opportunities, and a thirst for stimulation rather than edification. "Never has youth been exposed to such dangers of both perversion and arrest as in our own land and day," he warned adults,[8] an assertion that observers of teen life were to repeat for decades to come. As historians note, the main legacy of Hall's book is the causal link it established between the developmental tumult of growing up and the potential breakdown of social traditions. By defining the adolescent psyche as distinct from the adult mind-set, Hall helped to popularize the notion that youth are at once troubled and troubling, their status as a unique social caste making the difference that they embody a danger to the preservation of mainstream mores. As Hall and the child-care advocates that he influenced insisted, American society could alleviate this threat only by allowing young people to treat their teen years as a moratorium, or "repose," from adult obligations, a period in which they could indulge in leisure and art to cultivate their interests and discover their identities.

This new psychology of adolescence only partly explains why teens have proved such an object of scrutiny since the beginning of the twentieth century. Equally important are the sociological conditions fostering alienation among youth. The particular phenomena contributing to teenage disdain for adulthood since the 1950s can be categorized under the general heading of postmodernism, an umbrella term that connotes the beleaguering randomness, discontinuity, and sense of exhausted experience that characterized life in the post–World War II era.

HISTORICAL TRENDS

The increasingly corporate and bureaucratic character of American life devalued individual initiative in favor of bland conformity to values that endorse the status quo.

The affluence and high living standard that the American middle class enjoyed in the aftermath of World War II raised concerns that the average American was sacrificing selfhood to attain the status symbols of prosperity and leisure. Sociological tracts such as David Riesman's *The Lonely Crowd* (1950), C. Wright Mills's *White Collar* (1951), and Colin Wilson's *The Outsider* (1956) presented the argument that Americans were too willing to adopt the attitudes and ambitions of the institutions dispensing the gains of prosperity by blindly pursuing received standards of success. Transformed into a corporate drone, a cog in the system of capitalist productivity, the individual had become the stereotypical "man in the gray flannel suit"—indistinct, replaceable, and, in the eyes of social critics, spiritually unfulfilled.

The workplace was not the only realm of life in which individuality seemed to be waning in the 1950s. Conformity also penetrated the far more private space of personal politics. The virulent anti-Communism of the era, fueled by the Cold War between the United States and the Soviet Union, epitomized widespread intolerance for dissent and fear of radicalism as a threat to national security. Although unsubstantiated, Senator Joseph McCarthy's highly publicized allegations of Communist infiltration into the American government created an atmosphere of paranoia that discouraged free speech. At the same time, inquiries by the House Un-American Activities Committee (HUAC) into the Communist affiliations of Hollywood actors and writers demonstrated how even flimsy accusations of unpatriotic sentiment could destroy careers and reputations. For many observers, these disturbing spectacles recalled the infamous seventeenth-century Salem witch trials by making public excoriation the price for any expression of individuality.

Conformity was even writ large in the design of new American communities. The invention of the suburb shortly after World War II marked a mass exodus from cities to isolated oases in which the middle class found security in the generic orderliness of home design and decor. The prefabricated homogeneity of neighborhoods such as Levittown, the mass-produced Long Island community built in the late 1940s by the developer William Levitt, offended critics who believed that individuals express their dignity through the unique arrangement of their living space. The historian Lewis Mumford repeatedly condemned Levittown as indicative of the contagion of conformity:

> The new suburban ideal is a multitude of uniform, unidentifiable houses, lined up inflexibly, at uniform distances on uniform roads, in a treeless command of waste, inhabited by people of the same class, the same incomes, the same age group, witnessing the same television performances, eating the same tasteless prefabricated foods, from the same freezers, conforming in every outward and inward respect to a common mold manufactured in the same central metropolis.[9]

By dictating such unnegotiable sameness, the suburb confirmed critics' fears that conformity was fast becoming the standard measure of normality.

The pervasiveness of a mass-produced culture furthered the felt inauthenticity and disposability of life by perpetuating the belief that identity was a product of the commodities one consumed.

After the end of World War II, the American industrial capacity that enabled the United States and its allies to defeat Germany, Italy, and Japan switched from producing weaponry to articles of personal consumption. The ability of manufacturers to flood the market with an astounding array of purchasable goods changed the place from which culture originated. No longer coalescing from local, community-grounded sources, it was now mass-produced and disseminated through franchises and national chain outlets that offered the same products in the same environments, regardless of where they might be located. As one historian explains,

> Folk or oral culture completed its changes during the fifties to popular or mediated culture. Long produced anonymously at the local level, folklore had been *collected* in urban centers. People *make* popular culture in urban centers, however, and distribute it to the local level, where it usually dissipates uncollected. This was an important reversal of the cultural vector. Lore, which previous generations had absorbed at Grandpa's or Uncle Remus's knee or on the store porch, was now absorbed basking in the blue glow of the TV, from the car radio, from comics and theme parks. Instead of producing and participating in their own lore, fifties people began buying it ready-made, became its recipients.[10]

The value of "ready-made" culture was not the only aspect of this reversal that troubled critics. They also feared the power of manufacturers to shape the beliefs of the populace through the values that their goods embodied. Vance Packard's *The Hidden Persuaders* (1957) was one of many sensational exposés that portrayed producers and advertisers as conspiring to brainwash the public into subscribing to a consumer lifestyle in which happiness was proportional to one's purchasing power. A more erudite expression of this fear arose among academic leftists, particularly those belonging to the Frankfurt school of Marxist social theory. The writings of such prominent Marxists as Theodore Adorno and Herbert Marcuse introduced at least two terms into the vernacular, "culture industry" and "false consciousness," both of which dramatized marketeers' unfettered power to abolish individual choice and dictate how Americans should live their lives. Subsequent critics have challenged the Frankfurt School premise that consumers mindlessly adopt attitudes handed down by tastemakers, arguing instead that people attach their own meanings to the goods that they buy. Nevertheless, the suspicion remains that mass-produced culture is inauthentic because it is not indigenous to the communities that consume it.

An accelerated pace of life fractured the sequential flow of time into isolated, fragmented moments, leaving individuals feeling disconnected from history and tradition.

The technological advances of the latter half of the twentieth century forced people to accommodate an unceasing cycle of rapid change that weakened bonds to habits and customs once handed down from generation to generation. As one critic complains, "Our entire contemporary social system has little by little begun to lose its capacity to retain its own past, has begun to live in a perpetual present and in a perpetual change that obliterates traditions of the kind which all earlier social formations have had in one way or another sought to preserve."[11] Living in a perpetual present not only isolates the self from the continuity of history but also reduces one's ability to absorb this constant transitoriness. The speed of daily life leaves little time for analysis and reflection. Instead, people register experience as passive observers rather than active participants in unfolding events. For many authors, emotionally obtuse adolescents epitomize society's evaporating empathy, the passivity and withdrawal of youth indicative of a culture moving too fast for its population to know how to care.

The psychological redefinition of adolescence and the social conditions resulting from an accelerated pace of life suggest why representations of youth are so pessimistic about the possibilities of adulthood. Of course, novelists have been intrigued by the awkward age since long before the 1950s. Yet, the fictional youth of yesteryear often strike contemporary readers as blithely obedient (and thus unrealistic) in their eagerness to mature. Early British novels such as Samuel Richardson's *Pamela* (1740–1741) and *Clarissa* (1748–1749) portray adolescence as a series of preparatory challenges that teach youth the importance of reason, caution, and moderation. While not oblivious to elders' foibles and failures, such texts nevertheless demand that youth uphold their traditions, lest society slide toward chaos. The same is true in American literature before the 1920s. From Susanna Rowson's *Charlotte Temple* (1794) to Booth Tarkington's *Seventeen* (1916), the dominant narrative voice is that of a stern but understanding parent figure who pontificates on the benefits of being a grown-up. Even when a rebellious tone seeps into the storytelling, anti-authoritarian posturing is muted by inflected maturity. Such is the case with the nineteenth century's prototypical rebel without a cause, the "bad boy" hero of such popular novels as Thomas Bailey Aldrich's *The Story of a Bad Boy* (1869). Although the bad boy excited parental outrage for skipping school and pulling pranks, novelists invariably assured readers in the conclusions of their books that their prepubescent ne'er-do-wells had indeed grown up to become respectable adults. The major exception to this rule is Mark Twain's Huckleberry Finn, the literary godfather of Holden and his peers. Huck remains as suspicious of adulthood at the end of *Adventures of Huckleberry Finn* (1885) as at the beginning.

The first generation of modern youth emerged in American fiction in the 1920s as authors discovered that the coming-of-age story provided a dramatic vehicle for vivifying the welter of changes afflicting the early twentieth century. For writers such as F. Scott Fitzgerald, Ernest Hemingway, William Faulkner, and John Dos Passos, the anguish and indirection of youth were no longer just a passing stage. These tendencies were a part, rather, of the besiegement that their generation felt doomed to suffer at the hands of uncontrollable forces. In Fitzgerald's *This Side of Paradise* (1920) Amory Blaine expresses the dislocation that he and his peers suffer when he realizes that the creeds handed down by his parents and teachers are irrelevant to the new world around them. "I know myself. But that is all," the young man declares in the final line of the novel, thus admitting how ill-equipped he is for adult responsibilities.[12] This lack of resolution characterizes the endings of Hemingway's *The Sun Also Rises* (1926), Faulkner's *Absalom, Absalom!* (1936), and many other contemporaneous works. In each, growing up invites loss rather than growth, for the adult world offers young people little beyond a sense of failed promise and diminished expectations. In this way, these works exemplify Hall's central assertion in *Adolescence:* "Modern life is hard, in many respects increasingly so, on youth. Home, school, church fail to recognize its nature and needs and, perhaps most of all, its perils."[13] By and large, post–World War II authors continued this custom. They, too, saw the adolescent struggle as symbolic of the broader human problem of accommodating the uncertainty of contemporary life.

CHARACTERISTICS OF ALIENATED-YOUTH FICTION

In alienated-youth fiction young people's reluctance to mature dramatizes the rising generation's quest for a more meaningful existence, one in which success is not measured by professional achievement or material possessions.

In the early 1960s the social psychologist Paul Goodman popularized the phrase "growing up absurd" to characterize the goals of maturation that American society was instilling in postwar youth. Whereas the nation once espoused individuality and freedom of choice, a new vogue for standardization and efficiency had diminished opportunities for meaningful experience. As Goodman complained, America was teaching its youth to define their worth within a spiritually void circuit of production and consumption: "In our highly organized system of machine production and its corresponding social relations, the practice is, by 'vocational guidance,' to fit people wherever they are needed in the productive system; and whenever the products of the system need to be used up, the practice is, by advertising, to get people to consume them."[14] Rather than condemning rebels and juvenile delinquents for not taking their proper place in this system, Goodman and other social scientists interpreted adolescent alienation as evidence of the system's failure to stimulate the citizenry's intellect. From their perspective, adolescent discontent was less a threat to society than a corrective to its corrupted values. Indeed, as Goodman contemporary Erik H. Erikson insisted, youth should be encouraged to question their elders' values to ensure a better future: "It is the young who, by their responses and actions, tell the old whether life as represented by the old and as presented to the young has meaning; and it is the young who carry in them the power to confirm those who confirm them and, joining the issues, to renew and regenerate, or to reform and rebel."[15]

Most alienated-youth fiction endorses this function by portraying protagonists as frustrated idealists seeking spiritual sanctuary from various conformist settings. For privileged young men like Holden or the preparatory-school friends in Knowles's *A Separate Peace* (1960), alienation results from the emptiness of elitist educational traditions that equate contentment with career achievement and middle-class respectability. Other young people rebel against gender and race inequities. The heroine of Plath's *The Bell Jar* (1963) discovers that her artistic ambitions clash with the goals that proper young women are expected to pursue— most pressingly, marriage and motherhood. The African American protagonist of Ellison's *Invisible Man* (1952), meanwhile, discovers that the political agendas of white and black elders restrict his ability to assert his identity. Society renders him invisible because it can see a black man only as a threat or a problem, someone to be feared or pitied, but not respected as a unique individual.

In the absence of inspiring opportunities many alienated adolescents set out in pursuit of more fulfilling alternatives. For the Beat Generation, celebrated most famously in Kerouac's *On the Road* (1957), this search took the form of high-speed journeys across the highways and byways of America. In *On the Road* these continental joyrides allow narrator Sal Paradise and his pal Dean Moriarty to revel in the exuberant mobility that for them is the essence of the American spirit. For other adolescents, the quest was directed inward rather than outward. Franny Glass, the heroine of Salinger's "Franny" (1955), turns to Zen Buddhism as a remedy for the rampant self-interest that she believes plagues American culture. Regardless of the specific cure for teen discontent, alienated-youth fiction almost always depicts young people's restlessness as indicative of their refusal to follow the path that society has paved for them.

Alienated-youth fiction portrays adults as corrupt agents of socialization who are oblivious to the redemptive power of youth. As unworthy role models, parents, teachers, and other representatives of the grown-up world must be resisted, debunked, and stripped of their pretensions to authority.

In the eyes of most fictional youth, adults merit little respect. They are liars, hypocrites, conformists, drunks, and adulterers who embody everything distasteful about the social system that they ask teens to adopt. Even worse, they fail in their obligation to protect the innocence of youth, leaving their progeny vulnerable to the predatory violence of the world. Alienated-youth fiction's gallery of evil grown-ups includes several of the most compelling villains in recent literature. There is Mrs. Robinson, the unhappy, alcoholic housewife who seduces family friend Benjamin Braddock in Charles Webb's *The Graduate* (1963), which was adapted in 1967 as the seminal Mike Nichols movie of the same name, starring Dustin Hoffman and Anne Bancroft. Dr. Gordon in *The Bell Jar* is a psychologist who promises to cure adolescent patients of discontent by subjecting them to electroconvulsive shock treatments. In Robert Cormier's *The Chocolate War* (1974) Brother Leon is an assistant headmaster whose priestly vows do not preclude colluding with a gang of student bullies to enforce his power over his Catholic high school. Even the rare adult who merits a modicum of respect in the end finds himself besmirched. No sooner does Mr. Antolini, Holden Caulfield's former English teacher in *The Catcher in the Rye,* offer the boy sound advice than Holden accuses the man of making sexual advances toward him.

At its simplest, this vilification of adults reflects a generation-gap mentality indicative of the structural segregation of young and old in America. Since the early twentieth century, when industrialization and mandatory public-schooling laws removed children from parental control for most of the working day, elders have found their authority over young people supplanted by the peer group. As Beth L. Bailey notes, "In the late nineteenth and early twentieth centuries, youth were segregated increasingly by age and decreasingly by gender. Groups of young men and women came together in an intimacy of common experience, sometimes with relative freedom from the supervision of family and traditional community, and formed tight peer cultures. These local groups contributed to a revolution in the way youth defined themselves."[16] Adults serve as dramatic foils for fictional youth because they either devalue the importance of these peer values or they actively seek to police and repress them. It is striking to note that even in novels in which teens are depicted most threateningly—as in Evan Hunter's *The Blackboard Jungle* (1954), one of many Eisenhower-era exposés of juvenile delinquency—youth are portrayed as victims of unfounded adult prejudice. Although few works of alienated-youth fiction are optimistic about bridging the generation gap, they nevertheless imply that if adults made an effort to understand peer rituals rather than demonize them, young people might be more inclined to respect their elders.

While alienated-youth narratives criticize adult values, they do not blindly endorse adolescent rituals and pastimes as superior replacements for those mores. Instead, these works question whether the rites of passage that youth create through peer affiliations actually lead to maturity or whether they trap young people in "liminal" experiences that arrest their emotional development.

The anthropologist Victor Turner uses the term *liminality*—derived from the root word *limen*, meaning "threshold"—to describe the experience of transition inherent in adolescence. Although rites of passage are intended to initiate youth into maturity, they also dramatize the "in-between" nature of adolescence by providing socially sanctioned forms of experimentation and play by which teens act out behavior that would be considered inappropriate for their elders. In essence, liminality functions as a social pressure valve; it affords youth opportunities for letting off steam without disrupting the process of their socialization. Existing on the threshold can be dangerous, however, because rituals of contained rebellion may become fixed patterns of behavior, prolonging rather than resolving adolescence. Turner's assessment of the hippie movement of the 1960s applies to several previous and subsequent youth subcultures: "There is a tendency among many people, especially those under thirty, to create a life style contained within liminality. Instead of the liminal being a passage, it seems to be coming to be regarded as a state."[17]

The concern that teens will suffer from arrested development seems to be justified in modern novels, which are apt to leave their heroes stranded on the brink of maturity. *The Catcher in the Rye* concludes with Holden's expressions of impatience with the adults asking him whether he is ready to "apply" himself now that he has submitted to psychiatric care. (Salinger also provides a symbolic clue to the liminal nature of Holden's problems: although the boy is only a teenager, patches of his hair have gone gray). In the closing scene of *The Bell Jar*, Esther Greenwood prepares to leave the sanatorium where she has been hospitalized after a suicide attempt: "There ought, I thought, to be a ritual for being born twice," she says, but the lack of such a ritual means that she returns to the outside world without conclusively resolving her adolescent insecurities.[18] Holden's and Esther's predicaments are comparable to many of their fictional peers, who find themselves trapped by their desire to remain young forever.

Alienated-youth fiction examines the effects of mass culture on youth. As teens develop the rites and rituals by which they express their sense of self, they draw from the media-dominated world surrounding them. Just as they question how well liminal experiences prepare youth for adulthood, these works ask whether the images and attitudes that they borrow from movies, music, and books are beneficial or baleful.

Mass culture usually affects fictional teens in one of two ways. Along the lines of the Frankfurt School's culture-industry argument, it is said to sap the individuality and initiative of youth by transforming them into mindless consumers. Teenage heroes often resist this process by cultivating an acidic disdain for the diversions and entertainments distracting their peers. Throughout *The Catcher in the Rye*, Holden rails against the celluloid delusions of Hollywood. The movie business not only corrupts talented artists with the promise of easy money (including Holden's older brother, D. B., who has abandoned fiction for writing screenplays). Even worse, its glossy productions teach people "phony" behavior, encouraging them to respond to situations as though they were actors performing a part. Holden is no less susceptible to this mimicry than others. After a beating from a pimp named Maurice, he imagines himself as a gangster taking revenge by "plugging" the crook with an automatic pistol. "The goddamn movies. They can ruin you," Holden declares when he realizes the absurdity of his fantasy (136).

Such derogatory attitudes toward mass culture are not universal. In many other works, popular culture provides adolescents with positive models for developing a sense of identity. Kerouac's Beat Generation discovers in the bebop jazz of Charlie Parker and George Shearing an improvisational approach to life that emphasizes spontaneity and immediacy over calculated reasoning. So, too, the narrator of *Invisible Man* discovers that the blues and jazz traditions of his African American heritage are resources for understanding his sufferings in a racist society. Ultimately, whether a specific text celebrates or condemns mass culture depends on how the author regards it. Either way, alienated-youth fiction recognizes that young people exist in a world in which identities are considered an external apparatus that one can alter by purchasing a new product.

Alienated youth fiction is a product of American society's age consciousness. It reflects the cultural obsession with retaining youth and eluding the decay and erosion associated with growing older.

Although reverence for youth was a major characteristic of the Romantic movement of the late eighteenth and early nineteenth centuries, the twentieth century was a time of unprecedented redefinition of the meanings of youth and adulthood. Previously, the life cycle was portrayed as a journey toward enlightenment. The child passed from naiveté to knowledge, learning along the way to accept the limitations of being human. To be young was to be inexperienced and therefore undeserving of any status other than that of a dependent or apprentice. Adulthood, by contrast, conferred respect and authority. With modernity, however, arose the belief that *new* was synonymous with improvement and innovation, while *old* meant out-of-date and irrelevant. Advertisers and lifestyle advocates seized upon this transformation to sell their products, equating youth with energy and enthusiasm and senescence (old age) with deterioration and diminution. Since the 1920s, staying young has been something akin to a civic duty: people battle the aging process in order to retain their beauty and vitality.

The result of this ageism is a culture in which fear of aging often leads to the confusion of growing old with growing up. As the 1960s generation that advanced the slogan "Never trust anyone over thirty" reaches old age, the cult of youth it helped to establish encourages people to resist the notion of age-appropriate behavior. As a result, the norms of maturity are constantly redefined, with elders often adopting outwardly juvenile attitudes to prove that they are still young at heart. Joseph Epstein is one of many essayists to lament this trend: "This cult—more like a national craze—allows a very wide berth for youthfulness. Today one would not think to say that no one over thirty is to be trusted; that sentiment has been replaced by the notion that no one under forty needs to get serious."[19] For young people themselves, the consequences may be even more serious. By placing so much value on youthfulness, American culture risks teaching them that life peaks during the teen-age years, when freedom and leisure sanction the endless pursuit of fun. In contrast, the traditional rites of passage that follow—the milestones of marriage, parenting, and professional accomplishment—all seem a lockstep progression of prolonged dwindling, which can only be tolerated by reverting to one's adolescent past. In other words, the cult of youth may condone arrested development in the mistaken belief that any evidence of maturity foreshadows the supposed corruptions of adulthood.

YOUTH CULTURE AND "MORAL PANICS"

"'Moral panic' occurs when the official or press reaction to a deviant social or cultural phenomenon is 'out of all proportion' to the actual threat offered. It implies that public concern is in excess of what is appropriate if concern were directly proportional to objective harm."

John Springhall

From *Youth, Popular Culture and Moral Panics: Penny Gaffs to Gangsta-Rap, 1830-1966* (New York: St. Martin's Press, 1998), p. 7.

In light of the ageism of post-1950s America, alienated-youth fiction faces a major challenge: how to celebrate the idealism and enthusiasm that youth represents without condoning immaturity. Chapman's case offers an extreme yet illustrative example of why young readers must learn to critique the depiction of youth in these works, even while identifying with them. Only after more than a decade in prison could Lennon's murderer acknowledge how his arrested adolescent sensibility led him to misread *The Catcher in the Rye:* "It was a child that killed John Lennon. It wasn't a man. Even though I'd had twenty-five birthdays, inside I was sixteen years old like Holden Caulfield was. My only feelings were the feelings that came through that book to the sixteen-year-old Holden that was inside me."[20] The best and most enduring alienated-youth fiction urges teen readers both to appreciate and outgrow the sixteen-year-old inside themselves.

NOTES

1. See Jack Jones, *Let Me Take You Down: Inside the Mind of Mark David Chapman, the Man Who Killed John Lennon* (New York: Villard, 1992), pp. 6–23.

2. J. D. Salinger, *The Catcher in the Rye* (Boston: Little, Brown, 1951; reprint, Boston: Little, Brown/Back Bay, 2001), pp. 224–225. Subsequent citations of this work are given parenthetically in the text.

3. Jones, *Let Me Take You Down,* p. 177.

4. Priscilla Johnson McMillan, "An Assassin's Portrait," *New Republic,* 185 (12 July 1982): 17.

5. Grace Palladino, *Teenagers: An American History* (New York: BasicBooks, 1996), p. xiv.

6. Glenn Wallach, *Obedient Sons: The Discourse of Youth and Generations in American Culture, 1630–1860* (Amherst: University of Massachusetts Press, 1997), p. 7.

7. G. Stanley Hall, *Adolescence; Its Psychology and Its Relations to Physiology, Anthropology, Sociology, Sex, Crime, Religion and Education,* volume 1 (New York: Appleton, 1904), p. xiv.

8. Ibid., pp. xv–xvi.

9. Lewis Mumford, *The City in History: Its Origins, Its Transformations, and Its Prospects* (New York: Harcourt, Brace & World, 1961), p. 494.

10. W. T. Lhamon Jr., *Deliberate Speed: The Origins of a Cultural Style in the American 1950s* (Washington, D.C.: Smithsonian Institution Press, 1990), p. 9.

11. Fredric Jameson, "Postmodernism and Consumer Society," in *The Anti-Aesthetic: Essays on Postmodern Culture,* edited by Hal Foster (Port Townsend, Wash.: Bay Press, 1983), p. 125.

12. F. Scott Fitzgerald, *This Side of Paradise* (New York: Scribners, 1920), p. 282.

13. Hall, *Adolescence,* p. xiv.

14. Paul Goodman, *Growing Up Absurd: Problems of Youth in the Organized Society* (New York: Vintage, 1962), p. 4.

15. Erik H. Erikson, "Youth: Fidelity and Diversity," in *The Challenge of Youth,* edited by Erikson (Garden City, N.Y.: Doubleday, 1965), p. 24.

16. Beth L. Bailey, *From Front Porch to Back Seat: Courtship in Twentieth-Century America* (Baltimore: Johns Hopkins University Press, 1988), p. 78.

17. Victor Turner, *Dramas, Fields, and Metaphors: Symbolic Action in Human Society* (Ithaca, N.Y.: Cornell University Press, 1974), p. 261.

18. Sylvia Plath, *The Bell Jar* (New York: Harper & Row, 1971), p. 199.

19. Joseph Epstein, "Grow Up, Why Dontcha?" in his *Narcissus Leaves the Pool: Familiar Essays* (Boston: Houghton Mifflin, 1999), p. 280.

20. Mark David Chapman, quoted in Jones, *Let Me Take You Down,* p. 42.

REPRESENTATIVE WRITERS

INTRODUCTION

Authors who write about youthful alienation do not belong to a specific literary movement or school. Although their works may express a similar dread of adulthood, their teenage protagonists are products of a range of economic, educational, and familial backgrounds. Nor do these writers subscribe to one main style for telling their stories. Many (including J. D. Salinger in *The Catcher in the Rye*) employ a first-person narrative perspective that fosters empathy for the main characters, while others prefer a third-person approach that shrouds adolescents in an aura of remoteness. Novelists may even strike up different relationships with readers. Those categorized as "young-adult" writers—S. E. Hinton (*The Outsiders*, 1967) and Paul Zindel (*The Pigman*, 1968), for example—cater to a secondary-school-student constituency. Sensitive to their audience's moral impressionability, they fashion their plots as life lessons that illustrate important values. Still other authors view themselves as spokespersons for their peers by defending subcultural fads and fashions, thus subscribing to a dictum voiced by F. Scott Fitzgerald in 1920: "An author ought to write for the youth of his own generation, the critics of the next, and the schoolmasters of ever afterward."[1] Given the diversity of aims and approaches that alienated-youth fiction accommodates, isolating commonalities among its practitioners may seem a futile task. Indeed, at times it seems as though the only similarity that these authors share is their interest in adolescence.

Nevertheless, some tentative generalizations about youth's literary advocates can be offered. As W. Tasker Witham has noted, novels about adolescence are apt to be written by first-time authors mining autobiographical material: "A beginning novelist naturally writes about the people, places, and situations he knows best. Probably he has not lived long enough to have experienced many dramatic situations, but certainly he has experienced the promising yet terrifying adventure of growing into adulthood." After transcribing their youth into fiction, the more talented of

E·W·Kemble
·1884·

The character of Huckleberry Finn, portrayed here in an illustration from Mark Twain's 1885 novel, grew out of the nineteenth-century tradition of the "bad-boy" book, a forerunner of alienated-youth fiction. As Twain depicted him, Huck was a "wilful" youth.

these writers move on to other subject matter, while those who discover their inspiration exhausted lapse into prolonged silences, in some cases abandoning fiction for good. As Witham concludes, "Relatively few decide to settle in the field of fictional adolescence, and cultivate its soil assiduously season after season."[2]

ANTECEDENTS

The late nineteenth and early twentieth centuries were an opportune time for writers interested in the transition from youth to adulthood. Louisa May Alcott's *Little Women* (1868) inspired many lesser talents to take up the profitable genre of the "girl's book," which taught adolescent females the obligations of marriage and motherhood. Meanwhile, a one-time Massachusetts minister named Horatio Alger Jr. established the successful prototype for boys' fiction with a series of interchangeable novels about honest ragamuffins whose industry and virtue elevate them above their origins. Other popular authors of adolescent fiction included Burt L. Standish, who produced more than two hundred volumes in his Frank Merriwell series (1896–1916), about the exploits of a campus scholar-athlete; and Booth Tarkington, whose *Seventeen* (1916) told the story of a young "mooncalf" named Willie Baxter whose crush on a neighbor girl leads to slapstick misadventures. To differing degrees these writers subscribed to the conventions of the bildungsroman (the novel of development), which, by tracing a protagonist's passage from youth to adulthood, defines the values required for successful entry into the grown-up world. Yet, these authors' vision of maturation could be rather sentimental and condescending. As one reviewer complained in 1920, most writers depicted the teenager as an "amiable baby"—pious, compliant, and unerringly willing to assume the responsibilities of adulthood.[3]

At least one important nineteenth-century writer defied this tradition to develop a plot and character type that continues to influence alienated-youth fiction. Throughout his career, Mark Twain ridiculed the preachiness of the amiable-baby tradition. An early sketch, "The Story of the Good Little Boy Who Did Not Prosper" (1870), typifies Twain's satirical response to his era's youth literature. In this piece young Jacob Blivens discovers that life does not imitate art when the code of conduct prescribed by his favorite books results in humiliation rather than respectability: "And once, when some bad boys pushed a blind man over in the mud, and Jacob ran to help him up and receive his blessing, the blind man did not give him any blessing at all, but whacked him over the head with the stick and said he would like to catch him shoving him again, and then pretending to help him up. This was not in accordance with any of the books. Jacob looked them all over to see."[4] However patented Twain's familiar *faux naif* style may seem, it should be noted that such parody was hardly uncommon in its time. Many contemporary authors ridiculed the superficial morality of what was derisively known as the Sunday-school tract. Nor can Twain's depictions of maturation up through the mid 1870s be considered groundbreaking. To differing degrees, works such as *The Innocents Abroad* (1869) and *Roughing It* (1872) subscribe to the bildungsroman plot as they trace their main characters' passage from innocence to experience. In the mock memoir *Life on the Mississippi* (1883) young Cub takes to the river under the tutelage of Mr. Bixby, who teaches him that piloting requires professional training instead of derring-do. By the end of the narrative, Cub has outgrown his vision of riverboat life as a piratic diversion, appreciating instead the maturity needed to navigate its real risks and dangers.

As he conceived his most famous literary creations, Twain began to resist the traditional ending of the bildungsroman, which prescribed the hero's contented entry into adulthood. Both *The Adventures of Tom Sawyer* (1876) and *Adventures of Huckleberry Finn* (1885) mark the author's response to a variation of the novel of development known as the bad-boy book. This character type, popularized by works such as Thomas Bailey Aldrich's *The Story of a Bad Boy* (1869) and George W. Peck's *Peck's Bad Boy and His Pa* (1883), was an irreverent, puckish prankster, a rascal prone to mischief and misadventure. Although exciting outrage for glorifying hooliganism, these works concluded in bildungsroman fashion with the narrator, a rehabilitated bad boy, looking back at his misspent youth from the vantage point of well-adjusted maturity. Thus, while the bad-boy genre might mock sentimental notions of childhood, it did not repudiate the importance of growing up.

Twain, however, did. A quotation from his close friend William Dean Howells suggests the spirit that Twain invested in Tom and Huck: "He was a youth to the end of his days, the heart of a boy with the head of a sage; the heart of a good boy, or a bad boy, but always a wilful boy, and wilfulest to show himself out at every time for the boy he was."[5] Throughout *The Adventures of Tom Sawyer* and *Adventures of Huckleberry Finn* theatrical displays of childhood imagination prove essential to exposing adult falsities. The young protagonists act out a series of fantasies, in some episodes merely role-playing, in others going so far as to disguise themselves in elaborate costumes. (The final third of *Adventures of Huckleberry Finn* depicts Huck masquerading as Tom, for example.) Through these playful performances, the boys unknowingly reveal truths that the adult world seeks to obscure. Twain implies that the imagination of youth intuitively grasps toward truth, even when indulging in fiction. Adult codes of honor and forthrightness, meanwhile, steer elders to exploit the persuasiveness of appearances, thereby leading them into evasion and self-deceit. To differing degrees Tom and Huck remain entrenched in their "wilful" boyishness to elude initiation into the corruptions of adult society.

The growth of Twain's devotion to willful youth can be traced through the writing of *The Adventures of Tom Sawyer*. When he began the manuscript in early 1873, Twain intended for the action to carry Tom well beyond his boyhood enthusiasms into a disgruntled middle age. At the top of his manuscript, he outlined his hero's planned passage into adulthood: "1, Boyhood and youth; 2 y & early manh; 3 the Battle of Life in many lands; 4 (age 37 to [40?]), return & meet grown babies and toothless old drivelers who were the grandees of his boyhood."[6] After the first eight chapters Twain's inspiration waned, and he set the story aside for more than a year. Subsequent periods of inactivity delayed the completion of the manuscript until July 1875, when he abruptly ended the book with Tom still a boy. The effect was to omit the requisite character development that would have showed how Tom applied the lessons of his youth to the challenges of adulthood.

As a result, Tom remains the same raffish, self-centered show-off throughout his adventures, even though he undergoes such formative experiences as witnessing the death of Doc Robinson and testifying at the trial of Doc's killer, Injun Joe. Twain's refusal to follow his character's maturation beyond early adolescence is announced in the concluding chapter: "So endeth this chronicle. It being strictly a history of a *boy*, it must stop here; the story could not go much further without becoming the history of a *man*. When one writes a novel about grown people, he knows exactly where to stop—that is, with a marriage; but when he writes of juveniles, he must stop where he best can."[7] A later letter to Howells explains why Twain was uninterested in tracing Tom's growth in a sequel: "If I went on now and took him into manhood, he would just lie like all the one-horse men in literature and the reader would conceive a hearty contempt for him."[8] Twain believed that he was incapable of treating Tom's mature years without heaping his own scorn for the world of grown-ups upon his hero.

As he wrote *The Adventures of Tom Sawyer*, Twain realized that Tom's sometime companion Huckleberry Finn offered another perspective from which to explore the intuitive wisdom of youth. No sooner was the novel about Tom in print than Twain announced plans for Huck's autobiography. Yet, the relative failure of *The Adventures of Tom Sawyer*—the book sold a respectable twenty-three thousand copies in its first year but was ignored by critics—discouraged the author, and he set aside the preliminary chapters of *Adventures of Huckleberry Finn* for nearly seven years. When he finally returned to Huck in 1884, Twain invested the story with a mythic subtext that made it far more profound than the earlier book. Whereas the action in *The Adventures of Tom Sawyer* takes place largely around the fictional port town of St. Petersburg (based on Twain's childhood home of Hannibal, Missouri), Huck's adventures carry him down the Mississippi River. The river at once symbolizes the journey of life as well as the turbulent currents of American history, transforming Huck's moral passage from the tale of a single boy into the story of a nation's fall from innocence. Whereas *The Adventures of Tom Sawyer* revolves around juvenile diversions, *Adventures of Huckleberry Finn* tackles the defining political crisis of nineteenth-century America—slavery. As Huck travels the river south from Illinois to Louisiana in order to free Miss Watson's slave Jim from captivity, he must confront several ethical crises involving political commitment and the value of individuality. Because Twain explored the meaning of youthful innocence on many symbolic levels, *Adventures of Huckleberry Finn* remains the single most important precursor to twentieth-century alienated-youth fiction. As several critics have argued, the adolescent seekers of *The Catcher in the Rye, On the Road,* and *Invisible Man* might never have set off on their respective journeys without Huck's example.

Two famous episodes demonstrate how Twain infused his suspicion of adulthood with mythic significance. At a decisive moment, Huck must choose between conscience and culture. On the one hand, he believes that he will suffer damnation if he fails to inform Miss Watson of Jim's whereabouts. Yet, Huck's friendship with the runaway slave, with whom he has bonded during their river voyage, prevents him from betraying Jim. He finally decides to follow his loyalty: "All right then, I'll *go* to hell," he declares.[9] Huck's declaration fuses the child's intuitive recognition of the wrongs of slavery with the individual moral resolve necessary to question social conventions. The closing lines of the book offer another image of resisting adulthood. After helping Jim win his freedom, Huck is returned to Aunt Sally, the guardian charged with raising him. Huck declares his intent to escape the bonds of society: "I reckon I got to light out for the Territory ahead of the rest, because Aunt Sally she's going to adopt me and sivilize me, and I can't stand it. I been there before."[10] The pledge to "light out for the Territory" is the most influential image of the adolescent's flight from initiation into adulthood. As in *The Adventures of Tom Sawyer,* Twain presents willful youth as an antidote to the moral compromises that maturity demands.

As might be expected, *Adventures of Huckleberry Finn* inspired controversy in the mid 1880s. Several newspapers agreed with the assessment of *The New York World:* "The book's irreverence makes parents, guardians and people who are at all good and proper ridiculous."[11] Although reviewers recognized the morality beneath the satire, authorities proclaimed Huck a dangerous influence on children. In a move that made national headlines, the Concord Free Public Library in Massachusetts removed the novel from its shelves, setting a precedent that school administrators followed for more than a century. (In the 1980s authorities cited the frequent use of the racial epithet *nigger* in the book to justify its removal from school curricula.) Such bans demonstrate how alienated-youth fiction can discomfit adults when it encourages young readers to question authority.

Despite Twain's efforts, most of his contemporaries continued to depict adolescents as idealized, one-dimensional figures exuding mirth and moral rectitude. This tradition officially became outdated in March 1920 with the publication of Fitzgerald's first novel, *This Side of Paradise.* A semiautobiographical account of Fitzgerald's checkered undergraduate career at Princeton University from 1916 to 1918, the book was unlike any previous depiction of American college life. In this first half of the novel the protagonist, Amory Blaine, subscribes to the upper-class code of noblesse oblige. He reads all the right books, attends a prestigious prep school, and cultivates popularity among the in-crowd, all in the belief that he will be rewarded in adulthood with an aristocratic existence. Once Amory arrives at Princeton, however, his aspirations go awry, and he suffers a series of setbacks that precipitates a crisis. His family loses its wealth and prestige; he fails a crucial exam and leaves the prestigious Ivy League institution to join the army; and, shortly afterward, he loses the glamorous debutante Rosalind Connage to a wealthy competitor. In consolation Amory turns to drink, and he

OTHER IMPORTANT ALIENATED-YOUTH FICTION BEFORE 1950

"Paul's Case," from *The Troll Garden* (1905), by Willa Cather. A young man embezzles from his employer to escape his uninspiring working-class life and enjoy a luxurious weekend in New York City. When he discovers that his father is coming to bring him home, he commits suicide by hurling himself in front of a train.

Look Homeward, Angel (1929), by Thomas Wolfe. Moody Eugene Gant grows up in a small-minded world, eventually leaving his North Carolina hometown to discover his identity while attending the state university.

The Red Pony (1937), by John Steinbeck. Growing up on a California ranch and raising horses, Jody Tiflin undergoes a series of initiation experiences that teaches him the importance of responsibility, maturity, and compassion.

The Heart is a Lonely Hunter (1940), by Carson McCullers. Thirteen-year-old Mick Kelly confides her adolescent insecurities to deaf-mute John Singer, whose subsequent suicide makes Mick realize that she understood her friend far less than she presumed she did.

"The Bear," from *Go Down, Moses* (1942), by William Faulkner. In what many critics consider the quintessential initiation story of the modernist era, Isaac McCaslin witnesses the vanishing bounty of nature as he learns to hunt a legendary bear under the guidance of spiritual elder Sam Fathers.

As the dust-jacket illustration from his 1920 novel suggests, F. Scott Fitzgerald portrayed adolescents as more sophisticated and sexually mature than they appeared in nineteenth-century novels. Nevertheless, his flappers and collegians coveted their youth as a time of gaudy indulgence.

soothes his frustrations by self-consciously offending adults. He takes the rap for Rosalind's brother, Alec, who has smuggled a young woman up to his hotel room. Pretending that he is the one who hid the woman in the room, Amory scoffs at a hotel detective's threat of arrest on charges of indecency. Later, Amory denounces a wealthy capitalist who preaches the gospel of monetary success. In the end, however, Amory is unable to relieve his confusion. At the end of the novel he walks the Princeton campus, alone and uncertain of his future.

Upon publication, *This Side of Paradise* became a succès de scandale for Fitzgerald's candid depiction of collegiate drinking and "petting parties." Yet, the revelation that modern youth enjoyed consuming alcohol and necking somewhat obscured Fitzgerald's truest innovation. The novel presents the argument that when young people find that the world cannot fulfill their ambitions, they view their youth not as a preparatory apprenticeship to adulthood but as a time of glorious indulgence in which they seek to wring every possible ounce of fun out of it. While the novel, like *Adventures of Huckleberry Finn*, depicts the yearning to elude initiation, the tone is more pragmatic than nostalgic. As a disillusioned Amory confesses late in the book, "I don't want to repeat my innocence. I want the pleasure of losing it again."[12] If the beauty, vitality, and idealism that youth embodies are doomed to diminish over time, Fitzgerald insists, then one ought to exhaust them first through profligate pleasures.

The result of this ethos in *This Side of Paradise* is a representation of maturation that emphasizes its liminal or "on-the-threshold" nature. Unlike Alcott's or Alger's teenagers, who seem frozen in prepubescence, Amory and his fictional peers are like adults in their self-conscious sophistication. Yet, their narcissism and selfishness are also indicative of their resolute, almost petulant immaturity. This more complex rendering of the "in-betweenness" of adolescence struck a chord with young people eager for realistic depictions of their lives. In 1920 alone, *This Side of Paradise* sold nearly fifty thousand copies and inspired a slew of copycat works with provocative titles such as *Flaming Youth, Forbidden Fruit,* and *Wild Asses.*

Despite the gaudy romance and audacious energy that he associated with youth, Fitzgerald was fixated by its loss. In fact, most of his works pivot upon the moment that his protagonists must acknowledge the inevitable passage of youth. As Frederick Hoffman observes, "For Fitzgerald's youth the moment of beauty and serene self-confidence was short indeed. In his world of debutantes and young college men time was always reduced to a pinpoint present, and the task of maturing was a hard one, involving the need to give up that present." Hoffman only partly exaggerates when he adds, "Many Fitzgerald heroes are haunted by the reality that almost any day one might find oneself twenty-four instead of twenty-three."[13] Throughout Fitzgerald's fiction, the time to relinquish youth is indeed tied to a specific age milestone. *The Beautiful and Damned* (1922), Fitzgerald's second novel, depicts youth's obsessiveness over the significance of turning thirty. The main characters, Anthony and Gloria Patch, dread this particular birthday, the arrival of which they hope to stave off through drink and debauchery. Fitzgerald's intrusive narration also laments the onslaught of maturity, frequently interrupting the action to offer aphorisms on the aging process: "It is in the twenties that the actual momentum of life begins to slacken, and it is a simple soul indeed to whom as many things are significant and meaningful at thirty as at ten years before. At thirty an organ-grinder is a more or less moth-eaten man who grinds an organ—and once he was an organ-grinder!"[14] Critics dismiss *The Beautiful and Damned* as an immature effort. Yet, its preoccupation with maintaining the fieriness of youth was perfectly in accord with 1920s culture, in which advertising and self-help industries discouraged Americans from going gently into the dark night of middle age.

In his most sustained artistic achievement, *The Great Gatsby* (1925), Fitzgerald disassociates youth from age, equating it instead with the broader melancholy of mutability or change. Early reviewers praised the newfound maturity of the book; as many noted, Fitzgerald was memorializing not the fleetingness of youth but an even more mythic subject— the American dream. Despite favorable reviews, *The Great Gatsby* (which was not recognized as a literary classic for some thirty years) was not a commercial success, and financial woes forced Fitzgerald to resume writing fiction about young flappers and their boyfriends to support himself. Fitzgerald was generally contemptuous of his short stories written for magazine publication, but among them is a series of fourteen stories with a remarkably rich representation of adolescent coming of age. Collected in book form as *The Basil and Josephine Stories* (1973), the stories, dating from 1928 to 1931, explore the maturing minds of Basil Lee Duke and Josephine Perry as they endure various initiation experiences. In "Basil and Cleopatra" Basil realizes the frivolousness of popular schoolgirls who prove unworthy of his affection, inspiring a desire rare among Fitzgerald's heroes: "For the first time in his life he wanted passionately to be older, less impressionable, less impressed."[15] The six-story Josephine series ends on an even sadder note. In "Emotional Bankruptcy" the heroine must admit that her "vast, tragic apathy" and narcissism render her unfit for mature love. Her flippant attitude toward romance leads her to the realization that, although not yet eighteen, she "has nothing to give" and can't "feel anything at all": "One cannot both spend and have. The love of her life had come by, and looking in her empty basket, she had found not a flower left for him—not one."[16] In both cases Fitzgerald insists on the adolescent's capacity for epiphany. Basil and Josephine not only gain valuable insight into themselves, but the stories hint that they will never look upon the world as innocently as they once did.

Unfortunately, the emphasis on youth in Fitzgerald's work for many years stereotyped him in critics' eyes as a writer whose arrested development overwhelmed his artistry. Van Wyck Brooks's comments in 1953 regarding Fitzgerald's post–*Great Gatsby* belief that he had failed to fulfill his potential are typical: "Fitzgerald remained the college boy who could refer, in a story, to a 'fading but still lovely beauty of twenty-seven,' and what he felt as a betrayal of his gift was undoubtedly a sense that, for some reason, he had not grown up."[17] Similar prejudices surfaced in Brooks's estimation of Fitzgerald's colleague and rival, Ernest Hemingway, whom Brooks also credited with perpetuating "a cult of youth" that inspired "a fear of growing old that almost precludes at the outset any regard for the uses of growing up."[18] Like Fitzgerald, Hemingway wrote repeatedly about lost innocence, though in a quite different manner. Consider the conclusions of two stories about the demise of an adolescent romance. In "Winter Dreams" (1922) Fitzgerald's protagonist, Dexter Green, is stunned to learn that a former flame, Judy Jones, has lost the beauty that so enchanted him in his youth: "The dream was gone. . . . The gates were closed, the sun was gone down, and there was no beauty but the gray beauty of steel that withstands all time. Even the grief he could have borne was left behind in the country of illusion, of youth, of the richness of life, where his winter dreams had flourished."[19] In Hemingway's "The End of Something" (1924) Nick Adams breaks up with his girlfriend, Marjorie, during an outing in the Michigan woods. After the young woman departs, Nick's friend Bill happens upon their campsite:

"Did she go all right?" Bill said.

"Yes," Nick said, lying, his face on the blanket.

"Have a scene?"

"No, there wasn't any scene."

"How do you feel?"

"Oh, go away, Bill! Go away for a while."

Bill selected a sandwich from the lunch basket and walked over to have a look at the rods.[20]

The former passage is elegiac and mournful, while the latter is stark and stoic. Whereas Fitzgerald was apt to expound on the significance of loss, Hemingway preferred to vivify that emotional drama through characters' gestures and dialogue. Thus, while the final lines in Fitzgerald's story convey Dexter's anguish in detail, Nick Adams's unwillingness to discuss his feelings with Bill suggests an inability to articulate the pain. In the mid 1920s Hemingway's minimalist style, which does away with the rhetorical ornamentation that is a trademark of Fitzgerald's prose, proved highly influential. The rigorous terseness conveyed an image of hard-boiled youth shell-shocked by premature exposure to the violence and treachery of the modern world.

Hemingway never sought the role of generational spokesman as intently as Fitzgerald. His first major short-story collection, *In Our Time* (1925), is an autobiographical scrapbook of childhood and adolescent experiences. The stories were inspired both by the boyhood summers Hemingway spent hunting and fishing in upper Michigan as well as his service in World War I, during which he was wounded while working as a Red Cross ambulance driver in Italy in July 1918. Despite their autobiographical nature, the stories bespeak the general wariness and disillusionment felt by Hemingway's generation of wizened postwar youth. Fraught with war, marital strife, and the exposure of parental weakness and corruption, many of the pieces in *In Our Time* offer textbook examples of the initiation story, in which a young protagonist suffers a sudden realization of human powerlessness and frailty that strips him of his adolescent ideals. As one critic notes, "All Hemingway heroes must first become aware of the central fact of the universe, that at the very core of life there is 'nada.' Whether a boy or man, no Hemingway hero is 'mature' until he acknowledges defeat by the universe. Only in defeat is there victory."[21]

When *In Our Time* was published, Hemingway had been living for nearly four years in Paris amid a colony of American expatriates who found in the more liberal European ambience a welcome respite from the repressive morality of their native land. In late June 1925 he and several fellow expatriates traveled to Pamplona, Spain, for the annual San Fermín bull-fighting festival. The trip inspired the plot of Hemingway's *The Sun Also Rises,* a novel that, upon publication in October 1926, became a bona fide youth-culture phenomenon on a par with *This Side of Paradise* six years earlier. The story of Americans traveling from Paris to Pamplona and seeking to escape despair through drinking and promiscuity gave modern youth a sobriquet that conveyed their indirection. As Hemingway wrote (quoting Gertrude Stein, an older expatriate author, in the first of two epigraphs to the novel), they were a "lost generation." *The Sun Also Rises* had barely arrived in bookstores before young Americans embarked for Paris in droves to seek out the real-life cafés and bars described in it. Young people who remained in America also adopted the pessimistic poses of the main characters, Jake Barnes and Brett Ashley. As Hemingway's contemporary Malcolm Cowley recalled, "The Smith College girls in New York were modeling themselves after Lady Brett. Hundreds of bright young men from the Middle West were trying to be Hemingway heroes, talking in tough understatements from the sides of their mouths."[22]

Detractors complained that by glamorizing the decadence of expatriate life in *The Sun Also Rises,* Hemingway encouraged immaturity and escapism. Yet, the novel actually shows how conditions in the modern world prevented many in that lost generation from becoming adults. Although well into their thirties, the characters lack the rituals, traditions, and moral resources needed to establish happy, productive adult lives. For Hemingway's narrator, journalist Jake Barnes, manhood is a physical impossibility. Rendered impotent in an airplane crash on the Italian front, Jake is unable to consummate his sexual desires and is thus rendered unfit for marriage and parenthood. His love interest, Brett Ashley, has lost a fiancé to dysentery and a husband to madness, both tragedies also resulting from the war. These romantic losses have sent her into a series of affairs; their casual nature excuses her from the potential pain of a committed relationship. Only after ending an affair with a Spanish bullfighter fifteen years her junior can Brett assert adult responsibility. Significantly, she does so through a specific age reference. As she tells Jake, "I'm thirty-four, you know. I'm not going to be one of these bitches that ruins children."[23] While recognizing that her own hopes for love and stability are long lost, Brett refuses to destroy the innocence of another youth. For Hemingway, that sacrifice is the lone moral legacy available to members of the lost generation. Born into a world of eroded absolutes, flawed characters such as Jake and Brett can survive only by remaining true to their individual ethical instincts.

Of course, Twain, Fitzgerald, and Hemingway are merely three of the many authors before the 1950s to mythologize youth and demonize adulthood. Writers as diverse as John Dos Passos, Theodore Dreiser, James Joyce, Willa Cather, William Faulkner, Katherine Anne Porter, and Henry Roth also measured the effects of modernity on maturation. As the Salinger generation of authors emerged after World War II, however, its most obvious influences were Twain, Fitzgerald, and Hemingway. In differing proportions, writers of the 1950s combined Twain's sarcastic disregard for adults, Fitzgerald's lyric Romanticism, and Hemingway's stoic perseverance to create the modern image of the alienated youth.

SALINGER AND HIS CONTEMPORARIES

Salinger's literary career did not begin auspiciously. Between 1940 and 1947, the novice author published nineteen short stories, with titles such as "The Young Folks" (1940) and "A Young Girl in 1941 with No Waist at All" (1947). Although these early efforts foreshadowed a long-running fixation with adolescence, the characters are flat and the plots degenerate into overwrought sentimentality. Salinger's subsequent refusal to republish these stories suggests that they are best viewed as preparatory exercises rather than artistic accomplishments. As their scattershot quality reveals, Salinger knew from the start of his literary apprenticeship that he wanted to write about youth, but he was at first uncertain about his style and voice.

Two important exceptions deserve mention. In 1941 Salinger submitted a story called "Slight Rebellion Off Madison" to *The New Yorker*. The magazine accepted it but, for reasons that remain unclear, delayed publication for five years. The narrative follows a dapper young man named Holden Caulfield on a Manhattan date with Sally Hayes. While the couple watches ice-skaters at Rockefeller Center, Holden launches into a tirade against his various dislikes, including classmates, the movies ("Newsreels! There's always a dumb race horse and some dame breaking a bottle over a ship"), and, especially, his private school. When Holden's rant fails to incite Sally's passion, he insults her: "You give me a royal pain."[24] Eventually, the story was used for a key scene in *The Catcher in the Rye* reflecting Holden's withering disdain for his complacent peers. In his original incarnation, however, Holden comes off as a hotheaded snob rather than a wounded idealist. The reason is the distance that Salinger's third-person point of view imposes on the character. Because Holden's portrayal lacks emotional immediacy, the story seems more satirical than sympathetic.

I started running with my suitcases hanging the devil out of my legs. I ran all the way to the Gate, stopped, got my breath, and ran across Route 202

In this illustration for a short story by Salinger (*Collier's*, 22 December 1945) Holden Caulfield appears more cherubic than confused or tortured. Although the story includes scenes that later appeared in *The Catcher in the Rye*, Salinger had yet to create the image of the teenager as a saintly observer of social malaise that cemented his literary reputation.

In "I'm Crazy," another story featuring material later used in *The Catcher in the Rye*, Holden is the narrator. Published in *Collier's* in December 1945, the story includes embryonic versions of important scenes in the novel, but it, too, reveals that Salinger had only tentatively begun to attach to adolescence the mythic significance that turned the teenage protagonist into a saintly observer of social malaise. Early in "I'm Crazy," as Holden describes his imminent expulsion from preparatory school, Mr. Spencer, his history teacher, demands an explanation for his poor academic performance. Later, Holden's younger sister, Phoebe, grills him on his goals for the future. In *The Catcher in the Rye* both conversations provide Holden opportunities to vent against adulthood. The scene with Phoebe is especially important: in the novel it is the moment at which the young man articulates his dream of protecting children from falling into despair. Yet, in "I'm Crazy" Holden makes no mention of this aspiration. As the title of the story suggests, he accounts for his indirection by pleading insanity. Instead of blaming his unwillingness to mature on the culture's unsatisfactory definition of that process, he simply insists that he is mentally unstable. Warren French argues that "I'm Crazy" reveals Salinger's uncertainty over the causes of his main character's disaffection: "Somewhere between 1945 and 1951, Salinger dramatically changed his concept of his misfit hero from that of a pathetically misunderstood person who felt a need to apologize for himself and seemed doomed to an undistinguished life in New York's wasteland to that of one who has learned to transcend the morons and show his compassion for them by generous gestures."[25]

Salinger might never have transformed the adolescent into a "misfit hero" had he not affiliated himself with *The New Yorker* in the mid 1940s. Before accepting "Slight Rebellion Off Madison," the magazine had rejected seven previous submissions from him. If titles are indicative of tone, pieces such as "I Went to School with Adolf Hitler" were simply too outlandish for the patented slice-of-life approach to fiction characteristic of *The New Yorker.* A typical story in the magazine featured a sensitive protagonist protesting the alienation of his or her metropolitan environment. More often than not, this protest dramatized the character's despair but did not relieve it, leaving the reader to wrestle with the unresolved tensions.[26] In early 1947 Salinger adopted the *New Yorker* formula for an oblique tale of a World War II veteran named Seymour Glass who commits suicide after playing on a Florida beach with a young girl. "A Perfect Day for Bananafish" subsequently became a signature story for author and magazine alike. As critics have argued, Seymour's violent death symbolizes the futility of trying to protect childhood innocence in a brash, materialistic world. Between 1948 and 1953 *The New Yorker* published six more of Salinger's paeans to lost innocence, all of which feature angst-ridden adults who envy the purity of youth. (These seven stories, along with two others first published in other magazines, were collected in 1953 as *Nine Stories.*) So popular and influential was Salinger's short fiction that by the early 1950s he was hailed as a leading emissary of the *New Yorker* school.

As Salinger labored over his short stories intended for *The New Yorker,* he also struggled with an early, novella-length version of *The Catcher in the Rye.* The same qualities that made his stories captivating were not particularly suited to the novel genre, however. Neither his lack of interest in plotting nor his compact, symbolic style lent themselves to the dramatic breadth required by a longer narrative. Nor could he maintain the intensity of his characters' psychic woes outside the abbreviated space of the short-story genre. By mid 1949, however, Salinger discovered a narrative form congenial to his episodic sensibility. He recast Holden's story as a picaresque tale, a loosely connected series of adventures in which a hero encounters a succession of eccentric characters. This form allowed him, not unlike Twain, to document his protagonist's exposure to the hypocrisies of adulthood without forcing the boy into maturity, as the bildungsroman formula demanded.

Form was not the only impediment that Salinger faced. He also needed a sympathetic point of view to maintain readers' interest in the absence of a tightly paced plot. For most of his stories published in *The New Yorker* he had employed a third-person perspective that gave his insights into his characters' loveless existence an appropriately arch, laconic detachment. In *The Catcher in the Rye* such an approach would have interfered with readers' ability to identify with Holden. Accordingly, Salinger switched to the first person to create what many consider the most arresting trait in the novel, the narrative voice. What moves critics to praise the authenticity of Holden's voice are the rhetorical mannerisms that convey the defensive insouciance of adolescence. The stylistic repertoire Salinger gave to Holden includes humorous ad hominem (against the person) insults ("He hated it when you called him a moron. All morons hate it when you call them a moron" [57]), exaggeration (a "crappy" Broadway play is "about five hundred thousand years in the life of this one old couple" [163]), and slang ("The cab I had was a real old one that smelled like someone'd just tossed his cookies in it" [106]). Salinger also peppered his hero's narration with sufficient profanity to guarantee decades of uproar over the question of whether the novel was appropriate for teenage readers. While parents objected to Holden's anti-authoritarianism, many young people found (and continue to find) the voice compelling.

Although *The Catcher in the Rye* sold well when first published in July 1951, it was by no means a cultural phenomenon. Only after appearing in paperback a year later did the novel develop a cult following among high-school and college students. As its reputation grew, Salinger rose to the status of a literary avatar of adolescent idealism. His popularity even pushed *Nine Stories* onto the best-seller lists, a rare achievement for a collection of short stories. By the mid 1950s the appearance of a new work by Salinger was a bona fide cultural event. When *The New Yorker* published the short story "Franny" on 29 January 1955, a scandal concerning the titular heroine erupted. Over the course of a conversation about spirituality with her boyfriend, Lane Coutell, Franny Glass (the younger sister of Seymour, the protagonist of "A Perfect Day for Bananafish") discovers that Lane is a self-absorbed cad. The realization sends her to the ladies' room, where she suffers a crying spell. At the climax of the plot, she faints. For many readers, Franny's condition implied an unplanned pregnancy, which Salinger declined to confirm or deny. In his biography of the author, Paul Alexander describes the reaction among subscribers to *The New Yorker*: "The response to the story was greater than that received by any story Salinger had published so far. Indeed the magazine was flooded with even more letters than it got when it printed Shirley Jackson's 'The Lottery.' The story had immediately attracted widespread attention and went on to be regarded as a model of the form."[27] Six years later, when "Franny" was collected as one of the two stories in *Franny and Zooey* ("Zooey" was first published in *The New Yorker* in 1957), it sold one hundred thousand copies in two weeks.

Although Salinger enjoyed commercial success until his self-imposed exile from publishing in 1965, "Franny" heralded a sea change in his critical fortunes. His subsequent published fiction consists of just four novella-length stories—"Raise High the Roof Beam, Carpenters" (1955), "Zooey," "Seymour: An Introduction" (1959), and "Hapworth 16, 1924" (1965)—none of which possesses the observational precision or satirical edge of his earlier short fiction. In writing about Seymour Glass's younger siblings (Buddy, Boo Boo, the twins Walt and Waker, Zooey, and Franny), Salinger restricted himself to too small a cast of characters. In critics' eyes, the idealism that made Holden's yearning so compelling had degenerated into a barely concealed elitism, for the Glass family's alienation seemed to arise from the parents' certainty that their children were too good for the world. The storytelling strategies of these later works also proved problematic. Never much for plotting, Salinger did away with any semblance of narrative action, indulging instead in authorial asides and long-winded digressions on Zen Buddhism. Irving Howe's comments typify the critics' belief that style had come to overwhelm substance in Salinger's fiction: "Hopelessly prolix, these stories are marred by the self-indulgence of a writer flirting with depths of wisdom, yet coy and embarrassed in his advances. With their cozy parentheses and clumsy footnotes, their careening mixture of Jewish vaudeville and Buddhist prescription, they betray a loss of creative discipline, a surrender to cherished mannerisms."[28]

As similarly stinging assessments became commonplace in the mid 1960s, Salinger refused to publish any new material and withdrew further from public life. Over the subsequent decades, his silence has only heightened his celebrity, making him the most famous literary recluse of his time. (Aficionados continue to journey to Cornish, New Hampshire, hoping to encounter the elderly author, who has lived there since 1953.) Yet, despite the enduring popularity of *The Catcher in the Rye*, critics tend to view Salinger's aborted career as evidence of his inability to mature artistically. In the words of one commentator, "Despite its many virtues, its frequent drama and fluidity of style, the bulk of Salinger's fiction is seriously undermined by the fact that he is congenitally less interested in getting to the bottom of his characters' emotionally retarded behavior than he is in celebrating it."[29]

In *The Catcher in the Rye* Salinger fashioned the quintessential portrait of the adolescent as an outcast. Jack Kerouac also viewed postwar youth as alienated, but instead of depicting them as loners, he celebrated the community and generational fellowship that was possible when young people established alternative subcultures. In November 1948, at the age of twenty-six, Kerouac coined the term *Beat Generation* to convey the longing for adventure that he shared with a coterie of writers based in New York and including Allen Ginsberg, William S. Burroughs, and John Clellon Holmes. As Kerouac explained, "Beat doesn't mean tired, or bushed, so much as it means *beato,* the Italian for beatific: to be in a state of beatitude, like St. Francis, trying to love all life, trying to be utterly sincere with everyone, practicing endurance, kindness, cultivating joy of heart."[30] Being beat meant rejecting the conformity, efficiency, and materialism of 1950s culture to pursue new, invigorating forms of spiritual enlightenment. To help youth cultivate this aspect of their nature, the Beats prescribed several stimulants, from bebop jazz and Buddhism to marijuana and amphetamines, all of which ostensibly enabled one to achieve otherworldly wisdom.

Early in his career Kerouac struggled to develop a unique voice that could articulate this ecstatic spirit of rebellion. His first novel, *The Town and the City* (1950), is a promising but derivative homage to his literary idol, Thomas Wolfe, whose gargantuan coming-of-age novels, *Look Homeward, Angel* (1929) and *Of Time and the River* (1935), were notable for their epic scope and wild flights of verbosity. In November 1948 Kerouac embarked on a more original project: a story about two young men who take to the road seeking to discover America and, by extension, themselves. The immediate inspiration for the novel was a six-week cross-country trip that he had recently completed with a vagabond acquaintance named Neal Cassady, whom he had met in December 1946. Four years younger than Kerouac, Cassady was already the patron saint of writers affiliated with the Beat movement. They viewed this veteran of reform schools, pool halls, and flophouses as an embodiment of the outlaw temperament that inspired their free-spirit philosophy. (Cassady boasted of having hot-wired more than five hundred cars since he was fourteen.) Biographer Ann Charters describes how Kerouac viewed the charismatic drifter as an American archetype: "Kerouac's vision of Neal Cassady ('Dean Moriarty') in *On the Road* centered in one of the most vital fantasies of America, the dream of the cowboy, free and footloose, become a drifter with the crowding and commercialization of modern life. *On the Road* caught a sense of the American folk hero rebelliousness, the spirit of the wide, western plains in Cassady's colossal restlessness."[31] In Kerouac's eyes Cassady was a modern-day picaresque hero, not only restless but reckless in his all-consuming vision of the highway as the road to uninhibited enlightenment and fun.

As Tim Hunt has shown, the book that eventually emerged as *On the Road* evolved through five distinct permutations over four years. (The text as published in 1957 is the fourth version; the fifth and final one, which Kerouac considered his favorite, appeared in expurgated form as *Excerpts from Visions of Cody* in 1959.)[32] By early 1951, after several aborted efforts, Kerouac settled for an overtly autobiographical literary form known as the roman à clef (novel with a key), in which characters are based on real-life figures. Just as Hemingway had transcribed the expatriate travels of actual members of the lost generation in *The Sun Also Rises,* Kerouac decided that the true story of his Beat peers needed little fictional invention other than rechristening himself as "Sal Paradise" and Cassady as "Dean Moriarty." For the rest of his career, Kerouac described his novels as an extended roman à clef called "the Duluoz Legend," named after his alter ego, Jack Duluoz, the Sal Paradise–styled hero of *Big Sur* (1962) and *Desolation Angels* (1965).

However firm in his conviction that the truest literature is autobiographical, Kerouac continued to flounder with his style until April 1951, when he seized upon a technique that captured the sensation of life on the road. According to literary legend, he dashed off *On the Road* in a three-week sprint fueled by coffee and Benzedrine, a type of amphetamine. To avoid interrupting his creative flow, Kerouac even eschewed regular typing paper, instead taping long sheets from a drawing pad into a scroll that allowed him to put down as many as a hundred words per minute without stopping to insert fresh paper into the typewriter carriage. (He had once won a speed-typing championship in high school). For many of his contemporaries, the idea of writing without pause for revision was an affront to the very idea of art as craftsmanship. In the late 1950s Truman Capote described Kerouac's style in a famously acid quip: "That's not writing—it's typing."[33] The hypnotic breathlessness of *On the Road* more than compensates for the lack of reflection and deliberation in the novel, however. Just as Sal and Neal's quest is a ramble with no fixed destination, Kerouac's writ-

Jack Kerouac (right) with Neal Cassady, 1951. At the time, Kerouac had just completed a first draft of *On the Road* (1957), in which Cassady was portrayed as Dean Moriarty, the restless embodiment of the American spirit.

ing revels in the immediacy of its indirection, preferring the joys of discovery to structured suspense.

One passage in particular conveys what Kerouac was attempting to achieve with this technique:

> And for just a moment I had reached the point of ecstasy that I always wanted to reach, which was the complete step across chronological time into timeless shadows, and wonderment in the bleakness of the mortal realm, and the sensation of death kicking at my heels to move on, with a phantom dogging its own heels, and myself hurrying to a plank where all the angels dove off and flew into the holy void of uncreated emptiness, the potent and inconceivable radiances shining in bright Mind Essence, innumerable lotus-lands falling open in the magic mothswarm of heaven.[34]

As Kerouac insisted in his best-known aesthetic tract, "Essentials of Spontaneous Prose" (1957), his approach was comparable to that of a jazz musician improvising a solo. Just as the soloist invents a melody against a rhythmic backdrop, the writer should eschew a conscientious selection of words in favor of an offhand method: "Follow free deviation (association) of mind into limitless blow-on-subject seas of thought, swimming in a sea of English with no discipline other than rhythms of rhetorical exaltation and expostulated statement," Kerouac advised.[35] By riffing like a musician on an image or symbol, the writer could bypass the rational, cognitive realm of the mind where conventional meanings accrue and discover new insights by tapping into the creative unconscious.

When Kerouac completed the scroll version of *On the Road* in late April 1951, he was confident of its literary merit. Unfortunately, the publication of the novel proved to be as protracted a process as its composition. Over the next half decade, nearly every major American publisher rejected *On the Road*. Only firms specializing in cheap, drugstore paperbacks expressed interest in it, and then only because the sex and marijuana-smoking scenes could be sold as tawdry entertainment. Although Kerouac continued to write at a furious pace—at one point toting twelve manuscripts in a duffel bag—his frustration turned to anger as he discovered fictionalized portraits of himself in Beat-inspired novels such as Holmes's *Go*, which appeared to great acclaim in 1952. By 1954 the still-unpublished *On the Road* was such an underground legend that Cowley discussed it in his study of post–World War II literature, *The Literary Situation*. Cowley, whose *Exile's Return* (1934) was an early celebration of literature by members of the lost generation, recognized that Kerouac's novel was a generational totem on par with *The Sun Also Rises*. Acting as a de facto agent, Cowley devised a roundabout strategy for generating publisher interest. Placing excerpts from the manuscript (which Kerouac had briefly renamed "The Beat Generation") with two prestigious literary journals, *New World Writing* and *The Paris Review*, he proved the critical and commercial viability of the novel to his superiors at Viking Press. Cowley's faith in the work was well founded. When *On the Road* was finally published in September 1957, the first two pressruns sold out in less than two weeks. In the process Kerouac shed his underground cult-figure status and became a bona fide celebrity.

Not unlike Fitzgerald, Kerouac soon discovered that fame undermined his literary credibility. No sooner had the Beat Generation entered the public consciousness than the media began an unceasing slew of attacks, misinterpreting both its literature and its lifestyle as

HOWL-ING AGAINST 1950S CONFORMITY

"Allen [Ginsberg] was nervous and had drunk a great deal of wine. He read with a small, intense voice, but the alcohol and the emotional intensity of the poem quickly took over, and soon he was swaying to its powerful rhythm, chanting like a Jewish cantor, sustaining his long breath length, savoring the outrageous language. Kerouac began cheering him on, yelling 'Go!' at the end of each line, and soon the audience joined in. Allen was completely transported. At each line he took a deep breath, glanced at the manuscript, then delivered it, arms outstretched, eyes gleaming, swaying from one foot to the other with the rhythm of the words. . . . Afterward Jack said, 'Ginsberg, this poem will make you famous in San Francisco.' Kenneth Rexroth corrected him: 'No, this poem will make you famous from bridge to bridge.'"

Barry Miles

From *Ginsberg: A Biography* (New York: Simon & Schuster, 1989), p. 196. Miles describes Beat writer Allen Ginsberg's first public reading of his epic poem *Howl* (1955).

amoral. Norman Podhoretz's "The Know-Nothing Bohemians" (1958) epitomizes the revulsion that *On the Road* inspired among many intellectuals. For Podhoretz, Kerouac was a primitivist whose rejection of reason for spontaneous feeling, if enacted on a mass scale, could result only in anarchy: "Being against what the Beat Generation stands for has to do with denying that incoherence is superior to precision; that ignorance is superior to knowledge; that the exercise of the mind and discrimination is a form of death. It even has to do with fighting the poisonous glorification of the adolescent in American popular culture."[36] Other commentators viewed Kerouac's ideals as more risible than revolting. Borrowing the suffix from the name of the earliest Soviet satellites, Sputnik, a *San Francisco*

Chronicle columnist coined the term *beatnik* to illustrate just how "far out" the Beats were. Lampoons of Kerouac's writing proliferated in the pages of *Mad* magazine and on television sitcoms such as *The Many Loves of Dobie Gillis,* which featured a clueless beatnik named Maynard G. Krebs, whose long-winded cadences and "hepcat" lingo parodied the rhapsodic gusto of *On the Road.*

Because such satires depicted the literary and spiritual pretensions of the Beats as spacey, sex- and drug-addled high jinks, they guaranteed that Kerouac's subsequent novels, such as *The Subterraneans* (1958) and *The Dharma Bums* (1958), received little serious attention. His inability to secure critical esteem embittered him against his reputation as the "King of the Beatniks." Although he continued writing throughout the 1960s, he retreated from the public spotlight and died on 21 October 1969 from complications of alcoholism. Despite Kerouac's innovative style and his mythic use of the road as a quest motif, many critics continue to view him as an immature artist. As with Salinger, his fascination with youth and the coming-of-age process makes it easy to stereotype him as a case of arrested development.

Unlike Salinger and Kerouac, Ralph Ellison did not reject the bildungsroman formula in favor of the picaresque. Rather, his major work, *Invisible Man,* fuses these dichotomous genres by melding the loosely organized, episodic format of *Adventures of Huckleberry Finn* with an ending characteristic of the novel of development, in which the hero achieves maturity. Two explanations suggest why Ellison preferred to resolve his character's adolescence. First, his insistence on delivering his hero to adulthood arose from a dissatisfaction with how most American literature depicted people of color. As he argues in his essay "Twentieth-Century Fiction and the Black Mask of Humanity" (1953), few authors imbued their African American characters with "the full, complex ambiguity of the human": "Too often what is presented as the American Negro (a most complex example of Western man) emerges as an oversimplified clown, a beast or an angel. Seldom is he drawn as that sensitively focused process of opposites, of good and evil, of instinct and intellect, of passion and spirituality, which great literary art has projected as the image of man."[37] Ellison aimed to redeem African American males from the demeaning connotations of inferiority embodied in the racial slur *boy.* In his fiction he strove to illustrate the educational process by which his heroes could forge their manhood and establish mature identities in a culture that denied them the status of autonomous adults. Had Ellison sought to escape the adult world in the manner of Salinger or Kerouac, his characters would remain unsophisticated and one-dimensional, thereby perpetuating rather than abolishing the "oversimplified clown" stereotype.

Secondly, Ellison was drawn to the bildungsroman out of a conviction that American literature should affirm democratic participation rather than promote escapism. He denounced the idea (perpetuated by Salinger and Kerouac) that community compromises individuality because he believed that any African American rejection of culture would continue the exclusion of minorities from mainstream society. In several critical essays Ellison singles out Hemingway as a writer who failed to overcome his alienation and thus failed to achieve a mature vision. In his 1935 African travel narrative, *Green Hills of Africa,* Hemingway encourages readers of *Adventures of Huckleberry Finn* to halt at the point at which Jim is captured and sent back into slavery: "That is the real end. The rest is just cheating."[38] For Ellison, failing to appreciate the moral significance of Huck's pledge to save Jim from slavery negates the boy's developing moral sensibility, thus reducing the novel from a powerful commentary on the individual's power to effect social change to a bucolic lark: "It is exactly this part of the action which represents the formal externalization of Huck-Twain's moral position, and if one may speak of ritual here, it is in this part of the action that the fundamental American commitment, the myth, is made manifest. Without this attempt *Huckleberry Finn* becomes the simple boy's book that many would rather it be, a fantasy born of pure delight and not really serious at all."[39] Ellison never commented on either *The Catcher in the Rye* or *On the Road,* but one suspects that he would have criticized them as "boys' books" that encourage adolescent withdrawal rather than "fundamental American commitment."

Ellison developed his literary ideals over a twenty-year apprenticeship that exposed him to a cross section of African American experience, from segregation in the Jim Crow South to the political agitation common in Northern urban centers during the Depression era. Born in Oklahoma, he attended Tuskegee Institute, an all-black university in Tuskegee, Alabama, that was founded by Booker T. Washington, whose controversial curricula trained students for working-class trades and teaching posts rather than encouraging assimilation into the white middle class. (*Invisible Man* includes a satirical portrait of both Washington and Tuskegee's conservative stance on integration.) Initially, Ellison was more interested in music than writing. A jazz aficionado, he studied trumpet and composition at Tuskegee in hopes of producing a symphony that would blend classical forms with slave spirituals and blues. In 1936, however, financial difficulties forced him to abandon his education, and he moved to New York to earn a living as a musician. There Ellison met such influential African

American authors as Langston Hughes and Richard Wright, whose novel *Native Son* (1940) and autobiography, *Black Boy* (1945), are important works depicting disaffected youth. Ellison gravitated toward the literary life, at first producing book reviews for the fledgling leftist magazine *New Challenge,* which Wright was then editing. At Wright's urging, he embarked on a series of short stories that, over the next several years, found their way into various political and literary journals, including *New Masses, Tomorrow,* and *Cross Section.*

These early stories demonstrate how Ellison viewed knowledge of African American history and folklore as the key to black maturity. "Mister Toussan" (1941) tells of two Oklahoma boys, Buster and Riley, who discover an example of racial dignity and heroism in the story of Toussaint-Louverture, the black revolutionary who led a slave revolt in 1791 on the island of Saint-Domingue (now Haiti). Significantly, Ellison dramatizes the boys' growing self-perception through images of flight, which proved to be a cornerstone symbol in the author's works: "As Buster remembered a story his teacher had told him, he saw a car rolling swiftly up the street and the pigeon stretching its wings and lifting easily into the air, skimming the top of the car in its slow, rocking flight. He watched it rise and disappear where the taut telephone wires cut the sky above the curb. Buster felt good."[40] The pigeon's soaring represents Buster's awareness that black history provides him role models that can help him rise above negative stereotypes of his people. Elsewhere, Ellison balances the flight motif against other symbols that convey the more grounded recognition that racism is not so easily eluded. In "Flying Home" (1944), Todd, a member of the vaunted Tuskegee Airmen (an elite, all-black squadron of fighter pilots in the U.S. Army Air Forces during World War II), crashes his airplane on the land of a racist Alabama farmer. While awaiting rescue, he listens to a sharecropper named Jefferson, who relates a recent dream in which St. Peter cast him out of heaven for reckless flying. (The story is known among African American folklorists as the "Colored Man in Heaven" legend.) Through this self-deprecating tale, Todd recognizes that isolating himself in his airplane does not alleviate oppression, for he must inevitably come back down to earth. His fall from the sky marks his symbolic fall into the knowledge that he must confront racism before he can overcome it. Not unlike the story of Toussaint-Louverture, Jefferson's dream exemplifies the pride and perseverance necessary to challenge racism, and it teaches Todd both the value of black folklore and the community from which he has alienated himself. For other authors, the fall from innocence is a negative initiation experience, but Ellison treats it with characteristic optimism, insisting that it is essential to growth.

The imperative of initiation is also the central theme of *Invisible Man*, which Ellison began writing in 1945 after a stint in the merchant marine. As he later recalled, "It was a rather simple story about how a young man grew up, and about the conditions which it was necessary for him to confront as he grew up." Yet, in describing his unnamed protagonist's maturation, he was also probing an important political question:

> My little book starts out by taking a young man who has an infinite capacity for making mistakes (and being a fool, I think), and who—in his *passion* for leadership, in his *passion* to prove himself within the limitations of a segregated society—blunders from one point to another until he finally realizes that American society cannot define the role of the individual, or at least not that of the *responsible* individual. For it is our fate as Americans to achieve that sense of self-consciousness through our own efforts.[41]

Guiding the young man—or *misguiding* him, as the novel suggests—are various representative African American figures, including a corrupt college president; a Harlem activist who takes to selling Sambo dolls to tourists; and Ras the Destroyer, a black nationalist whose separatist vision Ellison condemns as antidemocratic.

Framing the plot are a prologue and epilogue in which the narrator summarizes what his encounters have taught him. In the prologue he makes it clear that the invisibility he suffers is only partly owing to the "bio-chemical accident to my epidermis." The narrator has chosen to disenfranchise himself from society by holing up in an abandoned basement, where he entertains himself by diverting electricity from the local power company to light the thousand bulbs he has wired into the ceiling: "It is incorrect to assume that, because I'm invisible and live in a hole, I am dead. I am neither dead nor in a state of suspended animation. Call me Jack-the-Bear, for I am in a state of hibernation."[42] While his self-imposed exile affords him the distance necessary to assess the failures of his role models, he also realizes that alienation does not resolve his invisibility. "The hibernation is over. I must shake off the old skin and come up for breath," he declares in the epilogue. In the famous final line of the novel, the narrator offers his own experience as a model of self-discovery: "Who knows but that, on the lower frequencies, I speak for you?"[43] In this way Ellison, unlike Salinger or Kerouac, provides a resolution to the maturation experience that may help subsequent readers—regardless of color—to redress their invisibility.

Invisible Man won the National Book Award in 1953 and vaulted Ellison to the forefront of the American intelligentsia. Over the next forty years, he struggled to complete a second novel equal to the promise displayed by his first effort. Several excerpts from the book were published in

various literary journals in the 1960s and 1970s. Yet, Ellison suffered setbacks (including a 1967 house fire, which was rumored to have destroyed several hundred pages of manuscript) that precluded completion of the novel before his death in 1994. *Juneteenth* (1999), a compendium of fragments from the long-delayed project, suggests that Ellison, in attempting to re-create the complexity of *Invisible Man,* was unable to rein in his ambitions. As is the case with many writers whose debut novels garner critical acclaim, Ellison was intimidated by his early success. Rather than publish a novel with which he was dissatisfied, he devoted his energies to nonfiction and produced two seminal essay collections on race and literature, *Shadow and Act* (1964) and *Going to the Territory* (1986).

Unlike Salinger and Kerouac, Ralph Ellison insisted on ending his novel of alienated youth, *Invisible Man* (1952), with the protagonist's acceptance of the need to mature.

SALINGER'S DESCENDANTS

When *The Catcher in the Rye* was published, John Knowles was a recent Yale University graduate, working as a reporter for *The Hartford Courant* in Hartford, Connecticut. Although Knowles did not read Salinger's novel until he was well into the writing of his own debut work, he appreciated Salinger's critique of the elite world of eastern preparatory schools. Knowles was a graduate of Phillips Exeter Academy in Exeter, New Hampshire, having attended the prestigious private institution between 1942 and 1944, at the height of World War II. His memories of his education were stamped by war, in fact. As he and his fellow students approached draft age, their education was accelerated and augmented with military training to prepare them for induction into their chosen branch of service. Although Knowles (unlike Salinger) never saw combat, he did enlist in the U.S. Army Air Forces in 1944 and was training to become an aviator when the war ended the following year. Knowles's ambivalence toward the prep-school system and his anxieties about war remained with him over the next decade and a half, eventually inspiring his best-known work, the 1960 novel *A Separate Peace.*

Knowles's first published short story, "A Turn in the Sun" (1953), introduces his fictional version of Exeter, the Devon School, which also serves as the setting for *A Separate Peace*. The story, about a student whose inferiority complex culminates in suicide, also establishes themes and images that later became trademarks of Knowles's writing. As the young protagonist, Lawrence, attempts to garner popularity through athletic achievement, intramural sports come to symbolize the competitiveness in American society that creates envy and jealousy. The reckless extremes to which the boy is willing to go to prove his heroism also convey the naive faith of young people in their own invulnerability. Lawrence first comes to the attention of the upperclassmen by diving from a bridge. Yet, his subsequent efforts to ingratiate himself with them fail, and he kills himself by drowning in the river after a second jump.[44] As a vivid image of the boy's loss of hope, the fall provides Knowles with an evocative symbol of youth's inevitable initiation into disillusionment.

An even more important precursor of *A Separate Peace* is the short story "Phineas," published in *Cosmopolitan* in May 1956. Knowles not only set the story on the Devon School campus but also employed many characters and events that later became key to the novel. In particular, the story depicts the jealousy that the narrator, Gene Forrester, harbors for his roommate, Phineas, or "Finny." As with "A Turn in the Sun," the plot centers around a symbolic fall, this time from a tree instead of a bridge. As a requirement for membership in the "Super Suicide Society," Phineas, Gene, and their friends must demonstrate their fearlessness by leaping from the tree into a river below. During one test, Gene bounces the limb on which Finny stands, spilling him from the tree and breaking his leg. Gene at first attempts to avoid blame for the accident, but he soon finds himself overwhelmed by guilt. At the end of the story the young man prepares to confess his actions, realizing what it is in Phineas's nature that aroused his jealousy: "I walked down the corridor of elms descending from the infirmary to the dormitories, and at every tree I seemed to leave something I had envied in Finny—his popularity, his skill at sports, his ease. It was none of these that I had wanted from him. It was the honesty of his every move and his every thought."[45]

As a story about responsibility and integrity, "Phineas" suggests that, however painful, maturity is necessary for keeping such primal emotions as envy in check. Yet, "Phineas" lacks one important thematic element that later accounted for the popularity of *A Separate Peace* during the turbulent 1960s: war. As Knowles expanded his story to create the novel, he likened his characters' emotional development to the burgeoning pacifist movement that led people to question the need for war, suggesting that the pride that initially caused Gene to maim his friend was an expression of the same impulsive evil that leads nations into battle.

To convey his antiwar message, Knowles chose as the title a phrase from a vignette in Hemingway's *In Our Time* in which a wounded World War I soldier faces his fear of death. As Nick Adams tells a bullet-riddled Italian comrade while they wait to be carried off on stretchers for medical treatment, "You and me we've made a separate peace. Not patriots."[46] Nick discovers that abstract notions of duty and valor are meaningless in the heat of battle and that the only consolation for mortality is the courage with which one confronts it. Although in *A Separate Peace* World War II ends before Gene can be sent into battle, he likewise learns that patriotism is a shallow excuse for conflict and that humanity's true duty is to resist its hostile impulses. Such a message possessed special urgency for a generation facing its own crisis of loyalty as the conflict in Vietnam began to cost thousands of American lives. Philip D. Beidler suggests that Knowles's allusion to Hemingway located *A Separate Peace* within a tradition of literary protest that encouraged young readers to articulate their own resistance to war:

> Here for many young people was an important missing piece of history: a revelatory account of the extremely complicated things one's *fathers* and one's fathers before them may have actually felt about their twentieth-century wars—the war that was supposed to end all wars but which was quickly succeeded by the even bigger one that was supposed to be the "good" one. Here too, given the sensitivity with which such feelings and choices were represented, might be founded at least the honest beginning for a critique of the values involved in their own choices concerning a war that was starting to look like the ultimate *bad* one.[47]

This critique of values is best expressed in the closing pages of the novel, in which Gene eulogizes Finny's essential good nature. Unlike Finny, Gene and his classmates succumb to feelings of antagonism aroused by war: "All others at some point found something in themselves pitted violently against something in the world around them. With those of my year this point often came when they grasped the fact of war. When they began to feel that there was this overwhelmingly hostile thing in the world with them, then the simplicity and unity of their characters broke and they were not the same again." The passage culminates in a final arresting metaphor that compares the internal divisions afflicting his fellow students to the geopolitical consequences of military conflict: "All of them, all except Phineas, constructed at infinite cost to themselves these Maginot Lines against this enemy they thought they saw across the frontier, this enemy who never attacked that way—if he ever attacked at all; if indeed he was the enemy."[48] The Maginot line was a network of defensive fortifications that the French built along their border with Germany in the 1930s in hopes of preventing a Nazi invasion (which nevertheless occurred when the Germans outflanked the line to the north). For Knowles the line served as a symbol of the absurd reality of modern life, in which peace is deemed possible only through extensive military buildup. As the reference to the Maginot line suggests, *A Separate Peace* implies that this defensive attitude causes more internal damage than it prevents.

When *A Separate Peace* was published in February 1960, almost all reviewers compared it to *The Catcher in the Rye*. Unfortunately, the link between the novels has obscured the uniqueness of Knowles's contribution to alienated-youth fiction. Not only does his concern with pacifism and personal responsibility make his story more allegorical than Salinger's; his critique of prep-school life is also more extended. (This is perhaps not surprising, given that only the first quarter of the events recounted by Holden in *The Catcher in the Rye* take place at his school, Pencey Prep). More important, Gene achieves greater insight into his failings than Holden does. The reason for this heightened self-awareness is the greater length of retrospection that informs the narrative stance through which the action unfolds. When the reader first meets Gene, he is a grown man returning to the Devon School fifteen years after graduation. Visiting his adolescent haunts inspires memories of Finny, whose life and death are then related in an extended flashback. (In the novel Finny dies from a second fall. He trips down a flight of stairs after bolting out of a student-led inquisition into Gene's culpability in the first fall.) By presenting the story as a remembered series of events, Knowles forces readers to acknowledge two Genes in the text: the young character who is prone to jealousy and the older, more reflective narrator who has been contemplating his actions for more than a decade. One critic describes how this narrative orientation distinguishes Knowles's storytelling from Salinger's: "In *Catcher* the reader, with Holden, tends to respond to the experience with feeling rather than knowledge; understanding exists for him in the novel only by implication. In *A Separate Peace* the reader, with Gene, remains partially detached from the experience, able to examine and reflect upon it."[49]

Although *A Separate Peace* was a modest hardback success, like most alienated-youth fiction it attained its status as a classic in paperback form. With nearly eight million copies in print, the book continues to sell upwards of a quarter-million copies per year. Knowles celebrated the twentieth anniversary of his antiwar classic with a companion book called *Peace Breaks Out* (1981). Set at the Devon School shortly after the end of World War II, the novel centers around the death of a Nazi sympathizer at the hands of a student mob. Just as *A Separate Peace* questions the causes of war, *Peace Breaks Out* explores the meaning of patriotism. Yet, while the book was a critical success, readers have continued to prefer its predecessor, and Knowles has long reconciled himself to the shadow cast by his literary debut.

Whereas the similarities between *The Catcher in the Rye* and *A Separate Peace* are nominal, Sylvia Plath's *The Bell Jar* (first published in England under the pseudonym Victoria Lucas in 1963) more overtly evinces Salinger's influence. Indeed, Plath borrowed specific plot elements from Salinger's novel so that the alienation of her autobiographical heroine, Esther Greenwood, parallels Holden's. *The Bell Jar* is by no means derivative, however. As Plath's many biographers have documented, the plot follows events in its author's life during the summer of 1953, during which she served as an intern at the women's magazine *Mademoiselle*. At once ambitious and insecure, she was ill at ease with the magazine's image of prim, compliant femininity. Nor could she reconcile herself to the overbearing attempts of her mother, Aurelia, to steer her away from her literary pursuits toward more traditional women's work, such as nursing or stenography. Additionally, Plath felt unresolved anger toward her father, Otto, whose sudden death in 1940 had left her with feelings of abandonment.

Upon completing her internship, Plath returned to her hometown of Wellesley, Massachusetts, where she succumbed to a debilitating depression. A journal entry from that summer suggests her precarious condition: "You are an inconsistent and very frightened hypocrite. You wanted *time* to think, to find out about yourself, your ability to write, and now that you have it: practically 3 months godawful time, you are paralyzed, shocked, thrown into a nausea, a stasis. You are plunged so deep in a little whirlpool of negativism that you can't do more than force yourself into a rote where the simplest actions become forbidding and enormous."[50] At her mother's insistence, Plath attempted to cure her depression with electroconvulsive shock therapy, a then-popular treatment designed to reduce anxiety by inducing short-term memory loss through massive jolts of electricity to the brain. The treatment only exacerbated her instability, and on 24 August 1953 she attempted to commit suicide with an overdose of sleeping pills. After a frantic two-day search, authorities discovered her alive in the crawl space of her mother's cellar. Plath was institutionalized at McLean Hospital in Belmont, Massachusetts, under the care of the psychologist Ruth Beuscher, the inspiration for the kindly Dr. Nolan in *The Bell Jar*. Although Beuscher also prescribed shock treatments, Plath regained sufficient stability to leave the hospital shortly before Christmas 1953.

The insecurities that overwhelmed Plath may seem incomprehensible, given that her writing had already been published in prestigious magazines by the onset of her depression. Before she turned twenty, she had won first place in a *Mademoiselle* short-fiction contest with "Sunday at the Mintons'" (1952), and *Seventeen* published "Initiation" (1953). Her poems had also been accepted by such important periodicals as *The Christian Science Monitor, The Atlantic,* and *Harper's.* By any measure, Plath was a prodigy. Yet, she felt her creative instincts hampered by conventional notions of femininity, and her unwillingness to confine her ambitions to what she called "the limitations of a woman's sphere" resulted in long-running feelings of confusion, self-doubt, and rage.[51] As many critics have noted, Plath's writing documents the adolescent struggle to establish an identity independent of parental expectation and social obligation, a struggle that characterized the condition of young women in mid-twentieth-century America.

After her release from McLean Hospital, Plath resumed her studies and graduated from Smith College in 1955. A Fulbright scholarship allowed her to pursue graduate work at Cambridge University in England, where she met the poet Ted Hughes, whom she married the following year. Over the next four years, in addition to two hundred poems, Plath wrote several short stories with themes and images that foreshadow those in *The Bell Jar.* Although critics have ignored these stories, posthumously collected in *Johnny Panic and the Bible of Dreams and Other Prose Writings* (1977), they are significant because they show Plath rehearsing formative autobiographical scenes while attempting to establish her literary voice. Stories such as "Tongues of Stone" (1955) include many fragments of scenes that she later incorporated into her account of Esther's hospitalization, including an unsettling dream in which the heroine imagines strangling her sleeping mother. Unfortunately, "Tongues of Stone" also evinces Plath's habit of overdramatizing emotion by conjoining dark, disturbing metaphors: "She had gone on circling at the brink of the whirlpool, pretending to be clever and gay, and all the while these poisons were gathering

THE PERILS OF PRECOCITY

Like John Knowles, other writers of alienated-youth fiction have had their careers defined by their early success:

Charles Webb. By the late 1960s, Webb's *The Graduate* (1963) had sold a half-million paperback copies, owing to the success of the Academy Award–winning movie adaptation. Yet, his subsequent novels such as *Love, Roger* (1969) and *The Marriage of a Young Stockbroker* (1970) failed to capitalize on the appeal of *The Graduate,* and Webb sunk into literary obscurity.

Richard Fariña. A colorful figure who counted Bob Dylan and the novelist Thomas Pynchon among his best friends, Fariña wrote *Been Down So Long It Looks Like Up to Me* (1966) when he was not busy making popular folk-music records with his wife, Mimi, the younger sister of singer Joan Baez. On the way home from a publication party for his debut novel, he died in a motorcycle wreck. Although *Been Down So Long It Looks Like Up to Me* was popular among youth in the mid 1960s, interest in Fariña faded by the early 1970s, and today he is mainly remembered for his early influence on Dylan's career.

Sylvia Plath in a Smith College yearbook photo taken in the same period as the events she later recounted in *The Bell Jar* (1963)

in her body, ready to break out behind the bright, false bubbles of her eyes at any moment crying: Idiot! Impostor!"[52] Before Plath could complete *The Bell Jar,* she had to learn to restrain her descriptive powers so not to overwhelm the plot.

After several aborted attempts Plath began her novel in earnest in late 1960 as her first poetry collection, *The Colossus,* garnered favorable notices in the British press. However autobiographical her material, she was not above relying on *The Catcher in the Rye* for a sense of development and pacing. Biographer Linda Wagner-Martin suggests how Plath borrowed elements and details from Salinger's novel as she shaped her story: "In many ways, *The Catcher in the Rye* was the model Plath was using for *The Bell Jar.* Sylvia turned to it for structure, and drew on it whenever she ran out of events that seemed to fit Esther's story. Holden meets a sailor and a Cuban; so does Esther. Holden walks forty-one blocks back to his New York hotel; Esther walks forty-eight. *Catcher* has its violent and bloody suicide in James Castle's death, which becomes the suicide by hanging in *The Bell Jar.*"[53]

Despite these parallels with *The Catcher in the Rye,* Plath (not unlike Knowles) created a work that stands on its own. *The Bell Jar* explores the issue of adolescent sexuality more openly than *The Catcher in the Rye,* with Plath critiquing the double standard that excuses the promiscuity of Esther's boyfriend, Buddy Willard, but demonizes Esther's own awakening sensuality. The problem of teenage suicide is also more prominent in Plath's novel, as is the pressure of parental expectations. Most important, the depiction in *The Bell Jar* of sanatorium life inspired a subgenre of alienated-youth fiction about the treatment of female adolescents in mental-health hospitals. Popular works such as Joanne Greenberg's *I Never Promised You a Rose Garden* (1964) and the anonymous *Go Ask Alice* (1971) owe the candor with which they depict young women's emotional problems to Plath's novel.

Plath's attitude toward *The Bell Jar* suggests that she had little pre-monition of its future influence. From an early age, she regarded poetry as a more serious art form than fiction; in one well-known letter she even calls *The Bell Jar* a "potboiler," insisting that it must be published under a pseudonym so as not to distract attention from her verse.[54] More-personal motives prompted Plath to use a pseudonym, however. Among the supporting characters in *The Bell Jar* are thinly veiled versions of her college boyfriend, Dick Norton (Buddy Willard), her mother, and *Mademoiselle* staff members, none of whom are depicted with sympathy. Fearing the pain that her portrayals could cause, Plath insisted that the book never be published in her native country.

During the years in which Plath labored over *The Bell Jar,* her life was mired in domestic crises that culminated in her suicide. The birth of her two children, Frieda and Nicholas, in 1960 and 1962, respectively, inspired bouts of postpartum depression that undermined her creative confidence. In 1961 she had suffered a miscarriage that further upset her emotional balance. Most devastating, she and Hughes separated in mid 1962 after the revelation of Hughes's infidelity. In her anger, Plath produced a group of poems, posthumously published as *Ariel* (1965), that established her as a leading poet. Fusing biblical and mythological allusions with nursery-rhyme rhythms, she created a disconcerting voice that is childlike in form but whose tone boils with complex emotions. It by no means diminishes the artistry of these poems to say that they resonate with the ire of adolescence, for their common theme is frustrated growth and revolt against authority. The best-known *Ariel* poem, "Daddy," links Plath's rage at her dead father with her philandering husband in a protest against paternal controls over women, which, in a controversial move, she likens to Nazi fascism:

> I have always been scared of *you,*
>
> With your Luftwaffe, your gobbledygoo.
>
> And your neat mustache
>
> And your Aryan eye, bright blue.
>
> Panzer-man, panzer-man, O You—[55]

As a fantasy of patricide, "Daddy" presents the view that only by killing off father figures can a young woman gain freedom of identity.

Plath's artistic breakthroughs could not alleviate her depression, however, and on 11 February 1963, a month after the publication of *The Bell Jar,* she committed suicide through a combination of sleeping pills and gas poisoning. (At the time of her death, she was working on a sequel to *The Bell Jar* that was to follow Esther's life through marriage, motherhood, and a liberating divorce.) Because of the tragic circumstances of Plath's death, interest in *The Bell Jar*—as well as her poetry—is impossible to separate from interest in her life story. Under the pseudonym Victoria Lucas, the novel garnered lukewarm reviews but sold poorly. The 1966 edition attributed to Plath, in contrast, was a best-seller in England. For several years Plath's family refused to allow the publication of *The Bell Jar* in the United States, for fear of offending the acquaintances depicted in it. Harper and Row finally published the book in 1971, when a loophole in international copyright laws threatened to allow legal circulation of pirated editions. Thirty years later, *The Bell Jar* continues to sell more than a hundred thousand copies per year, and Esther remains the most prominent heroine of alienated-youth fiction.

At first glance, describing Joyce Carol Oates as a Salinger descendant may seem misinformed. Unlike Knowles and Plath, Oates's reputation as a novelist does not rest upon a single work written in the manner of *The Catcher in the Rye*.[56] In fact, diversity has been the term most often used to characterize her writing over a long career distinguished by more than seventy volumes of prose, poetry, and criticism. Nevertheless, Oates merits a place among important authors of alienated-youth fiction for the simple reason that the unifying element of her work is young women's coming-of-age experiences. According to Ellen G. Friedman, "Oates has brought to life an enormous cast of female characters who come from virtually every station in life. She has perhaps the largest gallery of adolescent girls of any contemporary writer."[57] Most notable among this gallery are sixteen-year-old Connie, the heroine of "Where Are You Going, Where Have You Been?" (1966), one of the most anthologized short stories of recent decades, and Maureen Wendell in *them* (1969), Oates's best-known novel. In both cases, Oates's adolescents are immersed in hostile environments fraught with abuse, rape, and incest against which they must steel themselves if they are to survive to adulthood.

Like Plath, Oates was a writing prodigy. During her undergraduate years at Syracuse University, she won the 1959 *Mademoiselle* fiction contest and published short stories in prestigious literary journals. She was barely in her mid twenties when she published her first story collection, *By the North Gate* (1963), and her debut novel, *With Shuddering Fall* (1964). In March 1966 she was at work on her second novel, *A Garden of Earthly Delights* (1967), when she read a *Life* magazine article about an Arizona serial killer who preyed on teenage girls. Dubbed "The Pied Piper of Tucson" by the media, Charles Schmid had seduced three young women, luring them from their homes by aping the leather-jacketed charisma of Marlon Brando and James Dean.[58] The killer's story became the basis for

"Where Are You Going, Where Have You Been?" in which a rebel hot-rodder with the ironic name of Arnold Friend seduces the gullible Connie with contrived bad-boy gestures and talk.

The story has been interpreted variously as a naturalistic tale of rape, a Gothic seduction fantasy, and an allegory of good and evil. Yet, it might best be read as a commentary on American youth culture's habit of glamorizing risky behavior. Like most teenagers, Connie finds her suburban upbringing boring, and her only escape from monotony is the rock music that pours from the radio, inspiring "trashy daydreams" of romance and rebellion. Music is a major motif throughout the story. A passage describing the diner that Connie and her friends frequent conveys its role in teens' lives: "They sat at the counter and crossed their legs at the ankles, their thin shoulders rigid with excitement, and listened to the music that made everything so good: the music was always in the background, like music at a church service; it was something to depend upon."[59] Connie is so infatuated with the music that she likens the thrill of being pursued by young men to its illicit throb: "All the boys fell back and dissolved into a single face that was not even a single face but an idea, a feeling, mixed up with the urgent pounding of the music and the humid night air of July."[60] As Oates portrays it, rock music provides young people the rush of excitement that their environment curbs.

Through the character of Friend, Oates shows how the allure of rebellion can be manipulated. Everything about Friend is contrived, from his faux James Dean wardrobe to his souped-up roadster to his penchant for speaking in out-of-date slang. Yet, while Connie recognizes that he is no teenager, his image continues to attract her. However aware she may be of the danger that Friend represents, she allows herself to be drawn from her parents' home for a joyride that, as Oates implies, will end with her rape and/or murder. As if to emphasize the relevance of the story to 1960s youth culture, Oates replaced the original title ("Death and the Maiden") with a title inspired by "It's All Over Now, Baby Blue," a 1965 song by Bob Dylan, whose evocative tone Oates was attempting to emulate. (Oates also dedicated the story to Dylan). As such, "Where Are You Going, Where Have You Been?" has been read as a parable on the naiveté of the 1960s generation, whose flirtations with risk mired many in drug abuse and promiscuity. One need not analyze the story only in its historical setting, however. In a broader sense it challenges young people of every generation to be aware of the dangers that lurk in the adult world.

After "Where Are You Going, Where Have You Been?" Oates completed *A Garden of Earthly Delights* and a third novel, *Expensive People* (1968), both of which also feature adolescent protagonists. During the late summer of 1967, she and her husband, Raymond Smith, were living in Detroit when a race riot erupted. Drawing on her own memories of growing up poor, Oates embarked on a novel that examines the anger and futility associated with coming of age in an environment offering little hope for the future. To emphasize her characters' alienation from the American dream, Oates chose a simple, one-word title for the book: *them*. As she later explained, "The title *them* came to me as inspiration, with its sly suggestion that there is in fact a *them* and an *us;* in our democratic nation, a category of *them* at whom we can gaze with pity, awe, revulsion, moral superiority, as if across an abyss; a *them* not entirely civilized, yet eager to 'rise' in class; a *them* who constitute the ideal, impressionable, ever-naive and ever-hopeful consumers of American dream-products."[61] By granting her impoverished adolescents the psychological complexity denied them in most fiction, she set out to prove to readers that "them" is indeed "us."

Despite its epic ambitions, *them* is an initiation novel built around dramatic episodes documenting the protagonists' loss of innocence. The pattern of destroying characters' dreams begins in the explosive opening scenes, in which sixteen-year-old Loretta Botsford is forced to watch her brother murder her boyfriend in a fit of incestuous jealousy. Howard Wendell, the policeman who investigates the killing, seduces Loretta; for inexplicable reasons, she marries him and quickly produces two children, Jules and Maureen. When her husband later dies in an industrial accident, Loretta sinks deeper into poverty, surviving through favors from shadowy men who exploit her vulnerability. During her adolescence, Maureen suffers an equally horrific fate. After one of Loretta's boyfriends rapes her, she retreats into a comalike state and remains in bed for two years. Catatonia is an extreme version of the withdrawal to which Oates's female characters must surrender in order to survive. As Maureen explains, "Inside my body and face I am an old woman, not even a woman or a man but just an old person. I want to marry a man and fall in love and be protected by him. I am ready to fall in love. But my heart is hard and my body hard, frozen."[62]

Among the Wendell family members, only Jules emerges with his Romantic ideals intact. Despite merciless police beatings and an attempt by his lover, Nadine, to murder him, the young man transcends the defeat surrounding him to become a leading subversive in an underground anarchist movement. Jules's notoriety is cemented by his actions in the Detroit riots: he kills a policeman, thus becoming a hero to the city's radical fringe. As many critics have noted, the conclusion of *them* subverts the endings that traditionally distinguish the male and female bildungsroman. Although Maureen marries a middle-class college professor, Oates casts doubts on her claims that she is happy. To gain the financial security she craves, she has resorted to stealing her husband from his first wife. No sooner are the couple married than Maureen cuts all ties with her mother, insisting that she can no longer abide the squalor associated with her youth. As for Jules, although he is a wanted man, his act of violence proves liberating, for it allows him to escape the cruelty of Detroit. Indeed, in the closing scene Jules sets out for California, where he will adopt a new identity and begin a new life.

Upon publication, *them* proved to be both a commercial and critical success, climbing the best-seller lists and winning Oates the 1970 National Book Award in fiction. In the years following this achievement, her portfolio of alienated youth has continued to expand to include several more memorable characters. The much-anthologized story "How I Contemplated the World from the Detroit House of Correction and Began My Life Over Again" (1970) and novels such as *Childwold* (1976) and *Marya: A Life* (1986) include strong female protagonists who survive the perils of adolescence by resisting the withdrawal that endangers both Connie and Maureen. In fact, scholars have argued that more-recent works by Oates,

Joyce Carol Oates in the mid 1960s, shortly before she wrote "Where Are You Going, Where Have You Been?" (1966)

such as *Foxfire: Confessions of a Girl Gang* (1993), about a group of aggressive young women who refuse to be victimized by male violence, redress the passivity of the female characters in *them* and "Where Are You Going, Where Have You Been?" This feminist updating of her earlier fiction has not dimmed the controversy that surrounds Oates. When the Milton, Ontario, school system included *Foxfire* in its high-school curriculum in 1997, parents strenuously denounced the violence and sexual content in the novel and campaigned to ban it.[63]

Such censorship incidents have hardly diminished Oates's reputation—or her productivity. As she publishes at least one, if not two, novels per year, she continues to explore the teenager's lot in life. Her fiction provides adolescents with an important resource for conceptualizing their divided loyalties to family and freedom on the one hand and fun and danger on the other. Alienated-youth fiction endures, in fact, because its writers encourage young readers to acknowledge both the thrills and risks of growing into their own identities. As Oates herself might say, the author's challenge is to ply his or her literary skills to urge teenagers to account for what they have learned from where they have gone and where they have been.

NOTES

1. F. Scott Fitzgerald, "The Author's Apology," in *F. Scott Fitzgerald on Authorship*, edited by Matthew J. Bruccoli with Judith S. Baughman (Columbia: University of South Carolina Press, 1996), p. 35.

2. W. Tasker Witham, *The Adolescent in the American Novel, 1920–1960* (New York: Ungar, 1964), p. 18.

3. See Burton Rascoe, "A Youth in the Saddle," in *F. Scott Fitzgerald: The Critical Reception*, edited by Jackson R. Bryer (New York: Franklin, 1978), pp. 3–4.

4. Mark Twain, "The Story of the Good Little Boy Who Did Not Prosper," in *Collected Tales, Sketches, Speeches, & Essays*, edited by Louis J. Budd, volume 1 (New York: Library of America, 1992), p. 376.

5. William Dean Howells, "My Mark Twain," in *A Selected Edition of W. D. Howells*, volume 32: *Literary Friends and Acquaintance: A Personal Retrospective of American Authorship*, edited by David F. Hiatt and Edwin H. Cady (Bloomington: Indiana University Press, 1968), pp. 257–258.

6. Twain, quoted in Hamlin Hill, "The Composition and Structure of *Tom Sawyer*," *American Literature*, 32 (January 1961): 386.

7. Twain, *The Adventures of Tom Sawyer* (New York: Penguin, 1994), p. 247.

8. Twain to Howells, 5 July 1875, in *Mark Twain–Howells Letters: The Correspondence of Samuel L. Clemens and William D. Howells, 1872–1910*, edited by Henry Nash Smith and William M. Gibson, volume 1 (Cambridge, Mass.: Harvard University Press, 1960), p. 91.

9. Twain, *The Adventures of Huckleberry Finn* (New York: Penguin, 1994), p. 283.

10. Ibid., p. 386.

11. Quoted in Steven Mailloux, *Rhetorical Power* (Ithaca, N.Y.: Cornell University Press, 1989), p. 125.

12. Fitzgerald, *This Side of Paradise* (New York: Scribners, 1920), p. 282.

13. Frederick Hoffman, *The Twenties: American Writing in the Postwar Decade* (New York: Viking, 1955), pp. 107–108.

14. Fitzgerald, *The Beautiful and Damned* (New York: Scribners, 1922), p. 169.

15. Fitzgerald, "Basil and Cleopatra," in *The Basil and Josephine Stories*, edited by Bryer and John Kuehl (New York: Scribners, 1973), p. 207.

16. Fitzgerald, "Emotional Bankruptcy," in *The Basil and Josephine Stories*, pp. 326–327.

17. Van Wyck Brooks, *The Writer in America* (New York: Dutton, 1953), p. 71.

18. Ibid., p. 69.

19. Fitzgerald, "Winter Dreams," in *The Short Stories of F. Scott Fitzgerald: A New Collection*, edited by Bruccoli (New York: Scribners, 1989), pp. 235–236.

20. Ernest Hemingway, "The End of Something," in *The Complete Short Stories of Ernest Hemingway* (New York: Scribners, 1987), p. 82.

21. Barton C. Friedberg, "The Cult of Adolescence in American Fiction," *Nassau Review*, 1 (Spring 1964): 27.

22. Malcolm Cowley, *Exile's Return: A Literary Odyssey of the 1920s* (New York: Viking, 1951), pp. 225–226.

23. Hemingway, *The Sun Also Rises* (New York: Scribners, 1926), p. 247.

24. J. D. Salinger, "Slight Rebellion Off Madison," *New Yorker*, 22 (21 December 1946): 84.

25. Warren French, *J. D. Salinger, Revisited* (Boston: Twayne, 1988), p. 37; see also Salinger, "I'm Crazy," *Collier's*, 116 (22 December 1945): 36, 48, 51.

26. For a discussion of Salinger and the *New Yorker* school of fiction, see Maxwell Geismar, *American Moderns: From Rebellion to Conformity* (New York: Hill & Wang, 1958), p. 197.

27. Paul Alexander, *Salinger: A Biography* (Los Angeles: Renaissance, 1999), p. 183.

28. Irving Howe, "More Reflections on the Glass Menagerie," *New York Times Book Review*, 7 April 1963, p. 5.

29. Bruce Bawer, *Diminishing Fictions: Essays on the Modern Novel and Its Critics* (St. Paul, Minn.: Gray Wolf Press, 1988), pp. 181–182.

30. Jack Kerouac, "Lamb, No Lion," in *Good Blonde and Others*, edited by Donald Allen (San Francisco: Grey Fox Press, 1993), p. 51.

31. Ann Charters, *Kerouac: A Biography* (New York: St. Martin's Press, 1994), p. 289.

32. Tim Hunt, *Kerouac's Crooked Road: Development of a Fiction* (Hamden, Conn.: Archon, 1981; revised, Berkeley: University of California Press, 1996), p. 77.

33. Truman Capote, quoted in Gerald Nicosia, *Memory Babe: A Critical Biography of Jack Kerouac* (New York: Grove, 1983), p. 357.

34. Kerouac, *On the Road* (New York: Viking, 1957), p. 173.

35. Kerouac, "Essentials of Spontaneous Prose," in *Good Blonde and Others*, p. 69.

36. Norman Podhoretz, "The Know-Nothing Bohemians," *Partisan Review*, 25 (Spring 1958): 318.

37. Ralph Ellison, "Twentieth-Century Fiction and the Black Mask of Humanity," in *The Collected Essays of Ralph Ellison*, edited by John F. Callahan (New York: Modern Library, 1995), p. 82.

38. Hemingway, *Green Hills of Africa* (New York: Scribners, 1935), p. 22.

39. Ellison, "Society, Morality and the Novel," in *The Collected Essays of Ralph Ellison*, p. 719.

40. Ellison, "Mister Toussan," in *Flying Home and Other Stories*, edited by Callahan (New York: Random House, 1996), pp. 25–26.

41. Ellison, "On Initiation Rites and Power," in *The Collected Essays of Ralph Ellison*, pp. 528–529.

42. Ellison, *Invisible Man* (New York: Modern Library, 1992), p. 9.

43. Ibid., pp. 502, 503.

44. See John Knowles, "A Turn in the Sun," in *Phineas: Six Stories* (New York: Random House, 1968), pp. 1–17.

45. Knowles, "Phineas," in *Phineas: Six Stories,* p. 117.

46. Hemingway, "Chapter VI," in *The Complete Short Stories of Ernest Hemingway,* p. 105.

47. Philip D. Beidler, *Scriptures for a Generation: What We Were Reading in the '60s* (Athens: University of Georgia Press, 1994), p. 122.

48. Knowles, *A Separate Peace* (New York: Macmillan, 1960), pp. 194, 196.

49. Ronald Weber, "Narrative Method in *A Separate Peace,*" *Studies in Short Fiction,* 3 (Fall 1965): 68.

50. Sylvia Plath, *The Unabridged Journals of Sylvia Plath,* edited by Karen V. Kukil (New York: Anchor, 2000), p. 185.

51. Plath to Aurelia Plath, 4 August 1951, in *Letters Home: Correspondence, 1950–1963,* edited by Aurelia Schober Plath (New York: Harper & Row, 1975), p. 72.

52. Plath, "Tongues of Stone," in *Johnny Panic and the Bible of Dreams: Short Stories, Prose, and Diary Excerpts,* edited by Ted Hughes (New York: Harper & Row, 1979), p. 276.

53. Linda Wagner-Martin, *Sylvia Plath: A Biography* (New York: St. Martin's Press, 1987), p. 187.

54. Plath to Warren Plath, 18 October 1962, in *Letters Home,* p. 472.

55. Plath, "Daddy," in *The Collected Poems,* edited by Hughes (New York: Harper & Row, 1981), p. 223.

56. Oates's biographer reports that she once pursued Salinger through the Dartmouth College library in hopes of meeting him, but her few public comments on him have tended to be curt and negative. See Greg Johnson, *Invisible Writer: A Biography of Joyce Carol Oates* (New York: Dutton, 1998), p. 76.

57. Ellen G. Friedman, "Joyce Carol Oates," in *Modern American Women Writers,* edited by Elaine Showalter, Lea Baechler, and A. Walton Litz (New York: Scribners, 1991), p. 355.

58. Don Moser, "The Pied Piper of Tuscon: He Cruised in a Golden Car, Looking for the Action," in *"Where Are You Going, Where Have You Been?"* edited by Showalter (New Brunswick, N.J.: Rutgers University Press, 1994), pp. 51–66.

59. Joyce Carol Oates, "Where Are You Going, Where Have You Been?" in *Where Are You Going, Where Have You Been? Selected Early Stories* (Princeton, N.J.: Ontario Review Press, 1993), pp. 122–123.

60. Ibid., p. 121.

61. Oates, afterword to *them* (New York: Modern Library, 2000), p. 541.

62. Oates, *them,* p. 332.

63. David Frum, "It's Not the Parents Who Are the Aggressors against Freedom: Teachers Shouldn't Be Allowed to Abuse the Ideals of Literature and Learning," *Toronto Financial Post,* 15 February 1997, p. 28.

THE LITERARY RELEVANCE OF
ALIENATED-YOUTH FICTION

INTRODUCTION

In a 1958 essay in *The New Leader* literary critic Leslie A. Fiedler makes the unconventional assertion that he prefers the amoral, antihero youth of novels such as William Faulkner's *The Hamlet* (1940) and Vladimir Nabokov's *Lolita* (1958) to Huckleberry Finn, Holden Caulfield, and similarly sympathetic ne'er-do-wells. The reason is that Huck and Holden (whom Fiedler calls "Good Bad Boys") exemplify a "cult of the child" that caters to an unhealthy fear of the demands of adulthood. According to Fiedler, "*Lolita* and the tradition to which it belongs represent a resolve to reassess the innocence of the child, to reveal it as a kind of moral idiocy, a dangerous freedom from the restraints of culture and custom, a threat to order." By corrupting their elders, villainous teens force readers to question why Western culture idealizes youth while denigrating maturity: "In the place of the sentimental dream of childhood, writers like Faulkner and Nabokov have been creating for us a nightmare in which the child is no longer raped, strangled or seduced, but is himself (better herself!) rapist, murderer, and seducer. Their books reflect a growing awareness on the part of us all that our society has tended (at least aspired) to become not a conspiracy against the child—but a conspiracy against the adult." In a concluding passage Fiedler dramatizes the need to end this literary "Age of Innocence" by calling for the violent overthrow of the "Good Bad Boy": "The gods of such an age, if not yet dead, must be killed however snub-nosed, freckle-faced or golden-haired they may be."[1] Despite the apparent blood lust of Fiedler's prose, his concern is valid: Why does so much literature—alienated-youth fiction in particular—lament the passage of youth?

Fiedler's essay is the best known of many attempts since the 1950s to assess the literary relevance of alienated-youth fiction. *Relevance* refers to the reasons that novels and short stories in the tradition of J. D. Salinger's *The Catcher in the Rye* have remained popular among scholars, students, and general audiences who teach, analyze, and, in some cases,

Illustrations from nineteenth-century novels in the bildungsroman tradition, such as this one by Hablot K. Browne for Charles Dickens's *David Copperfield* (1850), suggest how Victorian writers portrayed adolescents as aspiring adults rather than as members of a distinct, age-specific subculture.

even emulate them. These reasons are at once literary, historical, and sociological. They involve enduring, centuries-old myths about lost innocence as well as the rampant concern in the post–World War II era that teenagers were prematurely exposed to sex, drugs, and violence. Alienated-youth fiction also owes its prestige to its privileged place in the classroom, where teachers use it to encourage young people to contemplate the problems of growing up. One can divide the significance of alienated-youth fiction into three categories: the literary traditions from which the genre emerged, the myths of innocence and aging that it dramatizes, and the modern psychological and sociological conceptions of adolescence that it has both inspired and reflected.

LITERARY TRADITIONS

The most obvious reason for studying alienated-youth fiction is that it incorporates several traditional narrative types. In particular, authors blend elements from three older genres: the quest narrative, the picaresque tale, and the bildungsroman. The first and oldest of these forms, the quest narrative, concerns a journey that the hero must undertake to return his culture to a mythic golden age from which it has fallen. Among the oldest of quest stories are ancient Greek epics such as the *Odyssey,* in which the hero, Odysseus, undergoes a series of marvelous adventures while struggling to return to his homeland and quell the instability that has arisen in his absence. Later variations include chivalric romances from the medieval age, such as Chrétien de Troyes's *Perceval* (circa 1181–1190) and the anonymous *Sir Gawain and the Green Knight* (circa 1375), which fuse Arthurian legends of the knights of the Round Table with biblical imagery. In these works a knight sets out to accomplish some task deemed vital to maintaining order in the kingdom he serves. Along the way, he faces a series of temptations that challenge him to uphold his moral or spiritual beliefs. Through his commitment the quester not only redeems his culture but also learns to cope with human fallibility. In many quest narratives an object associated with a holy ritual or sacrament embodies the moral order that the hero seeks to preserve. Chivalric romances, for example, usually involve attempts to recover the holy grail, the chalice from the Last Supper with which the apostle John caught the blood of the crucified Christ.

The influence of the quest narrative on alienated-youth fiction is most obvious whenever protagonists journey across a vast spatial expanse in pursuit of something or someone just beyond their grasp. As Janis P. Stout notes, "The quest may be for spiritual enlightenment,

THE CATCHER IN THE RYE AS QUEST NARRATIVE

Arthur Heiserman and James E. Miller Jr. compare Holden Caulfield to an array of epic heroes, from Ulysses and Aeneas to modern protagonists such as Stephen Dedalus and Leopold Bloom (from James Joyce's *Ulysses*, 1922):

"It is clear that J. D. Salinger's *The Catcher in the Rye* belongs to an ancient and honorable tradition, perhaps the most profound in western fiction. The tradition is the central pattern of the epic. . . . It is, of course, the tradition of the Quest. . . .

"There are at least two sorts of quests, depending upon the object sought. Stephen Dedalus sought a reality uncontaminated by home, country, church; . . . he knew that social institutions tend to force what is ingenious in a man into their own channels. He sought the opposite of security. . . . Bloom, on the other hand, was already an outcast and sought acceptance by an Ithaca and a Penelope which despised him. And, tragically enough, he also sought an Icarian son who fled the very maze which he, Bloom, desired to enter. So the two kinds of quests, the one seeking acceptance and stability, the other precisely the opposite, differ significantly. . . .

"The protagonist of *The Catcher in the Rye,* Holden Caulfield, seems to be engaged in both sorts of quests at once; he needs to go home and he needs to leave it. So Salinger translates an old tradition into contemporary terms. The phoniness of American society forces Holden Caulfield to leave it, but he is seeking nothing less than stability and love. . . ."

Arthur Heiserman and James E. Miller Jr.

From "J. D. Salinger: Some Crazy Cliff," *Western Humanities Review,* 10 (Spring 1956): 129-137.

Truth, for a lost father, for an artistic or craftly secret, for social establishment, but in any case it is likely to involve a quest for the quester himself, through the discovery of selfhood or self-definition."[2] In this sense, travel is an emblem of personal growth, with the quester's physical movement from place to place symbolizing the journey through the life cycle. Interestingly, adolescent questers often come to question the viability of their goals rather than realize them. As Stout suggests, "Because the goal of a quest tends to be absolute or ultimate, it comes to appear, in a limited and skeptical world, impossible to attain. Yet aspiration for the unattainable is in itself an exalted moral condition, worthy of the hero's aspiration. Hence the questing process becomes both means and end."[3]

Nominally, picaresque fiction also concerns a journey. Unlike in the quest narrative, the hero's travels are rambling rather than organized, for there is no goal directing his movement. Indeed, the protagonist rarely benefits from any significant development or insight. A picaresque narrative involves the main character's encounters with various representatives of society, most of whom are revealed to be corrupt and hypocritical. The hero serves as a perspective through which the ills that the other characters embody can be observed. Because of the aimlessness of the journey, the structure of a picaresque tale is episodic rather than sequential. Each scene is a self-contained story rather than a point of dramatic action in a developing plot. The form is also distinct in style from the quest narrative, depicting events in a realistic rather than an idealized fashion. Most importantly, picaresque heroes differ from their chivalric counterparts in being outlaws rather than representatives of aristocratic nobility. (In six-teenth-century Spain, where the picaresque story first emerged, the word *picaro* meant *rogue*). In such works as the anonymous *La Vida da Lazarillo de Tormes* (1554) and Daniel Defoe's *Moll Flanders* (1722) the protagonists are petty criminals who turn to stealing, forgery, or prostitution while eking out an existence on the margins of culture. Because such works celebrate the main characters' rascality as the means by which they survive, the picaresque genre is often satirical. In fact, picaresque works often ridicule the way quest narratives depict humanity as worthy of redemption.

As W. Tasker Witham observes, many teenage picaros of post–World War II American fiction resemble their literary ancestors because their criminal adventures are born of need rather than malice. Such notable picaresque novels as Saul Bellow's *The Adventures of Augie March* (1953) and Nelson Algren's *A Walk on the Wild Side* (1956) attribute adolescent deviance to the hero's impoverished upbringing: "Most of the adolescent nomads in all of these novels steal and cheat not merely for the excitement of defying laws and con-ventions (although this is usually a contributory motive) but as a means of providing the necessities of life. Thus dishonesty is made necessary and hence forgivable."[4] At the same time, other critics have recognized that alienated-youth fiction adopts the roguery of the picaresque tradition in order to celebrate the American ethos of rug-ged individualism. Characters such as Dean Moriarty and Sal Paradise in Jack Kerouac's *On the Road* take up the vagabond life, defying laws and customs at every turn, to forge their identities without concern for conformity. In doing so they enact the American myth of the soli-tary self, the "I" who remains unattached to either family or commu-nity in the name of self-reliance and self-determination. Young American picaros are thus apt to be likened to frontiersmen, pioneers, cowboys, drifters, and hoboes, figures whose isolation from the main-stream grants them absolute freedom and independence.

Even more than the quest narrative or the picaresque tale, critics regard alienated-youth fiction as an outgrowth of the bildungs-roman tradition. *Bildungsroman* is a German word most often trans-lated as the "novel of development." At its most basic the genre traces the growth of young protagonists as they rise above antagonistic social circumstances to establish themselves in a profession. A bil-dungsroman begins with an overview of a troubled childhood fraught with parental conflict and poverty, followed by an escape to a city, where the dangers of urban life threaten to undermine the hero's intuitive sense of right and wrong. Other challenges include distinguishing true love from adolescent lust, committing to a career or an artistic calling, and overcoming personal faults and foibles. As Jerome Hamilton Buckley notes, the bildungsroman concludes with the hero's relinquishing the narcissism of youth and shouldering the burden of maturity: "Each protagonist experiences privileged moments of insight, epiphanies, spots of time, when the reality of things breaks through the fog of delusion. And each then feels a responsibility for change of heart and conduct. For each is what we should now call 'inner-directed': each is guided by a sense of duty to the self and to others."[5]

The prototype of the bildungsroman, Johann Wolfgang von Goethe's *Wilhelm Meister's Apprenticeship* (1794–1796), appeared during the Romantic movement, a period in the history of the arts emphasizing individualism, introspection, and self-expression. As the story of a foppish young man coming of age while traveling with a theatrical troupe, *Wilhelm Meister's Apprenticeship* established many of the formative conventions of the genre, including the protagonist's moody temperament. As Romanticism fell out of fashion in the mid nineteenth century, a succeeding generation of writers adopted the form to critique the lifestyle of the bourgeoisie (the middle class). Foremost among this generation was the Victorian novelist Charles Dickens, whose most accomplished works in the bildungsroman form, *David Copperfield* (1850) and *Great Expectations* (1861), explore the idea of middle-class gentility. As Dickens's young men rise from their lower-class backgrounds to reap the rewards of professional success and affluence, they learn that belonging to the middle class does not make them immune to pride or envy. Although Dickensian heroes look back with nostalgia on the naiveté of youth, they are nevertheless committed to the responsibility and integrity that maturity entails. As Patricia Meyer Spacks notes, "Novelists of the nineteenth century often reveal a conviction that growing up is regrettable as well as necessary. Moralists express anger at the reprehensible aspects of adolescence; novelists stress the sadness of relinquishment."[6]

When analyzing the literary affinities between alienated-youth fiction and the bildungsroman, critics examine how contemporary authors allude to the practitioners of this older form in order to contrast modern youth with their nineteenth-century predecessors. In *The Catcher in the Rye,* for example, Holden Caulfield makes two references to Dickens, including a prominent one in the opening line: "If you really want to hear about it, the first thing you'll probably want to know is where I was born, and what my lousy childhood was like, and how my parents were occupied and all before they had me, and all that David Copperfield kind of crap, but I don't feel like going into it, if you want to know the truth" (3). Few critics believe that Salinger shares Holden's quasi-profane disregard for Dickens's young hero. (In fact, several have suggested that Salinger pays tribute to Dickens by emulating his propensity for eccentric character names, with *Caulfield* echoing *Copperfield*.) Rather, such allusions stress the inapplicability in the modern age of the model of maturation found in the bildungsroman. If, as Spacks suggests, the traditional novel of development depicts growing up as regrettable but necessary, alienated-youth fiction refrains from accepting that necessity and does not show the heroes crossing the threshold of maturity, as Dickens's protagonists do at the conclusion of his novels. For this reason, one often finds *The Catcher in the Rye* or *The Bell Jar* described as an "anti-" or "aborted" bildungsroman.

Critics also recognize that the maturation process outlined in the nineteenth-century bildungsroman reflects the experience of white European men. Accordingly, modern commentators now explore how sociological variables such as gender and race affect the coming-of-age experience of young women and minorities. Linda Wagner-Martin argues, for instance, that Sylvia Plath's *The Bell Jar* employs the conventions of the novel of development in order to call attention to the limited opportunities available to women. These limitations are even conveyed by Plath's title, which distinguishes her narrative from novels of development by Dickens and the Irish author James Joyce: "*The Bell Jar,* with its sinister implications of airlessness, imprisonment, and isolation, is a far remove from *Great Expectations;* and in its most positive scenes cannot approach the ringing self-confidence of [Joyce's] *A Portrait of the Artist as a Young Man,* although it is surely that novel writ female."[7] Similarly, in a study of the black bildungsroman, Greta LeSeur explores why African American authors do not idealize childhood innocence in the manner of white authors: "African-American writers experience a different kind of exile. They are exiles in their 'own' country, and their motive for writing a *Bildungsroman* is not to rediscover a 'lost' domain or recapture an 'experience,' but to expose those conditions that robbed the writer of a memorable and happy childhood."[8]

The distinctions among the quest narrative, the picaresque tale, and the bildungsroman often blur together in practice. A cursory reading of the critical response to *The Catcher in the Rye* reveals that

Salinger has been celebrated for writing a quest narrative, a picaresque novel, *and* a bildungsroman. This inconsistency does not mean that critics are imprecise in applying these labels. Rather, multiple categorization reflects the reality that authors blend elements from various narrative forms. Thus, while Sal and Dean's journeys in *On the Road* do possess a spiritual dimension that recalls the quest, the overall episodic nature of the plot, coupled with the characters' vision of themselves as rebels, links Kerouac's novel to the picaresque narrative. The most useful criticism of alienated-youth fiction does not attempt to shoehorn a text into a particular definition of a genre. Rather, it recognizes that youth-oriented stories represent a confluence of these categories.

MYTHIC AND THEMATIC RELEVANCE

Critics deem alienated-youth fiction significant because it evokes ancient myths about youth and aging. Foremost among these myths is the fall from innocence occasioned by youth's initiation into adulthood. Adam and Eve's expulsion from the Garden of Eden is the best-known version of this fall. According to Frederick W. Dillistone, the biblical couple's passage from pristine grace into mortal suffering has proved a durable metaphor for growing up because the story encapsulates the struggle to reconcile human potential with human imperfection: "The fear of falling is one of the earliest forms of anxiety in the human psyche, and it is never fully overcome. In a certain sense all life is falling—a falling before and away from one's aspirations, one's ideals, one's hopes, and one's intentions."[9] Artists equate adolescence with the Fall because maturation is the period of life in which one must begin to cope with this sense of "falling short." Christian theology further teaches that Adam and Eve's sin is a *felix culpa,* or "fortunate fault," because the result is knowledge of the human fallibility that demonstrates humanity's dependence on God's blessing. By extension, adulthood is said to represent a beneficial fall from youthful delusions of grandeur to a more balanced acceptance of one's limited power over life.

When critics attempt to account for the peculiar resistance to growing up found in alienated-youth fiction, they often liken it to the literature of the Romantic era. In this period, writers such as Goethe, Jean-Jacques Rousseau, and William Wordsworth argued that youth should resist the Fall and strive to retain their innocence. These authors idealized childhood as the stage of life at which one is most in harmony with nature, which they saw as a source of divinity that could inspire the imagination to attain wisdom. In their view, maturation diminishes the imagination's relationship with nature as the socialization process encourages conformity to the world of human affairs. Romantic literature thus depicts the journey of life as a continual falling away from the spiritual origins of life. In "Ode: Intimations of Immortality" (1807) Wordsworth records the diminution that aging causes. He describes the splendor that accompanies newborn children into the world: "trailing clouds of glory do we come / From God, who is our home: / Heaven lies about us in our infancy!" Although adolescence casts "Shades of the prison-house" upon young people, they are nevertheless "Nature's Priest" because they retain reverence for the godly light of wisdom. By adulthood, however, that reverence has eroded, alienating the individual from his spirituality: "At length the Man perceives it die away, / And fade into the light of common day." A line from the epigraph to the ode (from another of Wordsworth's poems, "My Heart Leaps Up When I Behold" [1802]) encapsulates the Romantic belief that youth, because they are more attuned to nature, are the spiritual elders of adults: "The Child is father of the Man."[10]

The story of the Fall has been especially influential in American literature, where it serves as a motif for dramatizing characters' sudden awareness of the gap between the promise and the reality of the American dream. R.W.B. Lewis's *The American Adam: Innocence, Tragedy, and Tradition in the Nineteenth Century* (1955) is one of many critical works to present the argument that Adam and Eve's expulsion from the Garden of Eden provides writers with a symbol of America's fall from innocence:

> The "matter of Adam" is the primary stuff by which the American novelist has managed to articulate his sense of the form and pressure of experience. Most American novels share the same basic plot. They involve the ritualistic trials of the young innocent, liberated from family and social history or bereft of them; advancing hopefully into a complex world he knows not of; radically affecting that world and radically affected by it; defeated, perhaps destroyed—in various versions of the recurring anecdote hanged, beaten, shot, betrayed, abandoned—but leaving his mark upon the world.[11]

Adamic heroes resist initiation into adulthood by setting off on a journey. Their inevitable failure to preserve their prelapsarian (before the Fall) innocence suggests that paradise lost cannot be regained. Accordingly, these heroes symbolize the burden of the postlapsarian (after the Fall) Adam, who must cope with his human fallibility. Significantly, in the final chapter of *The American Adam* Lewis explicitly locates alienated-youth fiction of the 1950s in this Adamic tradition: "In most of what I take to be the truest and most fully engaged American fiction after the second war, the newborn or self-breeding or orphaned hero is plunged again and again, for his own good and for ours, into the spurious, disruptive rituals of the actual world. We may mention especially *Invisible Man,* by Ralph Ellison; J. D. Salinger's *The Catcher in the Rye;* and *The Adventures of Augie March,* by Saul Bellow."[12]

While Lewis examines the symbolic legacy of the Fall in American literature, he does not address the question of why so many postwar writers cast their young heroes as teenagers rather than prepubescent children, as was the tradition in Romantic literature. Taking up this question was Ihab Hassan, whose *Radical Innocence: The Contemporary American Novel* (1961) marked an effort to rehabilitate the "Good Bad Boy" after the critical assaults of Fiedler. According to Hassan, adolescents make for compelling protagonists because their moral passage embodies the larger struggle of America itself to come to grips with its direction in history: "The life of the adolescent or youth still in his teens mirrors clearly the ambiguities of rejection and affirmation, revolt and conformity, hope and disenchantment observed in the culture at large. In his life as in our history, the fallacies of innocence and the new slate are exemplified. His predicament reflects the predicament of the self in America."[13] In other words, because adolescence is a transitional stage, its turbulence and confusion provide dramatic correlatives of America's postwar anxiety over its national purpose. The befuddling indirection that many teenagers suffer encapsulates the confusion of a nation unsure of its future.

Not all critics believe that American writers' reliance on the lost-innocence myth has been healthy. As *The Catcher in the Rye, On the Road,* and other youth-oriented works gained popularity in the 1950s, commentators questioned whether their ambivalence toward adulthood might not reflect the innate immaturity of the American imagination. By far the most vocal proponent of this position was Fiedler. In several essays and books published in the late 1950s and the 1960s, he insisted that innocence was synonymous with evasion. Authors lamenting the initiation into maturity perpetuated the stunted growth of American writing by refusing to tackle issues relevant to adults, whether domestic relations or political concerns. As a result, Fiedler insisted, American fiction was doomed to appear simplistic and even childish when compared to European literature. The argument is stated succinctly in the introduction to *Love and Death in* the *American Novel* (1960), the most influential—and controversial—study of American literature of its time: "The great works of American fiction are notoriously at home in the children's section of the library, their level of sentimentality precisely that of a pre-adolescent. In a compulsive way, the American author returns to a limited world of experience, usually associated with his childhood, writing the same book over and over again until he lapses into silence or self-parody."[14]

More recently, critics have identified an unheralded American literary tradition that does, contrary to Fiedler's claims, depict adulthood as more consequential than adolescence. Linda A. Westervelt has coined the term *altersroman* to characterize novels such as Henry James's *The Ambassadors* (1904) and Toni Morrison's *Jazz* (1992) that revise the derogatory image of aging found in most American novels of development.[15] Yet, such works remain the exception rather than the rule. When assaying the relationship between maturity and aging, most fiction continues to idealize innocence and view experience as a mythical falling away from purity.

PSYCHOLOGICAL, SOCIOLOGICAL, AND PEDAGOGICAL RELEVANCE

The importance of alienated-youth fiction is not restricted to concerns with literary form and myth. The genre also reflects modern theories about the impact of adolescence on an individual's sense of identity. Post-1945 theories of adolescent development so complement the themes and issues in troubled-teen narratives that many scholars call on leading psychologists to support their interpretations of the literature. At the same time, psychologists and sociologists quote from *The Bell Jar* or *On the Road* to illustrate their claims. Equally important, alienated-youth fiction has had a marked influence on the methods and strategies for teaching young people.

When examining the psychological significance of alienated-youth fiction, critics focus on teenagers' struggle to discover their identities as they break away from their families and establish their independence. Commentators find the work of Erik H. Erikson, the leading developmental psychologist of the postwar era, particularly useful for understanding the drama of maturation. In the 1950s Erikson popularized the term *identity crisis* to describe the main conflict youth confront while growing up: "The identity crisis occurs in that period of the life cycle when each youth must forge for himself some central perspective and direction, some working unity, out of the

Paul Goodman, whose *Growing Up Absurd: Problems of Youth in the Organized System* (1960) explores the alienation of youth in American culture

effective remnants of his childhood and the hopes of his anticipated adulthood; he must detect some meaningful resemblance between what he has come to see in himself and what his sharpened awareness tells him others judge and expect him to be."[16] Concepts such as the identity crisis lend scientific authority to scholarly readings of *The Catcher in the Rye* and other works of young-adult fiction. Rather than generalize about the coming-of-age process, critics are able to apply detailed psychological models of maturation to the fiction in order to distinguish various stages in a character's growth. Similarly, psychologists find fiction a ready source for illustrating their theories. In *The Adolescent through Fiction: A Psychological Approach* (1959) Norman Kiell argues that novels and stories are more compelling than the case histories that psychologists normally study: "Most case histories are pedantic, pedestrian and boring. Experimental techniques remove persons from meaningful life situations and develop either artificial or confining pictures of the individual. The artist, on the other hand, has the gift of portrayal in recognizable, realistic fashion and has the capacity to marshall words to depict real people."[17] As Kiell suggests, case histories tend to reduce their subjects' actions to dry, formulaic patterns of behavior, whereas the ambiguity of literature offers complex situations that defy easy generalization.

Psychological analyses such as Kiell's are usually organized around major initiation experiences that shape a character's identity. (Kiell's chapters have titles such as "On Physical Development," "On Getting Along Socially," and "On Family Relationships.") These studies examine the crises of growing up from an ahistorical perspective—that is, without reference to the specific social conditions that shape a culture's idea of what constitutes "normal" maturation. Other commentators blend psychology and sociology by exploring how the state of society exacerbates teenage alienation. In *Growing Up Absurd: Problems of Youth in the Organized System* (1960), for example, Paul Goodman examines how *On the Road* and Beat Generation literature in general represent an influential but ultimately escapist response to the uninspiring system of postwar life. Kerouac and his peers may have rejected the rat race, Goodman argues, but they failed to establish any viable alternative to it and thus remained trapped in adolescent behavior, even as they entered their thirties: "Their principle is the traditional one of classical mysticism: by 'experiences' (=kicks) to transcend the nagged and nagging self altogether and get out of one's skin, to where no questions are asked. Resigning from society, they form peaceful brotherhoods of pure experience, with voluntary poverty, devotional readings, and a good deal of hashish."[18] Other social psychologists echoed Goodman's critique, arguing that the Beat subculture was a symptom but not a solution to the emerging generation's discontent. In this way these critics have used literature to critique the response of real-life youth to 1950s conformity.

Finally, critics study alienated-youth fiction for its pedagogical value. Adolescent psychologists have long recognized that coming-of-age stories provide teachers a useful tool for encouraging students to discuss the difficulties of growing up. According to G. Stanley Hall's landmark study, *Adolescence; Its Psychology and Its Relations to Physiology, Anthropology, Sociology, Sex, Crime, Religion, and Education* (1904), "ephebic literature" (an ephebe is a minor) encourages self-awareness among youth: "Much of it should be individually prescribed for the reading of the young, for whom it has a singular zest and is a true stimulus and corrective. This stage of life now has what might almost be called a school of its own. Here the young appeal to and listen to each other as they do not to adults, and in a way the latter have failed to appreciate."[19]

To maximize the educational potential of teen-oriented fiction, teachers have developed various instructional approaches. They may encourage students to analyze themes in a work, for example, in order to articulate what it says about the teenage experience. Instructors may also ask their classes to explore protagonists' growth (or lack of it) to evaluate how these characters respond to conflict. Most pedagogy addressing novels such as *The Catcher in the Rye* revolves around student identification with the texts. As the author of one teaching guide argues,

> Adolescent readers respond best to literature when discussion of it starts within the circle of their own experience, when they can begin their reading by relating to the work personally and emotionally. This is not the last level of response, certainly, but it is often the best to begin with, for once that affective link has been made—once students feel the connection between the

SILENCING ALIENATED YOUTH

Banned in the U.S.A.: A Reference Guide to Book Censorship in Schools and Public Libraries (1994), by Herbert Foerstel. Foerstel offers case histories of several banned books, including *The Catcher in the Rye.* As he notes, parents lobbying for the removal of the novel from classrooms and libraries typically have tallied Holden Caulfield's profanity as proof that the book is a negative influence on adolescents: "A complaining parent in California counted 295 occasions in which God's name was taken in vain, while another complainant in Kansas noted 860 obscenities."

Anatomy of a Book Controversy (1995), by Wayne Homstad. Homstad explores how one Northeastern school district dealt with a parent's objection to the use of *Go Ask Alice* in a seventh-grade class in 1987.

Censorship in Schools (1996), by Victoria Sherrow. Sherrow offers an evenhanded account of several types of censorship cases that arise in schools, including not only controversial literature but also textbooks and adolescent self-expression as well. The chapters on banned books include interviews with both protestors and defenders of authors such as J. D. Salinger, Robert Cormier, and Judy Blume.

work and their own lives—it is a great deal easier to get them to think about other ideas or connections in the novel.[20]

By comparing themselves to Holden Caulfield or Esther Greenwood, students can gain a better understanding of their own insecurities and uncertainties. By the same token, thinking about how they would respond to protagonists' dilemmas provides these young readers an analytical entry into the discussion of such literary issues as theme, symbol, and character.

The use of alienated-youth fiction in classrooms has also spawned an unexpected field of study. *The Catcher in the Rye,* the anonymous *Go Ask Alice,* and Robert Cormier's *The Chocolate War* are just a few of the works that have inspired censorship battles throughout American school systems. In the 1960s and 1970s teachers and administrators who assigned controversial works to underage classes risked censure and even, in extreme cases, dismissal. As justification for their censorship campaigns, parents and community leaders who still push for the banning of some youth-oriented books cite their fear that young people will be exposed prematurely to depictions of profanity, violence, or sexual activity. For the advocates of the novels, however, the reasons for repressing these books have less to do with their subject matter than their anti-authoritarian tone. In a study of several censorship cases involving *The Catcher in the Rye,* Pamela Hunt Steinle argues that what most offends adults is the indictment of elders found in the novel: "The lack of faith in the American character expressed in the *Catcher* controversies is rooted not in doubts about the strength of the adolescent Americans' character but in recognition of the powerlessness of American adults—as parents, professional and community leaders—to provide a genuine sense of the future for the adolescents in their charge."[21] While protestors demand the teaching of fiction that is optimistic about America and the adult world, defenders of alienated-youth fiction insist that, as the inheritors of that world, teenagers have not only a right but also an obligation to express their discontent with the way they are taught to live their lives.

The controversies surrounding alienated-youth fiction suggest that these works tap into a deep ambivalence toward youth in Western culture. This ambivalence is present in the older narrative traditions of the quest, the picaresque tale, and the bildungsroman that inspired this contemporary genre. It is apparent as well in myths of lost innocence, such as the story of the Fall, to which *The Catcher in the Rye* and other novels allude. On the one hand, Western literature lionizes the energy, enthusiasm, and potential of youth. At the same time, its drama typically centers around the moment at which these traits are irrevocably lost, whether through sacrifice or squandering. The result of this loss is a sense of unresolved transition, for which the adolescent experience is a perfect emblem. Caught between nostalgia for the past and fear of an uncertain future, the teenager represents the individual poised on the brink, hesitant to commit to a course of action. Pragmatic but not complacent, daunted but not defeated, fallen, perhaps, but not yet felled, the adolescent hero symbolizes a society unsure of where it is headed.

NOTES

1. Leslie A. Fiedler, "The Profanation of the Child," *New Leader,* 41 (23 June 1958): 29.

2. Janis P. Stout, *The Journey Narrative in American Literature: Patterns and Departures* (Westport, Conn.: Greenwood Press, 1983), p. 16.

3. Ibid., p. 91.

4. W. Tasker Witham, *The Adolescent in the American Novel, 1920–1960* (New York: Ungar, 1964), p. 95.

5. Jerome Hamilton Buckley, *Season of Youth: The Bildungsroman from Dickens to Golding* (Cambridge, Mass.: Harvard University Press, 1974), pp. 22–23.

6. Patricia Meyer Spacks, *The Adolescent Idea: Myths of Youth and the Adult Imagination* (New York: Basic Books, 1981), p. 206.

7. Linda Wagner-Martin, "Plath's *The Bell Jar* as Female *Bildungsroman,*" *Women's Studies,* 12 (February 1986): 65.

8. Greta LeSeur, *Ten Is the Age of Darkness: The Black Bildungsroman* (Columbia: University of Missouri Press, 1995), p. 27.

9. Frederick W. Dillistone, "The Fall: Christian Truth and Literary Symbol," in *Comparative Literature: Matter and Method,* edited by A. Owen Aldridge (Urbana: University of Illinois Press, 1969), pp. 156–157.

10. William Wordsworth, "Ode: Intimations of Immortality," in *William Wordsworth: Collected Poems,* edited by John O. Hayden (New York: Penguin, 1994), pp. 139–145.

11. R.W.B. Lewis, *The American Adam: Innocence, Tragedy, and Tradition in the Nineteenth Century* (Chicago: University of Chicago Press, 1955), pp. 127–128.

12. Ibid., pp. 197–198.

13. Ihab Hassan, *Radical Innocence: The Contemporary American Novel* (Princeton: Princeton University Press, 1961), p. 41.

14. Fiedler, *Love and Death in the American Novel,* revised edition (New York: Stein & Day, 1966), p. 24.

15. Linda A. Westervelt, *Beyond Innocence; or, The Altersroman in Modern Fiction* (Columbia: University of Missouri Press, 1997).

16. Erik H. Erikson, *Young Man Luther: A Study in Psychoanalysis and History* (New York: Norton, 1962), p. 14.

17. Norman Kiell, *The Adolescent through Fiction: A Psychological Approach* (New York: International Universities Press, 1959), p. 18.

18. Paul Goodman, *Growing Up Absurd: Problems of Youth in the Organized System* (New York: Random House, 1960), p. 156.

19. G. Stanley Hall, *Adolescence; Its Psychology and Its Relations to Physiology, Anthropology, Sociology, Sex, Crime, Religion and Education,* volume 2 (New York: Appleton, 1904), p. 589.

20. David Peck, *Novels of Initiation: A Guidebook for Teaching Literature to Adolescents* (New York: Teachers College Press, 1989), p. xv.

21. Pamela Hunt Steinle, *In Cold Fear: The Catcher in the Rye Censorship Controversies and Postwar American Character* (Columbus: Ohio State University Press, 2000), p. 17.

EXEMPLARY WORKS OF
ALIENATED-YOUTH FICTION

INTRODUCTION

Alienated-youth fiction is a challenging literary form to define. To begin with, there is no one accepted name for it. Critics speak of the "coming-of-age novel," the "initiation novel," the "junior novel," the "novel of adolescence," and "young-adult fiction"; yet, little agreement exists as to whether these designations describe overlapping or opposing sets of characteristics. This confusion in terminology is indicative of the broader difficulty of ferreting out parallels among the plots, character types, and themes of representative works. Readers who presume that teen protagonists exhibit the same pathology of disaffection quickly discover that the causes of adolescent alienation are not consistent from one novel to the next. Even more perplexing, the ages of young heroes vary so widely that the traditional chronological boundaries defining the teen years offer little assistance in generalizing about the genre. Jack Kerouac's alter ego, Sal Paradise, is already in his mid twenties, divorced, and a veteran of the merchant marine when *On the Road* begins. By contrast, the heroine of Toni Morrison's *The Bluest Eye* (1970), Pecola Breedlove, has barely entered pubescence at the start of her story. Such discrepancies suggest the lack of consensus among fiction writers—or within American culture itself—about the actual age at which adolescents come of age.

Despite this diversity, critics recognize some basic similarities. According to Norman Kiell, most alienated-youth fiction documents the struggle to determine one's identity: "The adolescent's conflicts, insecurities and uncertainties stem from the conflicts between generations in a changing society, sexual frustrations arising out of physical maturation and societal restrictions, difficulties in emancipation from parents, inconsistencies in authority relationships, and discontinuities in socialization patterns."[1] Regardless of the range of genres, plots, character types, themes, and motifs found in alienated-youth fiction, most of it explores the conflicts and uncertainties identified by Kiell.

S. E. (Susan Eloise) Hinton was a teenager when her first novel, *The Outsiders*, was published in 1967. The book heralded a more realistic depiction of teenage life in young-adult fiction.

GENRES

In literary studies, the word *genre* (French for *genus* or *type*) refers to the descriptive categories by which critics differentiate forms of writing. Typically, a genre is defined by a set of conventions, whether thematic or stylistic, that constitutes its uniqueness. The boundaries between genres are notoriously permeable, however. Many artists violate generic norms by creating hybrid forms that include elements common to different genres. Because exceptions to generic rules are as plentiful as exemplars, one should view any definition of a literary form as a convenient but provisional tool. Although genres allow readers to group comparable works under a general heading, they are by no means universal or fixed laws. One can distinguish between three main subtypes of alienated-youth fiction: the initiation story, young-adult fiction, and youth-culture fiction.

THE INITIATION STORY

The term *initiation story* is by far the one most frequently used to describe texts with teenage protagonists. Appearing first in Cleanth Brooks' and Robert Penn Warren's textbook *Understanding Fiction* (1943), the phrase at its most general refers to works in which an adolescent comes to a new realization of the complexity of human relations through a sudden, unexpected revelation known as an epiphany. Brooks and Warren borrowed the concept of initiation from anthropology, where it describes the social process by which young people prove their worthiness to assume adult responsibilities. In many societies, these processes are composed of elaborate rituals or rites of passage. Many works of youth fiction thus emphasize the ritualistic nature of initiation by centering their drama around a formal social test or challenge. In other cases, initiation is a psychological rather than a ceremonial event, with the protagonist coming to some personal crossroads, whether loss of virginity, marriage, parenthood, or knowledge of death. Initiation stories differ not only in the types of rituals they dramatize but also in the levels of insight that main characters achieve. In his influential essay "What is an Initiation Story?" (1960), Mordecai Marcus defines three basic degrees of self-knowledge that characters may attain—"tentative," "uncompleted," and "decisive":

> Some initiations lead only to the threshold of maturity and understanding but do not definitely cross it. Such stories emphasize the shocking effect of experience, and their protagonists tend to be distinctly young. Second, some initiations take their protagonists across a threshold of maturity and understanding but leave them enmeshed in a struggle for certainty. These initiations sometimes involve self-discovery. Third, the most decisive initiations carry their protagonists firmly into maturity and understanding, or at least show them decisively embarked toward maturity.[2]

REBELLION AND THE ADOLESCENT HEROINE

"It is difficult for adolescent heroines to put up any effective opposition to society's plan for girls. If they are stubborn enough to resist indoctrination and clever enough to escape constant surveillance, they may attempt to rebel against accepting a subordinate role in society. But the restrictions placed on women are so pervasive and so thoroughly institutionalized that girls' revolt can be easily contained. Moreover, adolescent heroines have to contend with what is probably the greatest hindrance to girls' rebellion—their own internal conflict. Many protagonists find it hard to trust their own feelings and perceptions. Adolescent females very seldom meet adult women who have not accepted their position as the 'second sex,' and until very recently rebellious women have been all but absent from history books. Hence it often seems to the girl that she stands alone in her predicament, and she fears being 'abnormal.'"

Barbara A. White

From *Growing Up Female: Adolescent Girlhood in American Fiction* (Westport, Conn.: Greenwood Press, 1985), p. 154.

According to Marcus's criteria, J. D. Salinger's *The Catcher in the Rye* exemplifies the uncompleted initiation. As is revealed in the final chapter, Holden Caulfield, despite having accepted the futility of his desire to protect children's innocence (and despite having entered a psychiatric clinic), has yet to overcome his disaffection: "A lot of people, especially this one psychoanalyst guy they have here, keeps asking me if I'm going to apply myself when I go back to school next September. It's such a stupid question, in my opinion. I mean how do you know what you're going to do till you *do* it?" (276). The novel thus ends on an inconclusive note, with Holden having accepted the intangibility of his ideals yet uncertain about how to move on with his life. The tentative initiation, meanwhile, usually involves prepubescent children who lack the emotional equipage to comprehend the implications of formative experiences. In Morrison's *The Bluest Eye*, Pecola is not mature enough to recognize how her parents' inability to love precipitates her insanity. Told from an early age that she is ugly, she absorbs the hatred heaped upon her by her mother and father. Rather than seek reassurance elsewhere, she takes refuge in the fantasy that blue eyes will make her as beautiful as the white baby dolls with which she plays. Her alienation ultimately leads her to create an imaginary playmate, whose companionship she fears losing: "Suppose my eyes aren't blue enough. *Blue enough for what?* Blue enough for . . . I don't know. Blue enough for something. Blue enough . . . for you. *I'm not going to play with you anymore.* Oh. Don't leave me."[3] Novels depicting tentative initiations make the presumption that readers will compensate for the main characters' naiveté by speculating on the future consequences of the children's experiences.

Marcus's final type of passage, the decisive initiation, is relatively rare, substantiating the critic Leslie A. Fiedler's complaints that American writers fail to push their protagonists past the threshold of adulthood. A notable exception is William Wharton's *Birdy* (1979), in which the disturbed hero eventually emerges from the shell-shocked fantasy that he is a bird, a condition brought about by combat in World War II. With the help of his boyhood friend Al, Birdy comes to recognize that his psychotic delusion is his way of coping with despair: "Maybe crazy people are the ones who see things clear but work out a way to live with it. We're crazy because we can't accept the idea that things happen for no reason at all and that it doesn't mean anything. We can't see life as just a row of hurdles we have to get over somehow. It looks to me as if everybody who isn't crazy just keeps hacking away to get through."[4] Instead of accepting that pain is inevitable, Birdy believes that the human imagination can transform reality, and he encourages Al to transcend the sadness of lost innocence. Thus, there is little worry at the conclusion of the novel that Birdy will suffer a relapse. He has learned from his problems, and he is a better person for having suffered through them.

As Marcus cautions, there is a basic danger in calling a work an initiation story: "The idea of initiation is so broad that almost any story of developing awareness or character can fit it."[5] Nor should it be assumed that narratives feature only a single initiation experience. In Sylvia Plath's *The Bell Jar*, Esther Greenwood leaves her family home, seeks out a career, and loses her virginity, all dramatic incidents affecting her identity. Works with several initiation experiences demonstrate that maturity does not pivot upon a single event but involves multiple tests and challenges.

YOUNG-ADULT FICTION

Unlike *initiation story*, the term *young-adult fiction* was not coined by scholars. It entered the critical vernacular through the efforts of the American Library Association (ALA), which established its Young Adult Services Division in 1958 to improve service to teenage library patrons. (The division is now known as YALSA, the Young Adult Library Services Association.) Eight years later the ALA incorporated the term *young adults* into the title of its annual recommended-reading list for secondary-school students, calling it "Best Books for Young Adults" in hopes of distinguishing adolescent fiction more clearly from children's fiction. Since first publishing the list in 1930, the ALA had employed a host of terms in the title, including *junior novel* and *juvenile fiction,* all of which seemed to denote an inferior art form. *Young-adult fiction* (often abbreviated as YA fiction) eventually became the accepted designation, in part because it sounded the least judgmental.[6]

The long search for a suitable name for young-adult fiction indicates the difficulty of establishing its central characteristics. One of the less-contested definitions suggests the qualifiers required to define the genre: "Young-adult literature is that realistic and contemporary American fiction which young adults as well as more mature and critical readers can find aesthetically and thematically satisfying and which is, implicitly or explicitly, written for adolescents."[7] "Implicitly" and "explicitly" are necessary qualifications: while one might assume that a young-adult novel is simply any book aimed at a twelve- to eighteen-year-old readership, many classic young-adult titles were in fact written for adult audiences. *The Catcher in the Rye, The Bell Jar,* and John Knowles's *A Separate Peace* are only three of many works intended for adults that have become identified with teen readers because of their popularity in secondary-school classrooms. Some authors even resent it when their work is classified as young-adult fiction, believing its association with adolescent audiences will detract from its critical reputation.

In addition to problems with naming and defining this form, there is a great deal of disagreement as to when young-adult fiction came into vogue. Some historians argue that works frequently classified as children's literature, including Louisa May Alcott's *Little Women* and Mark Twain's *Adventures of Huckleberry Finn,* are early exemplars. Others cite Maureen Daly's *Seventeenth Summer* (1942), noting three characteristics that make Daly's depiction of youth more modern than Alcott's or Twain's. Nine years before *The Catcher in the Rye,* Daly's first-person point of view allowed readers to experience an authentic-sounding adolescent voice in all its indirection and immediacy. The plot also includes scenes of teenage rituals (drinking and smoking) that show youth to be neither naive nor angelic. Finally, Daly's age (twenty-one at the time the novel was published) allowed her book to be publicized as an insider exposé of adolescence. Yet, despite its slang and putative candor, *Seventeenth Summer* (and the imitators it inspired) refrained from trespassing into the darker territories of adolescent confusion and despair. As Michael Cart notes, "These works were set in a *Saturday Evening Post* world of white faces and white-picket fences surrounding small-town, middle-class lives where the worst thing that can happen would be a misunderstanding that would threaten to leave someone dateless for the junior prom."[8]

As such comments suggest, most critics believe that the best young-adult fiction does not idealize youth but willingly addresses teen problems. The realism with which mainstream authors such as Salinger treated adolescence did not enter young-adult writing until the late 1960s with the publication of S. E. Hinton's *The Outsiders* and Paul Zindel's *The Pigman.* In a 1967 essay in *The New York Times Book Review* Hinton—like Daly, a teenager when she began her writing career—called for young-adult reading that reflected the treacheries of teen life: "The world is changing, yet the authors of books for teen-agers are still 15 years behind the times. In the fiction they write, romance is still the most popular theme, with a horse-and-the girl-who-loved it coming in a close second. In short, where is the reality?"[9] For Hinton, realism lay in the disadvantages suffered by working-class youth vilified as juvenile delinquents. *The Outsiders* and her next two novels, *That Was Then, This Is Now* (1971) and *Rumble Fish* (1975), feature scenes of gang life, including rumbles, shoplifting, joyriding, and drugs. They also celebrate the fraternal bonds between unpopular outcasts. Revisionists have recently denounced Hinton for perpetuating a sentimental view of her delinquent heroes; yet, it is undeniable that her novels introduced previously taboo topics that have become de rigueur in young-adult fiction.

The same is true of Zindel's *The Pigman*, in which two disaffected teens, John and Lorraine, betray the trust of a lonely old man named Mr. Pignati. The book's main legacy rests in the lesson about responsibility that it teaches. When Pignati is hospitalized for an ailing heart, John and Lorraine throw a party at his residence, during which his deceased wife's collection of glass and ceramic pigs is destroyed. Amid the chaos of the party, the old man returns home, and his grief at discovering his shattered possessions precipitates a fatal heart attack. For John and Lorraine, the Pigman's death demonstrates the consequences of teenage callousness. Only by outgrowing their selfishness can the pair hope for forgiveness. As John decides, "There was no one else to blame anymore. Our life would be what we made of it—nothing more, nothing less."[10]

The popularity of Hinton's and Zindel's books inspired a wave of unflinching examinations of teen violence, drugs, and sexual abuse. The most celebrated example of this realism is Robert Cormier's *The Chocolate War*, published in 1974. Essentially a fable, *The Chocolate War* presents the argument that teen hazing and violence epitomize the strife of the world at large. When a young man named Jerry refuses to sell chocolate bars in his parochial school's annual fund-raiser, he becomes a target of the Vigils, a gang sanctioned by the school's ambitious assistant headmaster, Brother Leon. In the hands of another writer of young-adult fiction, Jerry's innate goodness and respect for individuality would probably triumph over the callow hooliganism of the Vigils and their thuggish leader, Archie. Yet, Cormier refuses to conclude the story with an easy affirmation. In the final scene Jerry discovers Brother Leon's complicity in the beatings he has suffered, and he comes to believe his protest was not worth the pain it caused him. As he tells his friend

Robert Cormier, whose novel *The Chocolate War* (1974) has inspired many censorship battles because of its pessimistic, downbeat ending, in which the hero renounces his attempts to stand up to bullies and manipulative adults in his parochial school

Goober, "They tell you to do your thing but they don't mean it. They don't want you to do your thing unless it happens to be their thing. It's a laugh, Goober, a fake. Don't disturb the universe, Goober, no matter what the posters say."[11] This pessimistic conclusion continues to arouse parental objection when the book is taught in schools. Yet, *The Chocolate War* has the qualities that embody the best young-adult fiction—realistic but not melodramatic, concerned but not condescending, and educational but not didactic. Nearly thirty years after its publication, the novel remains a staple of secondary-school curricula because its complexity challenges teens to view their adolescent afflictions as representative of the larger dilemmas of the human condition.

The similarly downbeat endings of *The Catcher in the Rye* and *The Chocolate War* raise what remains the most befuddling question about young-adult fiction, here posed by Dagmar Grenz, a scholar of children's literature: "To what degree does the novel of adolescence specific to young people (meaning the novel that was especially written or published for a young audience) differ from the novel of adolescence in literature in general?" Grenz's answer reflects a general agreement among critics, who, despite *The Chocolate War*, view young-adult fiction as more prone to happy endings than mainstream literature tends to be: "The novel of adolescence written (or published) specially for young people does not achieve the same degree of modernity in that it is on the whole more traditionally written: It evinces a tendency toward greater unambiguity and toward harmonization; it follows the *Bildungsroman* more than the novel of adolescence; and when it does take on the model of the novel of adolescence, it more readily adopts that from the turn of the century than that of contemporary literature."[12] Although Grenz views this "greater unambiguity" as a literary detriment, a writer of young-adult fiction might argue that it reflects a sense of responsibility toward the impressionable audience of the genre. In a world already fraught with cynicism and apathy, most writers addressing teens seek to inspire rather than to perpetuate gloom and despair.

YOUTH-CULTURE FICTION

Youth-culture fiction is a recently established genre describing alienated-youth novels that bespeak a generational or subcultural sensibility. Previously, when critics sought to characterize young audiences' attraction to *On the Road* or Kerouac's following novels, such as *The Subterraneans* and *The Dharma Bums*, they dubbed these novels "cult classics." That term is far too general, however, for it can apply to any work—not just those about disaffected youth—the enduring popularity of which flies below the radar of scholarly esteem. The term *youth-culture fiction* more properly acknowledges that novels can inspire fads, fashions, and even the occasional illegal pastime. (Kerouac's fiction, for example, helped popularize recreational drug use among middle-class teens.) While adults regard works of youth-culture fiction as field guides for understanding teenagers, youth may adopt such books as lifestyle manuals instructing them in the slang, dress, and attitudes necessary for membership in a subculture.

Ample references to *The Catcher in the Rye* in sociological studies of the 1950s demonstrate how youth-culture fiction can serve as a generational totem. No sooner was Salinger's novel published than critics seized upon Holden as proof that the era's young people, said to belong to the "silent generation," were discontented with American conformity. Such influential studies as David Riesman's *The Lonely Crowd* (1950), Edgar Friedenberg's *The Vanishing Adolescent* (1959), and Kenneth Kenniston's *The Uncommitted: Alienated Youth in American Society* (1965) all cite *The Catcher in the Rye* for exemplifying the detachment of postwar youth. More-recent commentators, such as John Seelye, have even argued that Holden inspired resistance to the Vietnam War in the late 1960s: "The Vietnam War converted Salinger's novel into a catalyst for revolt, converting anomie into objectified anger. It was a threshold text to the sixties, ten years after it appeared at the start of the fifties, when it was a minority text stating a minor view. *Catcher* likewise supplied not only the rationale for the antiwar, anti-regimentation movements of the sixties and seventies but provided the anti-ideological basis for many of the actual novels about Vietnam."[13]

Despite such assertions, *The Catcher in the Rye* lacks one essential ingredient for inspiring a full-fledged subculture, replete with its own slang and fashion: the peer group. Because Kerouac's Beat Generation novels celebrate youth's desire to belong to age-defined tribes, they better exemplify how fiction can lay the foundation for alternative youth cultures. Before 1957 the Beat ethos was

St. Louis youth model varsity-style Beat Generation jackets sold in 1959. Such items demonstrate the ability of mainstream culture to appropriate subcultural slogans and phrases, diminishing the threat of youthful rebelliousness.

largely unknown outside the isolated bohemian enclaves of New York's Greenwich Village and San Francisco. As *On the Road* garnered media notoriety, however, teenagers throughout America began adopting the accoutrements of Kerouac's hipster characters. Within a short time, *Life* magazine was publishing articles on how to be Beat. By 1959 one could not only read Beat novels but also listen to Beat authors perform their work, accompanied by jazz music, on a series of record albums. One manufacturer even produced a line of varsity jackets with a "Beat Generation" insignia in place of a high-school logo. Such products indicate the power of mainstream society to appropriate the symbols by which a subculture declares its rebellion. As the culture industry cashes in on a new youth movement by producing goods that make affiliation with the subculture available to anyone with enough money, what started out as threatening or frightening is transformed into a mere fad.

One might assume that the ability of alienated-youth fiction to inspire adolescent subcultures has diminished at the hands of music and movies. Yet, novels such as Bret Easton Ellis's *Less Than Zero* (1985) and Douglas Coupland's *Generation X* (1991) played integral roles in shaping the perceptions of the generation that came of age in the 1970s and 1980s. Unfortunately, youth-culture fiction is such a new area of study that the process by which fiction affects the identity of youth remains relatively unexamined.

PLOTS

While the term *genre* designates the general class to which a text belongs, *plot* refers to the events within it that constitute the main action. Three main plot types dominate alienated-youth fiction: the journey of self-discovery, in which the protagonists set out to resolve their identity confusion; the rehabilitation story, in which main characters undergo some clinical therapy designed to remedy their disaffection; and the at-risk narrative, in which adolescents succumb to self-destructive behavior that dramatizes their lack of hope.

THE JOURNEY OF SELF-DISCOVERY

The journey of self-discovery is the most traditional storyline among works of alienated-youth fiction because it fuses elements of the quest, the picaresque tale, and the bildungsroman. At its most basic, the journey narrative follows a protagonist who sets out from home in search of some salve for a befuddling personal dilemma. The drama of these outward-bound stories arises from a lingering uncertainty of motive, with authors asking readers to ponder whether a hero's travels are a quest or an escape. Janis P. Stout describes the inherent ambiguity of these journeys: "Is the action an escape from a corrupt society to solitary beatitude? Or is it, as it repeats the pattern of exploratory ventures, a search for a righteous society? Both. Escape and quest are related, the difference arising from the question of which motivation is stronger, the repellant force or the attracting goal."[14] Heroes may embark on a quest only to realize that they are running away from their demons, or, midway into an escape, they may discover a goal that gives their journey purpose. Either way, the uncertainty of their intent dramatizes the anxiety of adolescent indirection. Because the journey motif symbolizes the broader journey of life, with individual episodes representing stages of the protagonist's emotional development, the lack of surety reflects young people's confusion over whether they should follow the crowd or take the road less traveled.

The Catcher in the Rye exemplifies the journey that begins as an escape but becomes a quest. Although Holden rambles throughout New York to avoid his parents' wrath over his expulsion from a third preparatory school, he slowly discovers a purpose to guide him, the viability of which he must ultimately question. This purpose is to protect the innocence of children. Holden's ambition becomes apparent when he discovers an obscenity scrawled on the wall of the elementary school his sister, Phoebe, attends: "Somebody'd written 'Fuck you' on the wall. It drove me damn near crazy. I thought how Phoebe and all the other little kids would see it, and how they'd wonder what the hell it meant, and then finally some dirty kid would tell them—all cockeyed, naturally—what it meant, and how they'd all *think* about it and maybe even *worry* about it for a couple of days. I kept wanting to kill whoever'd written it" (260). Despite his anger, Holden feels defeated by the impossibility of this task, especially after coming across two similar graffiti curses. As he despairs, "It's hopeless, anyway. If you had a million years to do it, you couldn't rub out even *half* the 'Fuck you' signs in the world. It's impossible" (262). Because these profanities symbolize the hostility of modern life, their omnipresence is for Holden a sign of both the vulnerability of innocence and the futility of trying to protect it. Because he cannot abide his own powerlessness against this brutal ugliness, he hatches a rather far-fetched plan to run away and become a reclusive hermit.

The conflict between Holden's desire to go on a quest and to escape comes to a head in the penultimate chapter. As he prepares to depart for California, he suddenly realizes the effect that his leaving will have on Phoebe. Having already lost her brother Allie several years earlier to leukemia, she refuses to let Holden disappear from her life, going so far as to lug a suitcase to what is supposed to be the siblings' farewell encounter. Knowledge of Phoebe's love fills him with a sudden sense of joy, which he acknowledges while watching her ride a carousel in Central Park: "I felt so damn happy all of a sudden, the way old Phoebe kept going around and around. I was damn near bawling, I felt so damn happy, if you want to know the truth" (275). As with many heroes of journey narratives, Holden discovers that individualism exacerbates alienation and that community can bring contentment as much as it enforces conformity. The famous final lines of the novel imply that Holden—almost against his will—realizes his need for human interaction: "About all I know is, I sort of *miss* everybody I told about. . . . Don't ever tell anybody anything. If you do, you start missing everybody" (277).

On the Road, by contrast, begins as a quest but ends in escape. Initially, Sal Paradise and Dean Moriarty pursue several goals: women, sex, drugs, jazz, "kicks," assorted Beat comrades, Dean's father, and America. As Sal puts it when he first embarks for the West Coast, "Somewhere along the line I knew there'd be girls, visions, everything; somewhere along the line the pearl would be handed to me."[15] Later, Sal and Dean identify that pearl of wisdom simply as "IT." During a rare eastward swing in their travels, Sal begs Dean to clarify this imprecise term. Dean responds with a rather long-winded description of the "soul-exploratory" effects of jazz, leading Sal to realize that "IT" is a feeling of jubilation that comes when the mind is allowed to wander freely: "The car was swaying as Dean and I both swayed to the rhythm and the IT of our final excited joy in talking and living to the blank tranced end of all innumerable riotous angelic particulars that had been lurking in our souls all our lives."[16] Such passages reveal that Sal and Dean seek the perpetual elation of "IT"; they are questing for experiences that elevate them beyond the dreary, convention-bound world to a more spiritual realm of intuitive wisdom. What drives Sal and Dean's constant movement is nothing less than their desire to discover what "IT" means to truly be alive.

By the end of *On the Road,* however, Sal comes to question the value of his journeys as he realizes that this uninterrupted bliss cannot be attained. During an excursion to Mexico, Dean impulsively returns to America to one of the many women in his life, leaving Sal to suffer a bout of dysentery alone. Dean's actions demonstrate for Sal that his friend's indirection is incurable. Because Dean is driven to keep moving, he can never settle down long enough to hone his talents. He is, in effect, running away from his responsibilities, and he is doomed to squander his prodigious energies until they are exhausted. In the final scene Sal declines Dean's invitation to join him on a cross-country caravan to San Francisco. As Stout suggests, he does so because he understands that he has been on a "journey to no end": "*On the Road,* the definitive fictional expression of the Beat Generation, clearly displays a No Exit sign. It suggests that in the modern closed-in world of alienation and irrationality, motion deteriorates into a 'frantic' zigzagging between arbitrary terminal points on linear reaches into emptiness."[17] The downbeat ending of *On the Road* reflects Sal's recognition that life on the road has led only to the end of his and Dean's friendship.

Not all journeys end in ambivalence. Ralph Ellison's *Invisible Man* concludes on an optimistic note, with the protagonist summarizing the significance of his experiences: "My world has become one of infinite possibilities. What a phrase—still it's a good phrase and a good view of life, and a man shouldn't accept any other; that much I've learned underground."[18] The heroes of Saul Bellow's *The Adventures of Augie March* (1953), James Baldwin's *Go Tell It on the Mountain* (1953), and Nelson Algren's *A Walk on the Wild Side* (1956) all experience similar epiphanies. Even when these heroes fail to realize their ambitions, they can at least admit that their experiences make them wiser. As such, this type of plot suggests that, whether questing or escaping, heroes will arrive at some degree of self-knowledge.

THE REHABILITATION STORY

In an essay on post-1945 trends in American fiction, Richard Ohmann identifies the "illness story" as a prominent genre: "Through the story of mental disorientation or derangement, novelists transform deep social contradictions into a dynamic of personal crisis, a sense of there being no comfortable place in the world for the private self." Stories featuring emotionally unstable protagonists, such as Plath's *The Bell Jar* and Joanne Greenberg's *I Never Promised You a Rose Garden,* are pervasive because they explore the power struggle between the adolescent self and society to decide what constitutes healthy maturation. As Ohmann explains, "Society has the power to label one as sick, if one is unable to make the transition into a suitable combination of adult roles. So the representation of malaise and neurosis in the novels of the period incorporates an ambiguity, sometimes explicit, sometimes latent: I seem to be crazy, but again, it's *society* that's crazy."[19] Typically set in a sanatorium, the rehabilitation story focuses on wayward youth's response to the various therapies by which authorities treat their woes. At their most beneficial, curatives such as psychoanalysis or counseling encourage adolescents to overcome their desire to withdraw. At worst, the intended remedies prove invasive and even torturous (electroconvulsive shock therapy and frontal lobotomy). Either way, the treatments symbolize the pressure that society places on young people to subscribe to existing standards of normalcy.

As Ohmann notes, *The Bell Jar* is the best-known example of the rehabilitation plot because of its vivid description of the electroshock regime that Esther Greenwood undergoes. For contemporary readers accustomed to pharmaceutical remedies for depression, the idea of applying high-voltage jolts of electricity to the brain probably seems barbaric and akin to torture. Yet, the practice was an accepted procedure in the mid twentieth century because it was supposed to alter the electromagnetic patterns in the mind that caused discontent. Writers such as Plath viewed electroshock therapy as a powerful symbol of the forced conformity to which society subjects those deemed "different." (In addition to *The Bell Jar*, other important literary works equate electroshock treatment with punishment, including Allen Ginsberg's epic Beat poem *Howl* [1955] and Ken Kesey's novel *One Flew Over the Cuckoo's Nest* [1960].) Plath likens electroshock therapy to electrocution by referencing the 1953 execution of Julius and Ethel Rosenberg, a couple sentenced to death for passing military secrets to the Soviet Union. (The Rosenbergs' sentence was a highly contested issue at the time, with many commentators viewing them as victims of America's Cold War paranoia). In the opening paragraph of the novel Esther imagines the Rosenbergs' pain as they died in an electric chair: "The idea of being electrocuted makes me sick. I couldn't help wondering what it would be like, being burned alive all along your nerves."[20] Later, her first electroshock treatment answers her question: "Then something bent down and took hold of me and shook me like the end of the world. Whee-ee-ee-ee-ee, it shrilled, through an air crackling with blue light, and with each flash a great jolt drubbed me till I thought my bones would break and the sap fly out of me like a split plant." Esther's final words in the scene suggest that she equates the experience with unwarranted punishment: "I wonder what terrible thing it was that I had done."[21] Although she does not specifically refer to the Rosenbergs here, her vivid description of the experience recalls her empathy for them, implying that she believes herself to be as unjustly persecuted as the condemned couple.

Ultimately, Esther learns that no institutional remedy—be it electroshock therapy or more-benign forms of treatment, such as counseling—can cure her adolescent confusion. As she prepares to depart from a second hospital, where she has been treated by the more sympathetic Dr. Nolan, she recognizes the inability of mental-health facilities to rid young patients of disaffection: "I had hoped, at my departure, I would feel sure and knowledgeable about everything that lay ahead—after all, I had been 'analyzed.' Instead, all I could see were question marks."[22] Rather than relying on external authorities, Esther understands that coping with life depends on attaining confidence in her own hopes and not on fulfilling society's expectations of her.

Unlike *The Bell Jar*, *I Never Promised You a Rose Garden* does not depict the sanatorium as a symbol of adult conformity. Since the publication of the novel in 1964, Greenberg (who originally published it under the name Hannah Green) has insisted that her intent in telling the story of sixteen-year-old Deborah Blau's battle with schizophrenia was to repudiate the facile associations between adolescence and madness found in many troubled-teen narratives. Although praised for the clinical accuracy of her portrayal of mental illness, Greenberg nevertheless attributes her heroine's psychological instability at least in part to a dread of adulthood. As an American Jew in the late 1940s, Deborah is haunted by stories of the Nazi extermination of Jews during World War II. She has also suffered from the racist taunts of her schoolmates, who doubt the legitimacy of the Holocaust. Deborah's caring psychiatrist, Dr. Clara Fried, recognizes that her patient's psychotic spells are a defense mechanism against anti-Semitism. Having witnessed firsthand the barbarism of Germany under Adolf Hitler, Dr. Fried views self-destructive behavior as a preemptive strike against others' hatred: "I once had a patient who used to practice the most horrible tortures upon himself, and when I asked him why he did such things, he said, 'Why, before the world does them.' I asked him then, 'Well, why not wait and see what the world will do?' and he said, 'Don't you see? It always comes at last, but this way at least I am master of my own destruction.'"[23] In a similar vein, Dr. Fried encourages Deborah to understand that she creates the demons that populate her delusions in order to harm herself before the outer world can.

Despite their differences, *I Never Promised You a Rose Garden* shares with *The Bell Jar* the insistence that young people must develop their own strengths rather than depend on adults. In one counseling session Dr. Fried encourages Deborah to recognize her own responsibility for her health rather than blame elders for the world's imperfections.

When hospital authorities accuse her of lying when she reports a staff member for striking another patient, Deborah asks, "What good is your reality, when justice fails and dishonesty is glossed over and the ones who keep the faith suffer?" Dr. Fried's response encapsulates the message of the novel: "I never promised you a rose garden. I never promised you perfect justice. My help is so that you can be free to fight for these things. The only reality I offer is challenge, and being well is being free to accept it or not at whatever level you are capable."[24] As Greenberg insists, teenagers must learn to make the world a better place rather than run from it.

In addition to *The Bell Jar* and *I Never Promised You a Rose Garden*, another often-studied rehabilitation narrative is *Go Ask Alice*, ostensibly a true-life account of a young girl's descent into drug abuse that was published in 1971. (Composed of what are described as excerpts from the girl's diary, the book is attributed to "Anonymous," although some historians suggest that the text is fictional). In a similar vein Wharton's *Birdy* takes place in a military hospital where physicians attempt to cure the hero's delusion that he is a bird. Despite the variety of emotional ailments afflicting youth, rehabilitation narratives share the belief that institutions charged with aiding troubled teens are more concerned with making them conform than with acknowledging the legitimacy of their discontent.

THE YOUTH-AT-RISK NARRATIVE

Like the journey and rehabilitation plots, the youth-at-risk narrative depicts adolescent alienation as symptomatic of society's ills. But whereas those story lines focus on introspective protagonists grappling with their problems, the youth-at-risk story involves detached young people who indulge in destructive behavior. This type of narrative originated from an unlikely source. In the 1950s American publishers seized on the rising preoccupation with juvenile delinquency to produce a barrage of novels about teenage hoodlums. Titles such as *The Thrill Kids*, *The Young Wolves*, and *Teen-Age Mafia* suggest that the intent of these novels was sensationalistic rather than serious, and most are long forgotten. Yet, at least two of these books transcended the exploitative nature of the genre to become important cultural touchstones. Both Irving Shulman's *The Amboy Dukes* (1947) and Evan Hunter's *The Blackboard Jungle* (1954) assessed delinquency from a sociological perspective. Because Shulman and Hunter attributed teen deviance to poverty, familial breakdown, and the American education system's neglect of working-class students, editorials on youth crime quoted from their novels as though they were nonfiction. This tendency is a basic effect of the youth-at-risk story: it blurs the line between fiction and sociology, first by warning adults that youth are caught in the throes of a crisis, and then by identifying the causes of their disaffection.

There are two basic variations to the youth-at-risk plot. The first insists that adult intervention can save fallen youth from self-destruction. Such texts attribute delinquency to elders' failure to provide their children with viable role models. The message is that young people turn to drugs or crime to blunt the pain of abandonment. Accordingly, the catalyst for redemption is either a concerned teacher or social worker who earns teens' trust by encouraging them to express their problems through affirmative rather than nihilistic means. The chief protagonist of *The Blackboard Jungle,* for example, is Richard Dadier, an idealistic former marine who battles institutional apathy and parental indifference while challenging students at a neglected New York trade school to care about education. Dadier endures insults, threats, and even a bloody beating to gain teens' grudging admiration. In a climactic scene, the teacher realizes that his dedication has moved his cynical classes to question their violent ways when one student stops another from stabbing him with a switchblade: "He remembered what he'd thought earlier, before the fight, remembered what he'd thought about just one kid, one kid, that's all, one kid getting something out of it all, one kid he could point to and say, 'I showed him the way,' and that would make it all right, if he could only say that."[25]

The youth-at-risk narrative arose from paperback novels that exploited postwar concerns over juvenile delinquency. Irving Shulman's *The Amboy Dukes* (1947) was one of the most popular.

In *The Outsiders* Hinton likewise portrays teen delinquents as worthy of redemption. Although ridiculed as "greasers" by the citizens of their hometown (Tulsa, Oklahoma), Hinton's disaffiliated youth pine for an opportunity to prove their inherent nobility. After Johnny Cade accidentally kills a rival member of the middle-class "Socs" (short for socials), he attempts to make amends by saving a group of children from a burning church. Hinton's narrator, Ponyboy Curtis, realizes what the opportunity to do good means to Johnny, who dies shortly after demonstrating his heroism: "That was the only time I can think of when I saw him without that defeated, suspicious look in his eyes. He looked like he was having the time of his life."[26] Ponyboy yearns to transcend a similar sense of defeat, a desire finally realized through the intervention of his English teacher, who encourages Ponyboy to write about his friends. In the final passages, Ponyboy recognizes the power of language to explain the greasers' predicament: "I could see boys going down under street lights because they were mean and tough and hated the world, and it was too late to tell them that there was still good in it, and they wouldn't believe you if you did. There should be some help. Someone should tell their side of the story."[27] Both *The Blackboard Jungle* and *The Outsiders* thus make the point that young people need only know that adults care about them to cure their disaffection.

In the second type of youth-at-risk plot, the adult intervention needed to save teens from self-destruction is lacking. As a result, the novels with this type of story line evince little optimism, portraying adolescent life as a teenage wasteland, a realm devoid of hope, where the only pleasure is the fleeting joy of a narcotic high. Ellis's *Less Than Zero,* the most notorious alienated-youth novel of the 1980s, exemplifies this more pessimistic type of plot. At one point the narrator, Clay, confronts his friend Julian, who must work as a male prostitute to finance his drug addiction: "Julian, his eyes all glassy, sad grin on his face, says, 'Who cares? Do you? Do you really care?' and I don't say anything and realize that I really don't care and suddenly feel foolish, stupid. I also realize that I'll go with Julian to the Saint Marquis. That I want to see if things like this can actually happen."[28] Clay's desire to witness Julian's degradation suggests that voyeurism, not empathy, is the dominant impulse among youth. Clay's inability to feel concern for any of his friends, not just Julian, bespeaks his incapacity for the self-awareness that Ponyboy gains by telling his fellow outcasts' story in *The Outsiders.* Only late in *Less Than Zero* does Clay account for his indifference: "I don't want to care. If I care about things, it'll just be worse, it'll just be another thing to worry about. It's less painful if I don't care."[29] Clay's response reveals that callousness is a form of self-defense. Having witnessed sundry forms of violence throughout their adolescence, Ellis's youth are so hardened that they believe detachment is their only option for survival.

As with the different genres of alienated-youth fiction, these plot types are not mutually exclusive. Although *Go Ask Alice* includes elements of the rehabilitation plot, it first gained notoriety as a youth-at-risk narrative that served as a warning against teens' recreational drug use. This overlap among plot types once again demonstrates that alienated-youth fiction comprises complex, multidimensional works that appeal to a range of readers.

CHARACTERS

Given that generation gaps are an inevitable fixture of troubled-teen narratives, one might presume that the cast of characters in alienated-youth fiction can be divided into two basic camps—young people and everybody else. In reality the range of plots and themes is so broad that neither teens nor adults can be grouped so facilely. Nevertheless, one can identify certain patterns of characterization that recur from novel to novel. Adults, for example, are defined by the power that they have over young people. Whether parents, teachers, or institutional figureheads (for example, a psychologist or a school administrator), elders are first and foremost authority figures, and their sympathetic or antipathetic depiction depends on how they exert their control over teens. As for adolescents, the main criterion of characterization is the degree of engagement with which they respond to their individual predicaments. Those incapable of addressing their problems succumb to self-destruction and, in extreme cases, suicide. Those who survive develop strategies for coping that allow them to overcome their disaffection and meet the demands of maturity.

LOOKING IN FROM THE OUTSIDE

"The very title of the book, *The Outsiders,* is an indication of its underlying myth as well as its sense of estrangement. All the Greasers are outsiders, alienated from the rest of the world by virtue of their hardships and deprivations and because the rest of the world (read 'The Sociables') looks down on them. It is a convention of teenage literature that these two extremes are always present, are always pitted against each other, and that the stories always take the side of the poorer, 'hoodier' elements, portraying them as projecting a toughness that conceals a basic goodness.

"What is curious is that readers, who come from all walks of teenage life, always identify with the 'Greaser' element, leaving one with the impression that the 'Sociables' do not really exist since no one claims to belong to them. If the reception of *The Outsiders* is any indication, just about all teenagers see themselves as Greasers. Obviously, there is a deep-seated wish to feel put upon, to identify with the underdog, to feel that one has to battle one's way out of an extremely disadvantageous position."

Thomas Reed Whissen

From *Classic Cult Fiction: A Companion to Popular Cult Literature* (Westport, Conn.: Greenwood Press, 1992), p. 186.

ADULT AUTHORITY FIGURES

Parents occupy the most immediate stratum of authority affecting youth; the family symbolizes the bonds of dependency that teens must break to achieve autonomy. At one extreme, alienated-youth fiction may explore parents' failure to nurture the young. In Morrison's *The Blu-*

est Eye Cholly Breedlove rapes and impregnates his daughter, Pecola, an experience that—coupled with the subsequent death of her fetus—initiates her incurable descent into insanity. Morrison does not simply vilify Cholly, however; she also attributes his inability to comprehend the immorality of raping his daughter to his own treatment as a child: "Abandoned in a junk heap by his mother, rejected for a crap game by his father, there was nothing more to lose. He was alone with his own perceptions and appetites and they alone interested him."[30] As Morrison insists, young people need the nurturing support of a family to develop not only knowledge of right and wrong but also a sense of personal dignity.

At the other extreme are parents who are too controlling. In Plath's *The Bell Jar* Esther's emotional problems are attributed to her domineering mother. Rather than empathizing with Esther's feelings of alienation, Mrs. Greenwood simply assumes that her daughter is choosing to be "different": "I knew you'd decide to be all right again," she says when Esther pleads with her to discontinue the electroshock regime.[31] Mrs. Greenwood even begs her daughter to pretend to be happy so that the hospital staff will not judge her to have been a bad mother. As Esther recalls, "She said she was sure the doctors thought she had done something wrong because they asked a lot of questions about my toilet training, and I had been perfectly trained at a very early age and given her no trouble whatsoever."[32] Most important, Mrs. Greenwood is oblivious to the guilt that Esther suffers for wanting more out of life than marriage and motherhood. The narrow possibilities that Mrs. Greenwood envisions for her daughter's future are the most formidable bell jar entrapping the girl. Although Esther wants to transcend these limitations, she believes that only by fulfilling them will she ever gain her mother's approval, and she thus remains incapable of making a definitive break from her family. By failing to grant Esther the freedom to define her own identity, Mrs. Greenwood guarantees her daughter's dependency on her.

Other works portray adults as emissaries of various social institutions responsible for guiding teens into maturity. Prominently featured among the cast of characters of rehabilitation narratives are psychologists and psychiatrists such as Dr. Gordon, who prescribes Esther's electroshock treatments in *The Bell Jar*. Not all psychologists are villains in alienated-youth fiction, however. Other medical authorities empathize with adolescent confusion and thus enable their patients' growth. Esther's second psychologist, Dr. Nolan, exhibits far more compassion than Dr. Gordon, in part because, as a woman, she recognizes that Esther's discontent is rooted in the restrictions imposed on young women. Another sympathetic psychologist is Dr. Fried in Greenberg's *I Never Promised You a Rose Garden*, who early on tells Deborah her goal for their therapy sessions: "Someday I hope to help you see this world as other than a Stygian hell."[33] She achieves this aim by establishing a bond with Deborah that allows the girl to see that the real world can offer friendship and security rather than isolation and pain.

An even more popular representative of adult authority in alienated-youth fiction is the school administrator. The reasons are obvious: aside from the family, school is the most influential institution charged with socializing adolescents, and administrators' manipulation of their own regulations symbolizes the hypocrisy of the adult world. Such is the case with Brother Leon in Cormier's *The Chocolate War*. To shore up his power as acting headmaster of Trinity High School, Leon conspires with a teen gang to terrorize any student who refuses to sell chocolate for the school's fund-raising drive. Cormier exposes Leon's conniving, duplicitous nature at his first appearance in the novel: "On the surface, he was one of those pale, ingratiating kind of men who tiptoed through life on small, quick feet. He looked like a henpecked husband, a pushover, a sucker." Yet, Leon's demeanor is deceiving: "In the classroom, Leon was another person altogether. Smirking, sarcastic. His thin, high voice

RECLUSE IN THE ROSE GARDEN

"I think it might have been the subject matter, with the confusion of the words sanity and insanity. We talk about an insane society, that war is insane, that this or that is insane. I think that very often young people are worried about their sanity. Particularly in their Western experience —and I don't mean American, I mean Western—which confuses creativity and insanity, which confuses imagination and insanity.

"I had given a little talk about creativity and insanity and I told my sister about it. And she said, you know it works the other way too. The idea of the talk was, when you are creative and mentally ill, it's almost impossible to differentiate the illness from the creative part, and our culture does very little to help you. My sister was right; it works the other way as well. If you want to be creative, you sometimes stop because you're afraid of its being insanity."

Joanne Greenberg

From Stephen E. Rubin, "Conversations with the Author of *I Never Promised You a Rose Garden*," *Psychoanalytic Review*, 59 (1972): 201-215.

venomous. He could hold your attention like a cobra. Instead of fangs, he used his teacher's pointer, flicking out here, there, everywhere."[34] Another malevolent school administrator is A. Herbert Bledsoe, the president of the all-black university attended by the narrator of Ellison's *Invisible Man*. In public Bledsoe acts deferentially toward the school's white benefactors. When Ellison's hero inadvertently exposes a white trustee to the black poverty that exists off campus, however, an enraged Bledsoe insists that the young man must learn "to act the nigger" if he ever hopes to succeed in a white-dominated world: "The dumbest black bastard in the cotton patch knows that the only way to please a white man is to tell him a lie!

What kind of education are you getting around here?" In his tirade Bledsoe reveals not only that he is duping the school's white supporters but also that he does so for his own benefit, not for that of fellow blacks: "I don't owe anyone a thing, son. Who, Negroes? Negroes don't control this school or much of anything else—haven't you learned even that? No, sure, they don't control this school, nor white folk either. True they *support* it, but *I* control it. I's big and black and I say 'Yes, suh' as loudly as any burrhead when it's convenient, but I'm still the king down here."[35]

The representation of adults in alienated-youth fiction is almost always negative. The tradition of portraying parents and role models as antagonists reveals the degree to which modern American culture equates growing up with corruption. Alienated-youth fiction portrays adults as responsible for a world that strikes youth as dangerous and demeaning. How young people respond to its treachery is an indication of their own characters.

LOST YOUTH

The term *lost youth* describes adolescent characters who are either oblivious to the wrongs of the adult world or are too disaffected to challenge them. Significantly, lost youth tend to be secondary characters whose problems mirror those of the main character. (Critics often use the term *doppelgänger,* a German word for someone's counterpart or double, to describe such a supporting player.) Lost adolescents thus allow writers to highlight the sensitive, searching nature of protagonists by placing these heroes against a backdrop of complacent contemporaries who cannot envision alternatives to the status quo. At one end of the lost-youth spectrum are teens who already exhibit adult malevolence. Such is the case with Lane Coutell in Salinger's 1955 short story "Franny." Coutell, a self-important Yale upperclassman and Franny's boyfriend, answers her professions of her spiritual aspirations with complaints about the negative effect of those aspirations on their sex life. When a distraught Franny faints after trying to explain her religious beliefs, he feigns compassion by promising to return her to her hotel. His real motive soon becomes clear, however: "'You're just going to *rest* this afternoon. That's all you're going to do.' He stroked her arm for a moment. 'Then maybe after a while, if you get any decent rest, I can get upstairs somehow. I think there's a goddam back staircase.'"[36] The fact that he can propose such intimacy after Franny's breakdown reveals that he has little concern for her problems.

Villainous youth such as Coutell tend to be caricatures rather than characters. More sympathetic are teens whose inability to cope with adult expectations leads to self-destruction. *The Catcher in the Rye* and *The Bell Jar* feature characters (James Castle and Joan Gilling, respectively) whose suicides move Holden and Esther to seek more-positive ways of expressing their own despair. Equally tragic is the fate of Tod Clifton, a young, black radical who befriends the narrator of *Invisible Man*. When Ellison's narrator first meets Clifton, he is the director of youth in a Communist organization called the Brotherhood, which competes against a black nationalist movement led by the mysterious Ras the Destroyer for the political loyalties of Harlem's disenfranchised African American population. Two events conspire to undermine Clifton's sense of identity. During a knife fight, Ras denounces him as an Uncle Tom, a black man who willingly serves his oppressors. (The Brotherhood, although attempting to organize African Americans, is led by white radicals.) In a subsequent street confrontation with local agitators Clifton inadvertently pummels a fellow Brotherhood member, thus turning the organization against him. When Clifton goes missing, the narrator tracks him down, discovering, to his horror, that he has taken to selling racist Sambo dolls on a street corner. The song that Clifton sings suggests the depths of his self-loathing: "*What makes him happy, what makes him dance, / This Sambo, this Jambo, this high-stepping joy boy? / He's more than a toy, ladies and gentlemen, he's Sambo, / The dancing doll, the twentieth-century miracle.*"[37] As the hero of a racist storybook, Sambo embodies the stereotype of blacks as happy-go-lucky, primitive beings incapable of comprehending their oppression. The doll is thus a perverse incarnation of Clifton's fate within the Brotherhood: he is a toy token, a marionette manipulated by the organization's white leadership. His crazed behavior represents the futility of one African American's attempts to establish an adult identity in America, a fate that the narrator recognizes when Clifton is later shot dead by a policeman: "He thought he was a man when he was only Tod Clifton. He thought he was a man and that men were not meant to be pushed around."[38] In order to avoid a similar fate, the narrator realizes that he must separate himself from both the Brotherhood and Ras the Destroyer and become secure in the knowledge of his own identity before he can address the larger political question of what it means to be young and black in America.

The fates of Castle, Gilling, and Clifton suggest that lost youth give into suicide and despair because they cannot envision any resolution to their discontent. For the main characters of troubled-teen narratives, the chief challenge is to discover some ray of hope or optimism that will allow them to transcend their alienation.

SAINTLY ADOLESCENT SEEKERS

The protagonists of alienated-youth fiction typically possess two main characteristics. Philip D. Beidler describes the first:

> It is astonishing to count the number of youth-scriptures that are about somebody going crazy in America. Significantly, that somebody in question is often a young person, sensitive, intelligent, well brought up (as they used to say), born to a comfortable life, sometimes actually privileged. Yet that same young person invariably finds himself or herself estranged to a deep heart's sickness from a culture that seems to have offered virtually everything possible materially and institutionally and virtually nothing morally and spiritually.[39]

Beidler voices the critical consensus when he suggests that teen heroes are flustered by a conspiracy of nature and nurture. On the one hand, they must cope with the emotional storm and stress inherent in the developmental drama of adolescence. On the other hand, society's corrupted values exacerbate this mental upheaval, driving many young people to the brink of breakdown. To emphasize the psychological nature of this "deep heart's sickness," Beidler draws on 1960s slang to dub this personality type the "juvenile head-case."

While Beidler's colorful coinage captures teen heroes' maladjustment, it fails to acknowledge a second, equally important trait, one suggested by the title of Jonathan Baumbach's influential essay "The Saint as a Young Man: A Reappraisal of *The Catcher in the Rye*" (1964). As Baumbach argues, suffering ennobles adolescent protagonists to the point that they become quasi saints or saviors whose quest for authenticity redeems their fallen culture: "Holden not only suffers as a victim from the effects of the evil in the world, but for it as its conscience—so that his experiences are exemplary. In this sense, *The Catcher in the Rye* is a religious or, to be more exact, spiritual novel. Holden is Prince Mishkin as a sophisticated New York adolescent; and like Mishkin, he experiences the guilt, unhappiness, and spiritual deformities of others more intensely than he does his own misfortunes."[40] (Mishkin is the hero of Fyodor Dostoevsky's 1868 novel *The Idiot,* a saintly sufferer who, like Holden, yearns to save children from evil.) In this sense, the "craziness" of disaffected adolescents is not a psychological aberration but a mark of spiritual wisdom from which the rest of society has fallen away. To say, however, that writers of alienated-youth fiction depict their heroes as contemporary Christ figures is an overstatement. Authors such as Salinger do not glorify teenage alienation as a metaphorical martyrdom. Rather, the adolescent outcast's sickness is meant to index the degree to which adult culture fails to feed the soul of youth.

From the opening paragraph of *The Catcher in the Rye,* Holden makes it clear that he sees himself as insane: "I'll just tell you about this madman stuff that happened to me around last Christmas before I got pretty run-down and had to come out here and take it easy" (3). Whenever he is accused of not growing up, Holden pleads insanity because he believes that dissatisfaction is a far more natural response to the state of modern society than obliging acceptance. In scene after scene he happens upon people who lack any understanding of themselves because their actions and emotions are entirely divorced from each other. Only children possess the uninhibited spontaneity that Holden believes is an honest expression of human nature. Adulthood, by contrast, confounds one's motives by encouraging dishonesty. As he explains when his sister, Phoebe, asks why he could not be happy as a lawyer like their father, "Even if you *did* go around saving guys' lives and all, how would you know if you did it because you really *wanted* to save guys' lives, or because you did it because what you *really* wanted to do was be a terrific lawyer, with everybody slapping you on the back and congratulating you in court when the goddamn trial was over, the reporters and everybody, the way it is in the dirty movies? How would you know you weren't being a phony? The trouble is, you *wouldn't*" (223–224). In Holden's eyes childhood represents the purity of instinct, while adulthood marks a confusion of motive.

Holden's disturbed condition parallels that of the title character in Salinger's "Franny." Like Holden, Franny is disgusted by the guises that adults assume to further their own self-interest. As an aspiring actress, she has even been trained to manipulate appearances and create the illusion of sincerity, but her ambivalent feelings about this training have led her to drop out of the university's theater department. When Franny's boyfriend, Lane, accuses her of lacking the competitive spirit necessary to succeed at her chosen craft, she corrects him: "I'm afraid I will compete—that's what scares me. That's why I quit the Theater Department. Just because I'm so horribly conditioned to accept everybody else's values, and just because I like applause and people to rave about me, doesn't make it right. I'm sick of it. I'm sick of not having the courage to be an absolute nobody. I'm sick of myself and everyone else that wants to make some kind of splash."[41] She once believed that art would provide a refuge from the self-absorption afflicting contemporary society, but both her drama and literature classes are populated by narrow-minded egotists pursuing fame. Searching for more meaningful motives for existing, Franny is studying a book about prayer and spiritual enlightenment. As she tries to describe her enthusiasm for this form of worship, she realizes that Lane has no interest in religion. Although his callousness drives Franny to a breakdown, the final image in the story suggests that she remains committed to her spiritual pursuits: "Alone,

Franny lay quite still, looking at the ceiling. Her lips began to move, forming soundless words, and they continued to move."[42] Franny's "soundless words" are the prayer outlined in her book, which has provided a respite from the self-preoccupation beguiling her.

Not all "crazy" youth suffer in as alienated a fashion as Holden and Franny. In novels such as *On the Road, A Separate Peace,* and *Birdy* the authors employ a doppelgänger, a saintly peer who helps the protagonist come to maturity. In *A Separate Peace* the young scholar-athlete Phineas (nicknamed "Finny") symbolizes innocence incarnate, for he is incapable of hatred, envy, and other human flaws. In contrast, Gene Forrester, the narrator, is plagued by these failings. Resentful of Phineas's purity, Gene bounces him off of a tree limb, breaking his leg and thereby maiming him for life. Tortured by guilt, Gene struggles to gather the courage to confess his role in the accident. Although Knowles never makes the point explicit, Phineas's pacifistic nature teaches Gene that he does not have to accept the war-justifying truism that strife and savagery are inherent in the human condition. An older, wiser Gene summarizes his friend's effect on his life: "During the time I was with him, Phineas created an atmosphere in which I continue now to live, a way of sizing up the world with erratic and entirely personal reservations, letting its rock-like facts sift through and be accepted only a little at a time, only as much as he could assimilate without a sense of chaos and loss." These "entirely personal reservations" are the core of the "separate peace" denoted by the title of the novel. Through Phineas's example Gene ends the battle between good and evil within himself by making a personal vow not to succumb to the latter. As he now understands, "It seemed clear that wars were not made by generations and their special stupidities, but that wars were made instead by something ignorant in the human heart."[43]

The gallery of "crazy," saintly main characters in alienated-youth fiction also includes the titular hero of *Birdy,* whose traumatic wounding in World War II teaches his friend Al how to cope with brutality; Benjamin Braddock in Charles Webb's *The Graduate,* who befuddles his parents by refusing to accept a graduate-school scholarship that could ensure his professional future; and the narrator of Frederick Exley's *A Fan's Notes: A Fictional Memoir* (1968), who struggles to prove that he is not a spectator doomed to observe other men's achievements. In these examples, "madness" is a product of young people's desire for a vision of the saner, more spiritual future. In the end, the aberrancy of these main characters is meant to move readers to the same epiphany as Dr. Fried in *I Never Promised You a Rose Garden:* "We must someday make a test to show us where the *health* is as well as the illness."[44]

THEMES

Interpreting the main theme of a narrative is perhaps the most challenging aspect of literary analysis. Because compelling literature shrouds itself in ambiguity, the audience must assume responsibility for articulating the implicit statement that the work is making. When describing the theme of a novel or story, it is best to respect this ambiguity by not reducing meaning to the literalness of an Aesopian moral. Rather than claiming that *The Catcher in the Rye* is about how people should stay young at heart, one might more appropriately assess Salinger's theme by stating that the novel depicts adolescent disaffection as a symptom of, but not a solution to, the spiritual apathy of modern American society. Similarly, one should recognize that narratives often include many themes. While it is correct to say that *A Separate Peace* is an anti-war novel, Knowles's book also explores such relevant issues as responsibility, loyalty, and friendship. The following themes should not be regarded as exhaustive. They represent only the most obvious assertions put forth in stories of troubled teens.

Alienated-youth fiction portrays rebellion as youth's response to adults' view of them as a social problem. Stereotyped as a potential threat to cultural stability, adolescents realize that the sole power they possess is their ability to fluster and frighten their elders. By defying convention, youth act out their status as "different" in order to insist that they exist beyond the norms of adult comprehension.

Dick Hebdige has described the predicament of teenagers in twentieth-century culture: "In our society, youth is present only when its presence is a problem, or is regarded as a problem. More precisely, the category 'youth' gets mobilized in official documentary discourse when young people make their presence felt by going 'out of bounds,' by resisting through rituals, dressing strangely, striking bizarre attitudes, breaking rules, breaking bottles, windows, heads, issuing rhetorical challenges to the law."[45] Authorities view teens as a social problem because they represent both the future and a threat to the future. While elders call on succeeding generations to maintain cultural continuity, they fear what will become of society should their charges decline this obligation. Adolescent rebellion seizes on this anxiety. As Hebdige writes, "Youth rebellion is a declaration of independence, of otherness, of alien intent, a refusal of anonymity, of subordinate status. Yet, it is also a confirmation of powerlessness, a celebration of the impotence of alienation. Both a play for attention and a refusal, once attention has been granted, to be read according to the Book."[46] If we cannot belong, teenagers insist, we cannot be known.

This theme is most apparent in narratives in which adults demand that teens account for their disaffection. As Holden prepares to leave Pencey Prep early in *The Catcher in the Rye*, he visits his history teacher, Mr. Spencer, who interrogates him about his academic failures. Holden's defense is succinct: "I'm a moron"(19). When pressed further, he admits (if not boasts) that he is immature, and he even offers a pat sociological justification for his indifference: "I'm just going through a phase right now. Everybody goes through phases and all, don't they?" (20–21). While Holden's detachment shocks Spencer, the boy's comments reveal that he does not really believe what he is saying. By his own admission to the reader, he is "shooting the bull" (18). Holden's behavior demonstrates how youth hide behind a veil of inscrutability, taunting adults with their inability to explain themselves. As he says when Spencer asks whether he cares about succeeding in life, "Oh, I feel some concern for my future, all right. Sure. Sure, I do. . . . But not too much, I guess. Not too much, I guess" (20). Similar scenes abound in other works of alienated-youth fiction. They suggest that whenever teenagers display flagrant disregard for their future, they do so knowing that their indifference will drive adults to distraction. As a result, youth remain a subject of cultural consternation, an enigma to both elders and themselves.

Although alienated-youth fiction celebrates teenage rebellion, it does not suggest that withdrawal will cure youth's discontent. Instead, teen readers are urged to recognize that they can begin to overcome the spiritual emptiness of modern America only by addressing these problems rather than running away from them. These works thus teach youth that they can transform the conditions plaguing them through engagement, not detachment.

Although authors such as Salinger, Plath, and Kerouac empathize with the teenage desire to impugn authority, they challenge readers to recognize that alienation is not an effective strategy for achieving social change. In effect youth must outgrow what Paul Goodman calls their "Either/Or" conception of their options, their belief that they must choose between two mutually exclusive paths: "Either they choose to conform to the organized system, reaping its rewards and feeling cynical about what they are doing. Or if they choose totally to dissent, they don't work at changing the institutions as radical youth used to, but they stop washing their faces, take to drugs, or become punch-drunk and slap-happy. Either way they lose the objective changeable world. They have early resigned."[47] As Goodman insists, withdrawal exacerbates feelings of futility in youth, leading to self-destruction rather than efforts to alter the system. Accordingly, alienated adolescents must acknowledge that only by returning home instead of running away, or by leaving the sanatorium instead of hiding in it, can they confront the conditions causing their despair.

Typically, alienated-youth novels make the case for engagement through an older, sympathetic adult figure who counsels the main character. In *The Catcher in the Rye* another of Holden's teachers, Mr. Antolini, serves this function. Late in his journey Holden visits his former English instructor's apartment, where the older man asks him to explain how such an intelligent pupil could become so disaffected that three different prep schools have expelled him. Holden responds with his usual complaints against phonies, but Antolini recognizes that such targets are a poor excuse for apathy. The teacher asks Holden to ponder a quote from the psychoanalyst Wilhelm Stekel: "The mark of the immature man is that he wants to die nobly for a cause, while the mark of the mature man is that he wants to live humbly for one" (244). As Antolini understands, Holden may be destroyed by his own behavior without having made any discernible dent in the system he detests. This advice is lost on Holden, however, for in a following scene he presumes that the teacher is making sexual advances toward him. Critics have long debated whether Antolini is indeed a closeted homosexual or whether Holden misinterprets the man's interest in him. In the end, the question is a red herring: Holden comes to a conclusion on his own that is similar to Antolini's. By abandoning his fantasy of running away from home, Holden acknowledges that cutting himself off from family and society will not cure his confusion. Furthermore, his submitting himself to psychiatric care signals at least a tentative desire to find more positive ways of dealing with his disaffection.

In *I Never Promised You a Rose Garden* the empathetic adult is Dr. Fried, who challenges Deborah to view the demonic hallucinations eroding her sanity as manifestations of the moral choices she is trying to elude in the real world. As Dr. Fried tells her, "You have to take the world first, to take it on faith as a complete commitment . . . on my word if no one else's. Then, on what you yourself build of this commitment you can decide whether it's a decent bargain or not."[48] In other cases the main character is the one who argues for engagement over withdrawal. At the conclusion of *Birdy,* the shell-shocked protagonist, who has retreated from his trauma by fantasizing that he is a pigeon, frees himself from his psychosis. His friend and fellow soldier Al believes that the hospital

Alienated-Youth Fiction   **101**

where they are recuperating will shelter them from the inhumanity that they have witnessed on the battlefields of World War II. Yet, Birdy insists that they return to the outside world and use the survival skills that their suffering has taught them. Dubious, Al demands to know how Birdy can simply will himself to heal. Birdy's response suggests that recuperation is an ongoing process that demands committed effort: "It's never that easy. Nobody gets off that way. But it's worth trying."[49] If the message of most alienated-youth fiction could be summarized in one word, it is the message in Birdy's advice to Al: try. As writers of this kind of fiction have argued, withdrawal merely perpetuates adolescent powerlessness. If young people truly find their elders' world intolerable, they must make the effort to initiate new modes of living.

Alienated-adolescent fiction presents the view that one key to the growth of self-understanding is the development of a unique voice. Through personalized forms of expression, young people are able to articulate and thus comprehend their disaffection.

Describing Holden's dilemma, Beidler suggests that the boy's woes arise in part from his "yearning inarticulateness," his inability to put his feelings into words: "Not only does this privileged character—as '60s parents were wont to call such young-adult offspring—agonizingly not know what he wants most of the time; even more desperately and heart-wrenchingly, he reveals in his greatest moments of loneliness that even if he did know he would possess no adequate discourse to communicate it, even to himself."[50] Many of Holden's fictional peers suffer the same affliction. Even garrulous protagonists such as Dean Moriarty go mute when challenged to account for themselves. When an acquaintance chastises him for running away from responsibility, he is unable to offer a defense: "Where once Dean would have talked his way out, he now fell silent himself, standing in front of everybody, ragged and broken and idiotic."[51] Those young people most successful in navigating the treacheries of growing up find the confidence to express their point of view through imaginative uses of language.

Because most alienated-youth fiction is autobiographical in origin, with authors basing their plots on their own coming-of-age experiences, this struggle for self-expression frequently takes the form of an artistic quest. Many protagonists are aspiring writers or, less frequently, musicians or actors who assert their individuality through their creativity. In *The Bell Jar* Esther must gain the confidence to pursue her literary ambitions, despite the pressure her mother exerts on her to secure gainful employment. (Mrs. Greenwood wants her to be a stenographer.) By the end of her hospitalization, Esther achieves her goal: "I was my own woman," she declares as she prepares to reenter the adult world.[52] Similarly, in *I Never Promised You a Rose Garden* Greenberg demonstrates the therapeutic value of artistic expression. Dr. Fried must help Deborah to understand that she herself is the author of the nightmarish world that undermines her sanity. By sketching images of this inner world, Deborah learns to externalize her fears. At a key moment she even realizes that the hallucinatory visions incapacitating her were inspired by an illustrated copy of John Milton's epic poem *Paradise Lost* (1667) that she pored over in childhood: "The nine-year-old had caught some of the ponderous thunder of the lines she did not know she had read, and while the artist in her had studied the etched angels and fire engraved lines that had blessed them with dimension, the secret-kingdom-seeker had subtly stolen the proud archangel for the first inhabitant of her world."[53] This epiphany assures her that her affliction is not unique to her own psyche but rather belongs to a tradition of human suffering that finds solace through expression. Deborah's artistry thus allows her to overcome her instability by venting her anxieties rather than succumbing to them.

As they depict the process of adolescent self-development, authors encourage teens to open themselves to new experiences, to experiment, and to make identifications across cultural boundaries. In particular, popular culture provides a resource through which young people can fashion their sense of who they are—and who they would like to be.

One popular-culture medium richly celebrated in alienated-youth novels is African American folk music. Whether spirituals, blues, or jazz, black musical idioms provide protagonists with themes and forms for articulating their identity. As more than one critic has noted, *Invisible Man* includes enough references to specific jazz and blues songs to compile a soundtrack to accompany the reading of the novel. In the prologue the narrator listens to Louis Armstrong's "Black and Blue." The chorus of the song ("What did I do / To be so black and blue?") poses the question the narrator must answer in order to understand how he has allowed himself to be duped by so many elders. During the public memorial service for Clifton, a Harlem singer spontaneously breaks into "There's Many a Thousand Gone," inspiring a large crowd to join him. As the narrator recognizes, the song speaks to the crowd's collective identity: "It was as though the song had been there all the time and he knew it and aroused it; and I knew that I had known it too and had failed to release it

Joanne Greenberg, whose *I Never Promised You a Rose Garden* (1964) which rivals Plath's *The Bell Jar* in popularity among adolescent female readers

out of a vague, nameless shame or fear."[54] Ellison's protagonist must recognize that this music embodies his own dilemma, as well as those of his fellow blacks. Far from being ashamed of his ethnicity, he learns that its traditions can teach him to express his confusion over his identity.

In other texts popular culture offers facile images of rebellion that endanger teens susceptible to the romance of self-ruin. In Joyce Carol Oates's "Where Are You Going, Where Have You Been?" the heroine, Connie, is bored by her parents' settled existence and turns for adventure to radio disc jockeys whose "hip" music and lingo equate adolescent exhilaration with risky behavior. She meets local hot-rodder Arnold Friend, whose self-styled "bad boy" mannerisms seem a transparent pastiche of James Dean and Elvis Presley: "Connie liked the way he was dressed, which was the way all of them dressed: tight faded jeans stuffed into black, scuffed boots, a belt that pulled his waist in and showed how lean he was, and a white pullover shirt that was a little soiled and showed the hard small muscles of his arms and shoulders."[55] She realizes too late how ill prepared she is to protect herself from the threat that the hoodlum poses. In this way, the ominous Friend—his name is a deliberate misnomer—symbolizes the manipulation of mass culture. By appealing to the same inclination to rebel that the music incites in Connie, he can lure her from her home, presumably to abduct and rape her. A dreamlike passage describing her confusion emphasizes the association between the music and Friend (who, Oates makes clear, is older than his prey): "Connie stared at him, another wave of dizziness and fear rising in her so that for a moment he wasn't even in focus but was just a blur standing there against his gold car, and she had the idea that he had driven up the driveway all right but had come from nowhere before that and belonged nowhere and that everything about him and even about the music that was so familiar to her was only half real."[56] Ultimately, Oates asks teens to view popular culture as a comparable form of seduction. Although promising freedom and fun, images of adolescent rebellion drive a wedge between young people and their families, placing them at the mercy of malevolent forces they may lack the maturity to resist.

Alienated-youth fiction does not speak exclusively to young people. It also addresses adults, seeking to energize their concern for teenagers by reminding them of their responsibility to provide youth a meaningful future.

Charles Acland argues that while teenagers may be the obvious audience for alienated-youth fiction, texts such as *The Catcher in the Rye* and *The Bell Jar* represent a plea to adults: "The plea is for that guiding hand that demonstrates the method of integration back into the realm of the normal youth, which in turn signifies the easy flow toward the adult."[57] In other words, the ideal reader of these works—the person to whom they seem to be addressed—is often an elder with the power to change the conditions causing the disaffection of youth rather than a teenager suffering from it. Discerning the ideal reader of any fictional text can be a difficult task, for one must infer the identity of this reader from clues in the storytelling that are not always overt. Writers often hint at who this addressee is by including in their cast of characters one member whose main function is to listen to the protagonist describe his woes. When Holden begins his monologue with the words "If you really want to hear about it . . ." (3), one ought to ask who this "you" is. Salinger provides sufficient evidence for readers to assume that Holden is speaking to a counselor at a clinic where he has been hospitalized. The doctor has neither name nor dialogue, yet his or her presence is evoked whenever Holden speaks to "you," as in this casual aside about Phoebe: "You should see her. You never saw a little kid so pretty and smart in your whole life" (87).

A fictional *you* is a common technique for placing an ideal reader in the story. The ephemeral listener in *The Catcher in the Rye* serves as a role model for actual readers by demonstrating the attitude they should take while interpreting what Holden says. In essence, Salinger asks readers to diagnose his narrator as a psychologist might. A therapist, after all, would presumably be empathetic and interested in helping Holden overcome his anguish. Such a person would not be judgmental or dismissive, nor—unlike other adults in the book—would he or she encourage him to conform without question. A therapist would also offer constructive criticism, challenging Holden to recognize faults and self-justifications. Most importantly, this authority figure would help him develop strategies for coping with discontent and avoiding self-destructive behavior. By specifying the context within which Holden's narration takes place, Salinger not only confirms that his protagonist is sick but also asks readers to prescribe a cure.

An even more obvious role model for the ideal reader is Mr. Antolini. Regardless of Holden's fears over the teacher's putative homosexuality, Antolini is compassionate, and his advice strikes many readers as sound: "Many, many men have been just as troubled morally and spiritually as you are right now. Happily, some of them kept records of their troubles. You'll learn from them—if you want to. Just as someday, if you have something to offer, someone will learn something from you" (246). Almost every piece of alienated-youth fiction includes a character like Mr. Antolini, whether it be Dr. Nolan in *The Bell Jar* or Dr. Fried in *I Never Promised You a Rose Garden*. The presence of such characters reminds adult readers (some of whom have even wanted to censor these books, fearful that they might inspire outbreaks of juvenile delinquency) of what youth both want and need: help. Allowing readers to view the dilemmas of Holden, Esther, and Deborah from the perspective of a concerned teacher or psychoanalyst means that expressions of disaffection are more likely to be interpreted as a crying out for understanding. In this way alienated-youth fiction defines a role for adults in the maturation process of adolescents.

MOTIFS

A motif is a recurring symbol or image within a text that conveys a theme. Sometimes referred to as a leitmotiv (a German word meaning "guiding motive"), its function is similar to that of a refrain in a poetic ballad or the chorus of a song. Through repetition a motif emphasizes the main idea of a narrative. More broadly, the term designates the stock elements that appear throughout different works in a particular genre. In effect, motifs are unifying devices. Within a novel or story they create internal coherence, while across a range of texts they allow critics to draw parallels and propose generalizations. The drama of much alienated-youth fiction arises from the tension between two specific motifs: flight and fall.

At their most basic, images of flight dramatize the desire to prolong initiation and stave off entry into adulthood. As Leslie A. Fiedler observes, flight from adulthood is a dominant impulse in American literature, particularly in fiction with male heroes: "The typical male protagonist of our fiction has been a man on the run, harried into the forest and out to sea, down the river or into combat—anywhere to avoid 'civilization,' which is to say, the confrontation of a man and woman which leads to the fall to sex, marriage, and responsibility."[58] For Fiedler and many other critics, the quintessential expression of this avoidance is Huck Finn's declaration in the closing paragraph of *The Adventures of Huckleberry Finn* that he plans to "light out for the Territory."[59]

Twain's image of the wilderness as a refuge from the social obligations of maturity suggests one popular variation of the flight motif: geographical flight. Especially in journey narratives, disaffected adolescents search for an unsettled territory where no custom or convention will impinge upon their freedom. Not unlike *The Adventures of Huckleberry Finn*, both *The Catcher in the Rye* and *On the Road* associate "lighting out" with the mythic American West. Holden dreams of escaping Manhattan for the West Coast, where he plans to assume the identity of a deaf-mute to separate himself from society: "That way I wouldn't have to have any goddam stupid useless conversations with anybody. If anybody wanted to tell me something, they'd have to write it on a piece of paper and shove it over to me. They'd get bored as hell doing that after a while, and then I'd be through with having conversations for the rest of my life" (257–258).

The West as a refuge for the independent spirit is even more important in *On the Road*. As Sal first travels across America, he encounters several characters whose solitary rambles assure him that such archetypes of American freedom as the cowboy and the hobo still exist. Yet, he also meets tourists and sightseers whose only knowledge of that freewheeling, footloose existence comes from kitschy, commercial roadside attractions that exploit their nostalgic feelings for independence. Venturing into Cheyenne, Wyoming, Sal finds the artificiality of the town's "Wild West Week" dispiriting because the event reveals just how anachronistic the unfettered self seems in an age of conformity: "Big businessmen, fat businessmen in boots and ten-gallon hats, with their hefty wives in cowgirl attire, bustled and whooped on the wooden sidewalks. Blank guns went off. The saloons were crowded to the sidewalk. I was amazed, and at the same time I felt it was ridiculous: in my first shot at the West I was seeing to what absurd devices it had fallen to keep its proud tradition."[60] Although Sal views Dean as an authentic embodiment of the Western tradition, he must eventually accept that both of them are searching for a territory that no longer exists. Rather than delivering them to freedom, their road trips become a race to keep their cowboy souls from being overrun by the status quo.

Other works eschew the motif of geographic flight for that of imaginative flight, in which heroes escape society's constraints by lighting out for an interior rather than exterior realm. As W. Tasker Witham explains, "Traditionally, the novel of adolescence presents a sensitive, often impractical youth surrounded by people who cannot understand his responses to stimuli that do not affect the majority of people, nor his failure to respond in ways that the majority consider natural if not inevitable. The difference tends to make the young protagonist more withdrawn from reality, and he is likely to find his pleasures in a dream world, from which he may or may not emerge."[61] The world of fantasy provides a safe haven from reality because it operates according to adolescent logic rather than adult rules. In *I Never Promised You a Rose Garden* Deborah's schizophrenic subconscious, however terrifying it may be, offers a retreat from the ostracization she suffers at the hands of parents and peers. One passage in the novel equates her delusions with escapism, which almost immediately proves illusory: "In the times of greatest joy, the happiness was so great that her feet could not bear the ground and she went to flight. The time of the pure flight, the joyful and perfect flight, had been pitifully short, and the Censor had begun to rule like a tyrant in both worlds. Yr [Deborah's imaginary world] still gave beauty and great joy, but the beauty and joy were at the tyrant's erratic whim."[62]

In *Birdy* Wharton makes similar use of flight as a metaphor for fleeing into the imagination. Throughout his adolescence Birdy is obsessed with the aerodynamic prowess of pigeons and yearns to experience the sensation of being lighter than air. In one scene he and his boyhood friend Al climb a coal tank to catch birds. Birdy slips over the edge, but instead of falling he stretches out his arms and, to Al's amazement, floats to safety. Birdy describes the resulting feeling: "The first time I flew, it was being alive. Nothing was pressuring under me. I was living in the fullness of it; air all around me, no holding place to break the air spaces. It is worth everything to be alone in the air, alive."[63] To maintain this exhilaration Birdy transforms his bedroom into an aviary, where he studies the motion of birds and designs mechanical wings. His family hopes that his induction into the service will cure him of his daydreams of flight, but when his plane is shot down while he is fighting in the Pacific theater, his only means of survival is slipping back into his delusion. When Al asks Birdy how he escaped from a Japanese massacre of wounded American soldiers, the young man tells an unlikely story, which he narrates in the present tense:

> There's a noise at the far end of the tent. It's a Japanese soldier cutting through with a bayonet. He goes down the line of cots. There's no screaming, only the thump of his rifle and the tear of the cot when the bayonet stabs through each time. I rip off the tubes, crawl under the edge of the tent, and start to run. Then,

> I begin to fly. I fly past the Japanese, over the tent, and into the jungle. I look back and see the tent on the edge of the sand and the water glistening. The next thing I'm here listening to you talk about pigeons.[64]

Wharton never supplies a more realistic explanation for Birdy's escape, forcing the reader to accept the improbability that the young man eluded death by defying gravity.

Whereas the flight motif dramatizes the desire to elude the pain associated with maturity, the motif of the fall suggests that the loss of innocence is inevitable. The evocative power of the fall arises from its symbolic association with the biblical story of Adam and Eve's initiation into mortality. As Fiedler notes, "An initiation is a fall through knowledge to maturity; behind it there persists the myth of the Garden of Eden, the assumption that to know good and evil is to be done with the joy of innocence and to take on the burdens of work and childbearing and death."[65] In alienated-youth fiction flight inevitably leads to fall, the latter tempering the protagonist's belief in his or her ability to evade initiatory experiences through a geographical or imaginative means of escape. (The exception to this rule is *Birdy,* in which Birdy's fall—symbolized by the shooting down of his airplane—leads to the renewed flight of his ambiguous escape.)

The Catcher in the Rye presents two images of the fall. The first occurs when Holden describes to Phoebe his dream of saving children at play in a rye field from tumbling over a cliff (the source of the title of the novel). Holden's ambition is a prelapsarian fantasy in which he preserves the purity of youth "before the fall." As Baumbach observes, "The metaphor of the title—Holden's fantasy-vision of standing in front of a cliff and protecting playing children from falling (Falling)—is, despite the impossibility of its realization, the only positive action affirmed in the novel. It is, in Salinger's Manichean universe of child angels and adult 'phonies,' the only moral alternative—otherwise all is corruption."[66] Yet, Mr. Antolini's advice to Holden suggests that the boy's devotion to this impossibility itself brings about a fall from innocence: "This fall I think you're riding for—it's a special kind of fall, a horrible kind. The man falling isn't permitted to feel or hear himself hit bottom. He just keeps falling and falling. The whole arrangement's designed for men who, at some time or other in their lives, were looking for something their own environment couldn't supply them with. . . . So they gave up looking. They gave up before they ever really even got started" (243–244). In effect Antolini urges Holden to question whether his disaffection might be a symbolic means of hurling himself from the cliff into the postlapsarian world of disillusionment. By flunk-

BIRDY AND THE LAUNCH OF AN UNLIKELY CAREER

Like J. D. Salinger and Joanne Greenberg, William Wharton, the author of *Birdy,* has steered clear of the literary spotlight and thus remains something of an enigma. Indeed, for many years he was so successful at obscuring his true identity that, in the early 1980s, rumors circulated in the publishing industry that Wharton was actually Salinger, who supposedly adopted the pseudonym so that his new book would not be compared with *The Catcher in the Rye.* That rumor was quickly quashed, and more recently Wharton has been more forthcoming about his origins.

Born Albert DuAmine in 1926 in Philadelphia, Pennsylvania, Wharton served in the U.S. Army's Eighty-seventh Infantry Division during World War II. Both his combat experiences (he was badly wounded and required a facial reconstruction) and his subsequent treatment at an Army psychiatric hospital inspired the plot of *Birdy.* After his discharge Wharton studied painting at the University of California, Los Angeles, where he also earned a Ph.D. before moving to Paris in 1959 to live as an artist. He was fifty-three when the semi-autobiographical *Birdy* was published in 1979; the unexpected success of the book inspired him to write a second initiation novel about war, *A Midnight Clear* (1982), as well as other novels about young adults, including *Tidings* (1987) and *Franky Furbo* (1989), which features Wharton's artwork. His popularity among young readers was also cemented by the successful movie adaptations of *Birdy* in 1984 and *A Midnight Clear* in 1991.

ing out of school and cutting himself off from his family, Holden isolates himself from the resources necessary for him to express his discontent through a positive rather than a self-destructive channel. In Antolini's view Holden's despair may benefit him by motivating him to seek out new knowledge and experience: "Among other things, you'll find that you're not the first person who was ever confused and frightened and even sickened by human behavior. You're by no means alone on that score, you'll be excited and *stimulated* to know" (246).

By insisting that Holden's disaffection can teach him an important lesson about humanity, Antolini invokes the biblical idea of *felix culpa* (the fortunate fault), which teaches the paradoxical idea that losing one's innocence is a blessing because it makes one more aware of human imperfection. In *A Separate Peace* the fall into knowledge is physical rather than metaphorical. As a test of courage Gene, Finny, and their friends leap from a tree into a nearby river. (As many critics have suggested, the tree evokes the biblical tree of knowledge.) By spilling Finny from a limb, Gene initiates himself into an awareness of his capacity for evil, and he must cope with his guilt over his inability to accept responsibility for his actions. If, as many critics argue, Finny is a sacrificial Christ figure whose death later in the novel redeems humanity, Gene represents that fallen humanity, which must bear the burden of its fallibility. However shameful Gene's actions, they are enlightening, for they force him to gain a deeper understanding of the nature of sin. In the end Gene learns to emulate rather than resent Finny's Christlike grace.

In *Invisible Man,* Ellison offers another important variation of the fall motif.

As in *A Separate Peace,* the fall is a literal one. While attempting to escape a racist mob, the protagonist tumbles through an open manhole near the boundary between the black- and white-populated sections of Manhattan. This fortuitous fall provides him with a sanctuary from the stereotypes that limit the self-development of African American youth. The hole grants the narrator a space within which his vision of himself will not be tainted by society's prejudices. From the preface he makes it clear that his fall is not an escape but an education: "Remember, a bear retires to his hole for the winter and lives until spring; then he comes strolling out like the Easter chick breaking from its shell."[67] He remains in hiding only as long as is necessary to learn how black and white elders have deceived him. In the closing paragraphs of the epilogue the invisible man confirms his growth by pledging to return to the world, secure in his identity: "I'm shaking off the old skin and I'll leave it here in the hole. I'm coming out, no less invisible without it, but coming out nevertheless. And I suppose it's damn well time. I've overstayed my hibernation, since there's a possibility that even an invisible man has a

John Knowles, whose *A Separate Peace* (1960), like Salinger's *The Catcher in the Rye,* has retained its popularity among student readers

socially responsible role to play."[68] Had the invisible man not fallen into the hole, Ellison implies, he would never have overcome the naiveté that made him a pawn of other men's politics.

The opposing motifs of flight and fall embody the core conflict that propels the drama of alienated-youth fiction. Each motif represents a basic choice that teen protagonists must make: should they withdraw from a way of life that offers little stimulation, or should they engage the conditions encouraging conformity and strive to change society for the better? Although flight appeals to the promise of endless youth, it exacts a heavy toll because it traps young people in their alienation. While the fall requires the sacrifice of innocence, the wisdom and perseverance acquired through experience compensate for that loss. If a basic purpose of the alienated-youth genre is to encourage young people to ponder their place in the world, it seems appropriate that the most enduring narratives of adolescence recognize the value of the fall. Novels such as *The Catcher in the Rye, The Bell Jar,* and *On the Road* may romanticize youth, but they also encourage readers to recognize that maturation leads to growth, not loss.

NOTES

1. Norman Kiell, *The Adolescent through Fiction: A Psychological Approach* (New York: International Universities Press, 1959), p. 17.

2. Mordecai Marcus, "What is an Initiation Story?" *Journal of Aesthetics and Art Criticism,* 19 (Winter 1960): 223.

3. Toni Morrison, *The Bluest Eye* (New York: Holt, Rinehart & Winston, 1970), p. 204.

4. William Wharton, *Birdy* (New York: Knopf, 1979), pp. 300–301.

5. Marcus, "What is an Initiation Story?" p. 227.

6. See Betty Carter, *Best Books for Young Adults: The Selections, the History, the Romance* (Chicago: American Library Association, 1994), pp. 1–24.

7. Maia Pank Mertz and David A. England, "The Legitimacy of American Adolescent Fiction," *School Library Journal,* 30 (October 1983): 119.

8. Michael Cart, *From Romance to Realism: 50 Years of Growth and Change in Young Adult Literature* (New York: HarperCollins, 1996), p. 20.

9. S. E. Hinton, "Teen-agers Are for Real," *New York Times Book Review,* 27 August 1967, p. 26.

10. Paul Zindel, *The Pigman* (New York: Harper & Row, 1968), pp. 148–149.

11. Robert Cormier, *The Chocolate War* (New York: Pantheon, 1974), p. 187.

12. Dagmar Grenz, "Literature for Young People and the Novel of Adolescence," in *Aspects and Issues in the History of Children's Literature,* edited by Maria Nikolajeva (Westport, Conn.: Greenwood Press, 1995), p. 179.

13. John Seelye, "Holden in the Museum," in *New Essays on J. D. Salinger's The Catcher in the Rye,* edited by Jack Salzman (Cambridge: Cambridge University Press, 1991), p. 24.

14. Janis P. Stout, *The Journey Narrative in American Literature: Patterns and Departures* (Westport, Conn.: Greenwood Press, 1983), p. 99.

15. Jack Kerouac, *On the Road* (New York: Viking, 1957), p. 11.

16. Ibid., p. 208.

17. Stout, *The Journey Narrative in American Literature,* p. 110.

18. Ralph Ellison, *Invisible Man* (New York: Modern Library, 1992), p. 567.

19. Richard Ohmann, "The Shaping of a Canon, 1960–1975," *Critical Inquiry,* 10 (September 1983): 213.

20. Sylvia Plath, *The Bell Jar* (New York: Harper & Row, 1971), p. 1.

21. Ibid., pp. 117–118.

22. Ibid., p. 199.

23. Joanne Greenberg (as Hannah Green), *I Never Promised You a Rose Garden* (New York: Holt, Rinehart & Winston, 1964), pp. 40–41.

24. Ibid., pp. 102–103.

25. Evan Hunter, *The Blackboard Jungle* (New York: Simon & Schuster, 1954), p. 301.

26. S. E. Hinton, *The Outsiders* (New York: Viking, 1967), p. 82.

27. Ibid., p. 155.

28. Bret Easton Ellis, *Less Than Zero* (New York: Simon & Schuster, 1985), p. 172.

29. Ibid., p. 205.

30. Morrison, *The Bluest Eye,* p. 126.

31. Plath, *The Bell Jar,* p. 119.

32. Ibid., p. 166.

33. Greenberg, *I Never Promised You a Rose Garden,* p. 25.

34. Cormier, *The Chocolate War,* p. 23.

35. Ellison, *Invisible Man,* pp. 137, 140.

36. J. D Salinger, "Franny," in *Franny and Zooey* (Boston: Little, Brown, 1961), p. 43.

37. Ellison, *Invisible Man,* p. 425.

38. Ibid., p. 450.

39. Philip D. Beidler, *Scriptures for a Generation: What We Were Reading in the '60s* (Athens: University of Georgia Press, 1995), p. 87.

40. Jonathan Baumbach, "The Young Man as Saint: A Reappraisal of *The Catcher in the Rye,*" *Modern Language Quarterly,* 25 (December 1964): 466.

41. Salinger, "Franny," p. 30.

42. Ibid., p. 44.

43. John Knowles, *A Separate Peace* (New York: Macmillan, 1960), pp. 194, 193.

44. Greenberg, *I Never Promised You a Rose Garden,* p. 19.

45. Dick Hebdige, *Hiding in the Light: On Images and Things* (New York: Comedia, 1988), pp. 17–18.

46. Ibid., p. 35.

47. Paul Goodman, *Growing Up Absurd: Problems of Youth in the Organized System* (New York: Random House, 1960), p. 135.

48. Greenberg, *I Never Promised You a Rose Garden,* p. 244.

49. Wharton, *Birdy,* p. 310.

50. Beidler, *Scriptures for a Generation,* p. 177.

51. Kerouac, *On the Road,* p. 195.

52. Plath, *The Bell Jar,* p. 182.

53. Greenberg, *I Never Promised You a Rose Garden,* p. 248.

54. Ellison, *Invisible Man,* p. 446.

55. Joyce Carol Oates, "Where Are You Going, Where Have You Been?" in *Where Are You Going, Where Have You Been? Selected Early Stories* (Princeton: Ontario Review Press, 1993), p. 125.

56. Ibid., p. 134.

57. Charles Acland, *Youth, Murder, Spectacle: The Cultural Politics of "Youth in Crisis"* (Boulder, Colo.: Westview Press, 1995), p. 121.

58. Leslie A. Fiedler, *Love and Death in the American Novel,* revised edition (New York: Stein & Day, 1966), p. 27.

59. Mark Twain, *The Adventures of Huckleberry Finn* (New York: Penguin, 1994), p. 386.

60. Kerouac, *On the Road,* p. 33.

61. W. Tasker Witham, *The Adolescent in the American Novel, 1920–1960* (New York: Ungar, 1964), pp. 167–168.

62. Greenberg, *I Never Promised You a Rose Garden,* p. 208.

63. Wharton, *Birdy,* p. 22.

64. Ibid., p. 302.

65. Fiedler, "From Redemption to Initiation," *New Leader,* 41 (26 May 1958): 22.

66. Baumbach, "The Young Man as Saint," p. 462.

67. Ellison, *Invisible Man,* p. 9.

68. Ibid., p. 503.

CRITICAL RESPONSE TO
ALIENATED-YOUTH FICTION

Alienated-youth fiction is something of a literary grab bag. Using various plot forms (the journey of self-discovery, the rehabilitation story, and the at-risk narrative) and borrowing from older narrative traditions (the quest, the picaresque tale, and the bildungsroman), it remains one of the most difficult types of fiction to define. Given the diversity of texts that this category can accommodate, it should not be surprising that the scholarly reaction to it is equally wide-ranging. In general, one can suggest three main currents of critical interest. Literary-historical critiques place contemporary representations of growing up in the context of American literary history, analyzing how, for example, Holden Caulfield's aversion to adulthood in *The Catcher in the Rye* compares with that of Huck Finn in *Adventures of Huckleberry Finn*. Thematic critiques enumerate the dramatic affinities between novels such as *The Catcher in the Rye*, *The Bell Jar*, and *A Separate Peace*. Cultural critiques explore the depiction of the social conditions affecting maturation in the historical period in which a particular novel or story is set.

An overview of the adolescent in American literature must acknowledge the influence of Leslie A. Fiedler. Beginning in the late 1940s Fiedler wrote a series of provocative essays critiquing America's mythic fascination with innocence. In his view the equation of youth with the prelapsarian purity of Adam and Eve bespoke artists' aversion to exploring the complex problems of adulthood. "Boys Will Be Boys!" is the third installment in a series of articles by Fiedler published in *The New Leader* in 1958. In it he insists that J. D. Salinger and Jack Kerouac extended the tradition of the "good bad boy" embodied by Huck Finn. The only difference between Huck's and Holden's generations is that, for modern youth, sex is no longer an initiation experience but merely another intuitive expression of naive innocence.

Kerouac (left) with Long Island fans in the late 1950s

From Leslie A. Fiedler, "Boys Will Be Boys!" *New Leader*, 41 (28 April 1958): 24–26.

    Huck Finn is in one sense the Really Bad Boy, a projection of insolence and contempt for authority; but he is also the persecuted orphan (blurring into the figure of Oliver Twist), a non-resisting rebel, gentle and scared and (alas!) cute. He emerges out of the earlier stereotypes of abused innocence and fades back into the later versions, one more forerunner of the grubby little boy and his dog, but also one more ancestor of the juvenile delinquent, whose badges of innocence are the switch-knife and hot-wiring kit. Before our own Hucks, the young hoods of the mid-20th century, we are disabled still by literature—unable to tell fact from myth, the real child from the projection of our own moral plight. The guilt of the JD seems to us somehow only one more sign of his innocence, of *our* guiltiness in failing to protect and cultivate his original purity with enough love and security. The "child of a broken home" replaces the orphan among our current stereotypes, as "psychic rejection" replaces old-fashioned bullying and flogging. We are, however, still attempting to appease the same unappeasable anguish which once wailed with Dickens over Oliver in the hands of Fagin or with Twain over poor Huck trapped in Pap's cabin; though now the villain is no longer projected as the evil Jew or the fishbelly-white village drunk, but as the harried bourgeois father oozing baffled good will.

Just as it is difficult for us to discuss our guilt toward Negroes and Indians, say, without really talking about our uneasiness over what we have done with our instinctive life, what reservations and ghettoes we have prepared for our darker impulses—so it is difficult for us (even more difficult perhaps) to consider the plight of our children as if they had independent existence and free will, and were not merely projections of our unconscious. We permit that unconscious (and the child) more sexual freedom now and are deeply troubled that this has made no difference, that each still blindly rebels. Perhaps, we sometimes think, we are paying the price for having restricted the child's range of aggression in return for his erotic freedom. The Good Bad Boy can have himself a girl these days even in the fiction of Anglo-Saxonism, but he is no longer permitted the glory of beating up the Jewish kid next door, or the minister's son or the overdressed stranger from the big city.

KEROUAC TAKES A "BEAT"-ING FROM *MAD*

Of the many attempts to ridicule the Beat Generation, perhaps none succeeded so brilliantly as the September 1960 issue of *Mad* magazine. In one column Seymour "Psycho" Getzoff purports to interview leaders of the Beat rebellion. The author of *On the Road* appears as "Kerr U. Ack, Part-Time Intellectual," extolling what *Mad* writers presumed was the real appeal of the Beat lifestyle:

"I joined the movement because I wanted culture. Not the commercial Madison Avenue kind of culture. Not the trite Bourgeois kind of culture. I wanted real culture. I was always on the intellectual kick, and I knew that this was the scene for me. So like, now, every night, there's beer, chicks, and wild parties ... and I tell you, Dad, this culture is the end!"

From "The Inquiring Hipster," reprinted in Fred W. and Gloria S. McDarrah, *Beat Generation: Glory Days in Greenwich Village* (New York: Schirmer, 1996), p. 42.

It is easy to exaggerate the difference a few generations have made in the basic concept of the Good Bad Boy. He is not to our moral imagination less innocent, but merely permitted a new innocence, that of sex. Yet even though he is allowed now a certain amount of good clean sex (not as the basis of a relationship but as a kind of exhibition of prowess) and forbidden in return an equivalent amount of good clean violence, his standard repertory of permitted crimes remains pretty much the same. What are winked at still as permissible expressions of youthful exuberance are crimes against school and against property. The hood can mock his teacher and play hookey like Tom Sawyer before him, though in our days of prosperity and the indefinite extension of adolescence he runs away (like the protagonists of J. D. Salinger or the speaker in Allen Ginsberg's poems) not from grade school but from prep school or the University. Similarly he is allowed still to "hook" things, though not in these more expansive times such meager loot as candles and a side of bacon but rather the neighbor's '58 swept-fin car. So much and so little have the spread of culture and health influenced our deeper mythical versions of our young selves.

Recently a group of writers in their late youth and early middle-age have appeared, who not only project in literature the image of the Good Bad Boy but even act out in life this standard role, as if they had just invented it. They think they are emulating Huck Finn, though in reality their model is Tom Sawyer, and even at times they rather resemble Becky Thatcher! Such writers range all the way from a suburban, upper-middle-class wing represented by Salinger and his image Holden Caulfield to Allen Ginsberg and Jack Kerouac with their transparent not-quite-fictional representations of themselves. Rural no longer in their memories or nostalgia, they yearn still for boyhood, and submit in their books to speaking through their masks in a language which simulates that of the Good Bad Boy himself whether in his prep-school or pseudo-hipster form. Unlike Twain who makes poetry of inarticulateness, his latter-day imitators produce only slick parodies of the silent generation pretending to talk—or are content with exclamatory noises: "And I said to myself, Wham, listen to that man. That's the West, here I am in the West. . . . Whooee, I told my soul, and the cowboy came back and off we went to Grand Island."

Such writers have found on their own upper-middle-brow or bohemian-*kitsch* levels a theme, a myth common at the moment to much of our society from its scarcely literate to its almost highbrow limits: the themes represented in the mass-arts by such wide-screen projections of the New Good Bad Boy as Elvis Presley, Jimmy Dean, Marlon Brando. The cornpone Romeo, the refugee from Broadway (half Tennessee Williams dream-boy, half stage-proletarian salvaged from the abandoned props of the Group Theater), the homemade Hollywood legend in jeans and horn-rimmed glasses (taught to mumble with the best by Elia Kazan) are all Boys together, pinned side by side on the walls of 14-year-old girls and indistinguishable from their dreams. They in the big features and their simulacra on a thousand TV programs and in a hundred quickie films act out stories of apparently causeless revolt (the cause is in the stereotype whose existence they fail to recognize) and accommodation, while the rock-and-roll fans roar approval. So the more literary exploiters of this theme, talking of "total rejection," actually rehearse the Tom Sawyer pattern once more, though this time for an audience that digs Miles Davis and worships the memory of the Bird.

In *The Catcher in the Rye,* Holden comes to the dead end of ineffectual revolt in a breakdown out of which he is impelled to fight his way by the Good Good Girl in the guise of the Pure Little Sister, from whose hands he passes directly into the hands of the psychiatrist. In *On the Road,* whose characters heal themselves as they go by play-therapy, the inevitable adjustment to society is only promised, not delivered; we must wait for the next installment to tell how the square hipster makes good by acting out his role (with jazz accompaniment) in a New York nightclub, or, even, perhaps, how he has sold his *Confessions of a Bad Boy* to the movies. In the book itself, all the stigmata of Tom Sawyer are already present except the return to Aunt Polly. . . .

Typically enough in our time, such Boys are also *plus religieux que le pape,* insisting on their dedication to God, their assumption of the Christ role (unlike poor Huck, who chose to "go to hell") in a way that would have made the anti-clerical Twain wince. To be sure, it is Zen Buddhism rather than Unitarianism or neo-Orthodoxy which attracts the square hipster and *New Yorker* contributor alike, binding together as improbable co-religionists Salinger and Kerouac; indeed, if James Dean had not yet discovered this particular kick before he smashed up in a sports car, it is because he died just a little too soon. Past the bongo drums and fiddling around with sculpture it was waiting for him, the outsider's religion in a day when there is room inside for the outsider himself, provided he, too, goes "to the church of his choice."

The fact that one is tempted, even impelled to speak of, say, Jack Kerouac at thirty-five as a Boy, the fact that he writes as one of the Boys, is symptomatic of the degree to which the image of Good Bad Boyhood has impinged upon adult life itself, has become a "career" like everything else in America. The age of Kerouac's protagonists is just as ambiguous as that of Twain's, though for quite opposite reasons. Twain blurred adolescence back into boyhood to avoid confronting the problem of sex; the newer writers, accepting the confusion of childhood and youth, blur both into manhood to avoid yielding up to maturity the fine clean rapture of "making out." The fictional counterparts of the provincial hipsters have crossed the borderline of genital maturity, but in all other respects they have not left Jackson's Island. *Plus ça change, plus c'est la même chose,* we sigh, capable only of banality in the face of such banality; and the American translation is, "Boys will be boys!"

Fiedler's essays in *The New Leader* were instrumental in establishing adolescence as a viable topic for literary study. By the early 1960s essay titles such as "The Adolescent in American Literature" and "The Cult of Adolescence in American Fiction" were common-

More than any other literary critic of the post-war era, Leslie A. Fiedler denounced American writers who lamented maturation as a loss of innocence. In his view the nostalgia for childhood reflected a fear of growing up ingrained in American life.

place. While many critics recognized that Fiedler's analysis of the "Good Bad Boy" offered a controversial perspective on the lost-innocence tradition, few shared his insistence that writers who mourned fallen youth risked artistic immaturity. Subsequent commentators instead viewed the coming-of-age process as a metaphor for America's struggle to define its identity in the post–World War II world. As critics insisted, the nation itself was caught in a prolonged state of "in-betweenness" similar to adolescence. The most influential critic to argue this view was Ihab Hassan. In *Radical Innocence: The Contemporary American Novel* (1961) Hassan showed how writers in the 1950s seized upon the teenager as the representative American. The following excerpt, drawn from a chapter on Salinger, can be read as a response to negative attacks such as Fiedler's on *The Catcher in the Rye.* Rather than condemn Salinger for creating characters who withdraw from society, Hassan describes alienation as a "rare quixotic gesture," an expression of naive idealism, the ultimate futility of which reflects the powerlessness of the individual in modern society. (The adjective *quixotic* is derived from the picaresque hero of Miguel de Cervantes's *Don Quixote,* who retreats into a fantasy world of knights and squires rather than tolerate the sordid reality of sixteenth-century Spain).

From Ihab Hassan, "J. D. Salinger: Rare Quixotic Gesture," in his *Radical Innocence: The Contemporary American Novel* (Princeton: Princeton University Press, 1961), pp. 259–263.

The worried hush with which each Salinger story is now anticipated in the pages of *The New Yorker* has become almost audible. Rumors seek the author in his stern retirement from the public glare and swell on his silences with the insistence criticism reserves to his speech. The satiric author of American adolescence in revolt already commands the authority of a prophet, the sanctity of a guru, and the teasing charm of a Zen Master. And yet it was only in 1951 that the apotheosis of *The Catcher in the Rye* as a Book-of-the-Month selection took place. Since then American youth has learned to speak of Salinger and Dostoevsky in the same breath, and to read them in the same measure, as a recent survey in *The Nation* claimed. This is all very well. James Dean and Elvis Presley have also had their moments. But we do Salinger ill-service to base his reputation on anything less enduring than his art.

Salinger, of course, has written some of the best fiction of our time. His voice is genuine, new, and startlingly uneven. In his work we find no showy or covert gesture in the direction of Symbolism or Naturalism, Gothic design or Freudian chiaroscuro; and indeed there was a time when we were unsure whether his intentions came closer to those of Fielding or Firbank, Twain or Chekov. If close to anything, Salinger's intentions are probably more in keeping with Fitzgerald's idea of self-created innocence and Lardner's biting renderings of corruption, with the spiritual assumptions of Martin Buber, and more recently, with those of primitive Christianity and Zen. Yet to speak of his uniqueness in these terms is simply to indulge in the small talk of criticism. We are more anxious, nowadays, to discover the opportunities of literary significance, the conditions of heresy, and protocols of formal excellence. We question *Kitsch* and middle-brow art to the extent that we consume it in prodigious quantities, and are adversely disposed to any serious work that carries the aura of either. It is in response to this line of criticism that the work of Salinger proves itself to be seriously engaged by a current and a traditional aspect of reality in America.

The traditional aspect wears no elaborate disguise. It is the new look of the American Dream, specifically dramatized by the encounter between a vision of innocence and the reality of guilt, between the forms love and power have tended to assume in America. The natural locus of that conflict in the work of Salinger is childhood and adolescence. In them the counterplay of hope and despair, truth and mendacity, participation and withdrawal, commands a full range of comic, that is ambivalent, reference: it is the old story of the self against the world in outlines blurred by mass society. To say as Fiedler does that the "images of childhood and adolescence haunt our greatest works as an unintended symbolic confession of the inadequacy we sense but cannot remedy" is to view a profound truth in a partial perspective.[1] Nostalgia, as we saw, is the result of our compulsion to reenact the story of the American fall. We do not always resist it well. But nostalgia, when it is known to itself, has its ironic and artistic uses. The retreat to childhood is not simply an escape; it is also a criticism, an affirmation of values which, for better or worse, we still cherish; and the need for adolescent disaffiliation, the refusal of initiation, expresses the need to reconceive American reality.

Yet it is hard for some critics to recognize that no act of denial in Salinger's work is without some dramatic and social correlative, which is more than we can generally say of equally serious novelists writing today. The urban, suburban, and exurban society which circumscribes Salinger's child and adolescent characters—the white dinner, not black leather, jacket circle—is usually well specified. About that society we have recently learned a good deal. We know that it exhibits a sad decay of genuine sensibility and even of simple truth. There are, no doubt, many opportunities of significant action still left in it, and we are justified in requesting our best writers to discover them. But the nature of action is such that its results are seldom commensurate with its motives. And the reverse is no less true. The anger of a child confronted for the first time with the force of anti-Semitism, the spirit of an adolescent who dons a red hunting cap in New York City, the tender cruelty of a woman, who is bereaved of her lover, toward her child, even the suicide of a misfit genius, can suggest possibilities of action which we hastily reject in favor of a mechanical gesture at the polling booth. Social realities are no doubt repressed in the work of Salinger—note how gingerly he handles Jews—and this puts a limit on the total significance we can accord to it. Yet it is by what an author manages to *dramatize* that we must finally judge him.

The dramatic conflict which so many of Salinger's stories present obviously does not lend itself to sociological classification. It is more loving and particular, and it partakes of situations that have been traditionally available to literature. The conflict, however, suggests a certain polarity between what might be called, with all due exaggeration, the Assertive Vulgarian and the Responsive Outsider. Both types recur with sufficient frequency to warrant the distinction, and their interplay defines much that is most central to Salinger's fiction. The Vulgarian, who carries the burden of squalor, stands for all that is crude, venal, self-absorbed, and sequacious in our culture. He has no access to knowledge or feeling or beauty, which makes him all the more invulnerable, and his relationship to the world is largely predicated by Buber's I-It dyad. . . . The Outsider, on the other hand, carries the burden of love. The burden makes of him sometimes a victim, and sometimes a scapegoat saint. His life is like "a great inverted forest / with all foliage underground."[2] It is a quick, generous, and responsible life, somehow preserved against hardness and corruption, and always attempting to reach out from its isolation in accordance with Buber's I-Thou dyad. Often there is something in the situation of the Outsider to isolate him, to set him off, however slightly, from the rest of mankind. He might be a child or an adolescent, might wear glasses or appear disfigured, might be Jewish, though seldom is he as crippled or exotic as the characters of Capote and McCullers often are. His ultimate defense, as Rilke, to whom Salinger refers, put it, is defenselessness. . . .

The response of these outsiders and victims to the dull or angry world about them is not simply one of withdrawal: it often takes the form of a strange, quixotic gesture. The gesture, one feels sure, is the bright metaphor of Salinger's sensibility, the center from which meaning drives, and ultimately the reach of his commitment to past innocence and current guilt. It is a gesture at once of pure expression and of expectation, of protest and prayer, of aesthetic form and spiritual content—as Blackmur would say, it is behavior that sings. There is often something prodigal and spontaneous about it, something humorous or whimsical, something that disrupts our habits of gray acquiescence and revives our faith in the willingness of the human spirit. But above all, it gives of itself as only a *religious* gesture can. In another age, Cervantes endowed Don Quixote with the capacity to perform it, and so did Twain and Fitzgerald endow their best creations. For the gesture, after all, has an unmistakably American flourish. The quest of American adolescents has always been for an idea of truth. It is this very idea of truth that the quixotic gesture is constantly seeking to embody. The embodiment is style in action: the twist and tang, the stammering and improvisations, the glint and humor of Salinger's language. Hence the examples of the deserted husband who memorizes his wife's farewell note backwards, the woman who, out of pity, starts smacking her husband at the sight of any dead animal, the man about to commit suicide who makes up a story about bananafish for a little girl, the lover who calls the sprained ankle of his sweetheart Uncle Wiggily, the young man who insists on giving half a chicken sandwich to a stranger, the college girl who trains herself to pray incessantly and does so in the toilet of a restaurant, and the bridegroom who is too happy to appear at his wedding. Out of context these may well sound trite or crazy; in their proper place they are nodes of dramatic significance.

Perceptive readers will note that both Fiedler and Hassan mention James Dean and Elvis Presley in the same breath as Salinger. Such references were by no means uncommon. As alienated-youth fiction came to prominence in the late 1950s, critics attributed its popularity to the same teenage audience that had elevated Dean and Presley to the status of youth-culture icons. For commentators who agreed with Fiedler that revering youth was detrimental to artistic maturity, likening Salinger or Kerouac to the rebel heroes of movies and rock-and-roll music was an easy means of minimizing the significance of these authors. If *The Catcher in the Rye* and *On the Road* had affinities with teen trends in popular culture, critics reasoned, they could not possess much literary value. This assumption is apparent throughout early estimations of the Beat Generation, such as James F. Scott's "Beat Literature and the American Teen Cult" (1962). Scott saw the Beat subculture as symptomatic of the baleful "adolescent-directedness" of modern culture, which, he argues in the essay, sanctions juvenile delinquency instead of offering mature alternatives to alienation.

From James F. Scott, "Beat Literature and the American Teen Cult," *American Quarterly,* 14 (Summer 1962): 150–156.

From a remarkable variety of sources we are now told that the so-called "Beat movement" in American literature is about to expire. Whether this forecast will ultimately prove correct is slightly irrelevant. The striking thing is the untoward haste with which the American public has sought to dispose of these postwar prodigals, who have already been honored with quite an array of wishfully premature epitaphs. Surely the presence of the scraggly citizens of Greenwich, North Beach and Venice West must be highly embarrassing. Perhaps even more embarrassing is that popular journalism seems at a loss to account for them. A typical observer wonders, "What have we done to deserve this?"[3] While in this frame of mind, we can do little more than wish the Beats embalmed and interred with all deliberate speed.

The Beats do not really defy analysis. It's just that the gasps of dismay are more heartening than close scrutiny. For in spite of their freewheeling eroticism and the vendetta they have sworn against both razor and scrub brush, the Beats are less alien to American culture than we would like to suppose. They are as unpopular among the rank and file of Americans as Benedict Arnold among the DAR, but society's strident outbursts against them often leave the impression of a harassed magician desperately trying to exorcise a demon without admitting, even privately, that his own magic has accidentally called it forth. This self-deception probably accounts for the irrelevance of much criticism of Beat literature.

Majority opinion notwithstanding, the failure of the Beats as literary artists has little to do with their widely publicized moral depravity and social negativism. Genius is not an exclusive possession of the righteous, nor is an artist obliged to edify the local chamber of commerce. No. The literary failure of the Beats is simply a bankruptcy of imaginative insight born of their unwillingness to nourish, direct or even properly motivate their creative faculties. But this failure of the Beat imagination, I fear, is related to a larger failure of American culture. More specifically, the Beat conception of the creative process, shot through with inconsistency and naivete, is an indirect yet almost inevitable result of powerful social forces now active beneath the surface of American life, forces which glorify immaturity and thus obscure an essential distinction between adolescent spontaneity and adult creativity. In other words, the Beat movement represents the first incursion into serious literature of an already well entrenched popular mystique which accords exaggerated significance to the vision and values of adolescence. Furthermore, the reluctance of many editors and supplement writers to refer Beat literature to this larger frame of reference is almost more disturbing than the Beats themselves, because it measures the reluctance of the American public to examine those cultural pressures that have caused the Beat movement to move.

The continuing popularity of the fuzzy and convenient "youth must have its fling" interpretation of the Beats typifies a general retreat from careful inquiry. This shibboleth is unsuitable because the Beats' rebellion is not merely a temporary evasion of responsibility. Rather, it is a way of art and life which permanently consecrates the pose and gestures of adolescence. For though most full-fledged Beats are well beyond teenage (some will never see thirty again), their patterns of behavior often reveal regressive adolescent traits, such as the use of special speech and dress as badges of identity and status or the compulsive hostility to authority, which causes all questions of value to be referred to the judgment of a select peer group. Going somewhat further, Ned Polsky identifies among many Beats of Greenwich Village a "persistence in more or less chronic form of some psychic state characterizing . . . adolescent pathology."[4] But even when pathology is not involved, the Beats—especially the literate and literary Beats—strenuously cling to an adolescent outlook which regards discipline or concentration as repressive and intelligence as a general nuisance. And though they profess to find this same view in the aesthetic radicalism of Whitman and the social iconoclasm of Thoreau, what the Beats really respect is not Whitman and Thoreau (neither of whom is immature) but an image of Whitman and Thoreau distorted by the eyes of adolescence. The tragicomic predicament of the Beats is that, having forsworn maturity, they have truncated their creative life.

Unfortunately, however, the self-conscious cultivation of juvenility is not restricted to the isolated cadres of Beatdom. In fact, the emergence of an American teen cult is one of the most disturbing events of our generation. Undergirded by popular psychology, exploited by commercial advertising, and dramatized by the public arts, the sentimental embodiment of adolescent values has come to touch nearly all areas of American life. Not only is the adolescent patronized in the permissive home and the "progressive" school; his attitudes and beliefs now threaten to become normative for the whole adult population.

The growing "adolescent directedness" of today's adults is reflected conspicuously in their almost obsessive concern with how the American teenager feels about the world. When Eugene Gilbert initiated his column, "What Young People Think," in the middle 1950s, he could hardly have foreseen that within five years this piece would become one of the most popular syndicated features of the Associated Press. And Gilbert's whirlwind success is certainly not an isolated event. Writing in 1958, Dwight MacDonald turned to the *Readers' Guide to Periodical Literature* to prove that the American people have developed an overblown interest in adolescence.[5] At that time, the number of entries under "adolescence" had jumped from 16 in 1911–1913 to 51 in 1955–1957, and the entries under "teenage" had mushroomed from 2 in 1941–1943 to 11 in 1955–1957. Already, little tidbits like "What Makes Teenagers Swoon" had become a regular part of American magazine fare. But the teen cult has since entered a new phase. The use of the word "adolescence," which sounds faintly clinical and has little commercial appeal, has declined in favor of the more attractive term "teenage." Although the *Readers' Guide* for 1950–1961 contains only 24 references to adolescence, a glance at the entries under "teen-age" reveals 13 cross references embracing the whole spectrum of adolescent activity—teen drinking, teen marriage, teen parties, teen reading, to cite only a few samples. If he so wishes, the American adult can now use even the most fashionable magazines to participate vicariously in the life of the teenager, whose every thought, deed and desire has been elaborately chronicled. . . .

The public, of course, indulges its esteem for adolescence only within a carefully circumscribed frame of reference, never permitting it to undercut consensually validated symbols of adult prestige. In most respects, the place of the parent, the teacher and the clergyman is still sacrosanct. But herein lies a paradox. For while we formally honor the home, the school, and the church, we continue to revel emotionally in a puerile worldview which renders those professed values meaningless, almost dishonest. And our divided loyalties cloud the development of mature insight into inherited codes of behavior, insight necessary to keep our institutions from turning into repositories of cultural fossils.

At the moment, the ambiguous commitment of the American people to the aggressive "spontaneity" of teendom on the one hand and to the reassuring stability of tradition on the other has its most adverse effect in the confused and confusing directives that devolve from it upon American youth. Currently fashionable counsel to the rising generation, disseminated through all the mass media, might (allowing for a trace of hyperbole) be summarized thus: Listen to mom and dad, even though their minds are darkened by middle age; study diligently in school, even though effective living requires only a bright, bacteria-free smile; respect Moses and the Commandments, even though a shiny, up-to-date Savior would at least have the decency to be beardless and would probably come only to lead a songfest at the local church. Obviously, this tissue of contradictions will withstand little battering, hardly the utterance of a cynical "pooh!" And this circumstance, I think, provides a clue to the coming of the American Beatnik.

Naturally, the current surfeit of adolescent sentiment cannot have caused the Beat movement directly. But it has contributed to the atmosphere in which Beat literature flourishes, because it gravely impairs genuine understanding of creative endeavor and thus deprives the adult world of all defenses against the Beats except aimless ridicule and ill-formulated disgust. For by comparison with what presently passes for the public conscience, even the logic of Beatdom looks cogent and persuasive. Confronted by the muddle of conflicting public values, the Beats have simply shattered the frame of moral reference imposed by convention and then deified the adolescent element already permeating American life. In this sense, at least, the Beats are very much our spiritual sons, though we may still prefer to regard them as something visited upon us by a peculiarly malevolent conjunction of the stars.

Despite such negative assessments, many critics deemed alienated-youth fiction worthy of study, and analyses of its themes, plots, and symbols proliferated throughout the 1960s and 1970s. *The Catcher in the Rye* garnered the bulk of this attention, with more than one hundred articles published on it during the first two decades the novel was in print. (As early as 1958, one detractor coined the phrase "the Salinger industry" to describe the factory-like regularity with which scholars churned out essays on Holden Caulfield.) Jonathan Baumbach's 1964 essay "The Saint as a Young Man: A Reappraisal of *The Catcher in the Rye*" is typical of this criticism. Focusing on the significance that innocence holds for Holden, Baumbach extends Hassan's notion of withdrawal as a "rare quixotic gesture" to include an overtly spiritual dimension. Baumbach argues that Holden is a symbolic saint who sacrifices his own innocence to protect the purity of children.

From Jonathan Baumbach, "The Young Man as a Saint: A Reappraisal of *The Catcher in the Rye,*" *Modern Language Quarterly,* 25 (December 1964): 461–463.

Like all of Salinger's fiction, *The Catcher in the Rye* is not only about innocence, it is actively for innocence—as if retaining one's childness were an existential possibility. The metaphor of the title—Holden's fantasy-vision of standing in front of a cliff and protecting playing children from falling (Falling)—is, despite the impossibility of its realization, the only positive action affirmed in the novel. It is, in Salinger's Manichean universe of child angels and adult "phonies," the only moral alternative—otherwise all is corruption. Since it is spiritually as well as physically impossible to prevent the Fall, Salinger's idealistic heroes are doomed either to suicide (Seymour) or insanity (Holden) or mysticism (Franny), the ways of sainthood, or to moral dissolution (Mr. Antolini), the way of the world. In Salinger's finely honed prose, at once idiomatically real and poetically stylized, we get the terms of Holden's ideal adult occupation. . . .

Apparently, Holden's wish is purely selfless. What he wants, in effect, is to be a saint—the protector and savior of innocence. But what he also wants, for he is still one of the running children himself, is that someone prevent *his* fall. This is his paradox: he must leave innocence to protect innocence. At sixteen, he is ready to shed his innocence and move like Adam into the fallen adult world, but he resists because those no longer innocent seem to him foolish as well as corrupt. In a sense, then, he is looking for an exemplar, a wise-good father whose example will justify his own initiation into manhood. Before Holden can become a catcher in the rye, he must find another catcher in the rye to show him how it is done.

Immediately after Holden announces his "crazy" ambition to Phoebe, he calls up one of his former teachers, Mr. Antolini, who is both intelligent and kind—a potential catcher in the rye: "He was the one that finally picked up that boy that jumped out of the window I told you about, James Castle. Old Mr. Antolini felt his pulse and all, and then he took off his coat and put it over James Castle and carried him all the way over to the infirmary" (226). Though Mr. Antolini is sympathetic because "he didn't even give a damn if his coat got all bloody," the incident is symbolic of the teacher's failure as a catcher in the rye. For all his good intentions, he was unable to catch James Castle or prevent his fall; he could only pick him up after he died. The episode of the suicide is one of the looming shadows darkening Holden's world; Holden seeks out Antolini because he hopes that the gentle teacher—the substitute father—will "pick him up" before he is irrevocably fallen. Holden's real quest throughout the novel is for a spiritual father (an innocent adult). He calls Antolini after all the other fathers of his world have failed him, including his real father, whose existence in the novel is represented solely by Phoebe's childish reiteration of "Daddy's going to kill you." The fathers in Salinger's child's-eye world do not catch falling boys—who have been thrown out of prep school—but "kill" them. Antolini represents Holden's last chance to find a father-catcher. But his inability to save Holden has been prophesied in his failure to save James Castle; the episode of Castle's death provides an anticipatory parallel to Antolini's unwitting destruction of Holden.

That Antolini's kindness to Holden is motivated in part by a homosexual interest, though it comes as a shock to Holden, does not wholly surprise the reader. Many of the biographical details that Salinger has revealed about him through Holden imply this possibility. For example, that he has an older and unattractive wife whom he makes a great show of kissing in public is highly suggestive; yet the discovery itself—Holden wakes to find Antolini sitting beside him and caressing his head—has considerable impact. We experience a kind of shock of recognition, the more intense for its having been anticipated. The scene has added power because Antolini is, for the most part, a good man, whose interest in Holden is genuine as well as perverted. His advice to Holden is apparently well-intentioned. Though many of his recommendations are cleverly articulated platitudes, Antolini evinces a prophetic insight when he tells Holden, "I have a feeling that you're riding for some kind of a terrible, terrible fall"; one suspects, however, that to some extent he is talking about himself. Ironically, Antolini becomes the agent of his "terrible, terrible fall" by violating Holden's image of him, by becoming a false father. Having lost respect for Antolini as a man, Holden rejects him as an authority; as far as Holden is concerned, Antolini's example denies the import of his words. His disillusionment with Antolini, who had seemed to be the sought-for, wise-good father, comes as the most intense of a long line of disenchantments; it is the final straw that breaks Holden. It is the equivalent of the loss of God. The world, devoid of good fathers (authorities), becomes a soul-destroying chaos in which his survival is possible only through withdrawal into childhood, into fantasy, into psychosis.

As critics began studying other disaffected-youth works, they acknowledged the formative influence of *The Catcher in the Rye* by using it as a benchmark for measuring other novels. Comparisons between Salinger's novel and John Knowles's *A Separate Peace* were particularly common. The two texts not only share a similar setting (the exclusive world of Eastern preparatory schools) but also employ a first-person narrator who renders adolescent confusion with vivid immediacy. Unfortunately, these comparisons worked to Knowles's disadvantage because *A Separate Peace* was judged to be derivative of Salinger's work. In "Narrative Method in *A Separate Peace*" (1968) Ronald Weber attempts to correct this perception by demonstrating the differences between the novels. In particular, he argues that Knowles's narrator, Gene Forrester, achieves greater insight into his failings than Holden does because of the greater interval of time separating events depicted in the novel and Gene's recounting of them.

From Ronald Weber, "Narrative Method in *A Separate Peace*," *Studies in Short Fiction,* 3 (1965): 64–67, 68–69, 71–72.

In both *The Catcher in the Rye* and *A Separate Peace* the narrative is presented from a first-person point of view; both Holden and Gene Forrester tell their own stories, stories in which they serve not only as observers but as narrator-agents who stand at the center of the action. Generally, first-person narration gives the reader a heightened sense of immediacy, a sense of involvement with the life of the novel. This surely is one of the charms of *Catcher* and one of the reasons for its immense popularity. The reader, particularly the young reader, is easily caught up in the narrative and held fast by a voice and an emotional experience he finds intensely familiar. With Knowles's novel, however, this is not the case. While the reader may greatly admire the book, it does not engage him quite as directly or perhaps even as deeply as *Catcher;* throughout it he remains somewhat outside the action and detached from the narrator, observing the life of the novel rather than submerged in it. The difference in reader response, taking place as it does within the framework of first-person, narrator-as-protagonist telling, is, I believe, a highly-calculated effect on Knowles's part. It indicates a sharply different thematic intention, and one that is rooted in a skillful alteration of the conventional method of first-person telling.

Holden Caulfield never comes to an understanding of his experience. He never quite knows what it means; he only feels certain things about it. In the final paragraph of the novel, responding to D. B.'s question about what he now thinks of his experience, he says: "I didn't know what the hell to say. If you want to know the truth, I don't *know* what I think about it" (276–277). At the end, as throughout the novel, Holden is much more aware of what he feels, in this case a broad sympathy for the people he has described. "About all I know is," he adds, "I sort of *miss* everybody I told about" (277). Gene Forrester, on the other hand, arrives at a clear understanding—a deeply felt knowledge—of the experience he narrates. At the end of the novel he knows, unlike Holden, precisely what he thinks about it.

Understanding means a measure of distance. We can seldom understand an experience, truly know it, until we are clearly removed from it—removed in time and removed in attitude. Holden achieves such distance only slightly, hence his understanding is slight at best. He tells his story at only a short remove in time from the actual experience of it. It all took place, the reader learns at the start, "around last Christmas" (3). Just as there has been some lapse of time between the experience and the telling, there has also been some shift in Holden's attitude. At the end of the novel, when we again return to the opening perspective, the recuperating Holden now thinks he will apply himself when he returns to school, just as he now sort of misses the people he has told about. In both cases, however, Holden is not sufficiently separated from his experience, either in time or attitude, to admit any real mastery over it. . . .

Unlike Holden, Gene Forrester is separated by a broad passage of time from the experience that he relates. "I went back to the Devon School not long ago," Gene says in the novel's opening sentence, "and found it looking oddly newer than when I was a student there fifteen years before."[6] That this lapse in time between the experience and the telling has brought understanding is also established early. "Looking back now across fifteen years," Gene says a few paragraphs later, "I could see with great clarity the fear I had lived in."[7] Although Knowles quickly leaves the distant perspective and turns to the immediate scene, he keeps the reader aware that Gene is looking back on the experience with a mature vision. At one point, for example, the distant perspective suddenly opens up at one end of a scene when Gene says: "But in a week I had forgotten that, and I have never since forgotten the dazed look on Finny's face when he thought that on the first day of his return to Devon I was going to desert him."[8] . . .

The distant point of the narration allows a detachment that permits Gene the mastery of his experience. Even when Knowles gives over the narrative wholly to immediate scenes the reader is reminded, sometimes with a phrase, at other times with an entire passage, of the perspective. The war, in addition, serves to create an increased sense of distance, a removal in attitude, within the story. Although the war touches Devon School only slightly—one of the joys of summer session is that it seems totally removed from the world of war—it cannot be forgotten or ignored for long; it exists not only as an event that stands between the experience of the novel and Gene's telling, but as an event that, at the very moment of the experience, dominates the life of each character. "The war," Gene says in retrospect, "was and is reality for me. I still instinctively live and think in its atmosphere."[9] The anticipation of war forces Gene and his companions into a slight yet significant detachment from their life at Devon—a life that, at times, seems unimportant and even unreal—and towards an unusual amount of serious, if carefully guarded, reflection. . . .

At this point we can begin to see some connection between Knowles's narrative method and his thematic concern. Again, comparison with *Catcher* is useful. Both novels, in a broad and very basic sense, are concerned with the response of the central character to an awareness of evil in the world; they are narratives in which the characters confront, during a concentrated period, part of the reality of life. In face of this reality Holden Caulfield suffers a severe physical and mental breakdown. At the end of the novel, when Holden admits he misses the people he has told about—the assorted phonies who represent the world—the reader is to understand that he now has begun to make some beginning accommodation with that world. Holden of course does not understand this change; it is, as we have said, merely a new feeling, a feeling of missing people he previously despised. Although it is clear that some change has taken place in Holden, it is important to see that it is explained in terms of other people; what must in fact be an inner change—Holden arriving at some peace within himself—is communicated in exterior terms.

In the course of his maturing process, Gene Forrester likewise must confront the fact of evil in the world. But in this case the location of that evil is quite different. At the very beginning of the novel, Gene, looking back fifteen years, says he can see with great clarity the "fear" he had lived in at Devon School and that he has succeeded in making his "escape" from. Even now, he adds, he can feel "fear's echo," and this in turn leads him back to the direct experience of the story.[10] The meaning of this experience is to be found in the development of the words *fear* and *escape*—in Gene's growing realization of what they mean as well as what they do not mean. . . .

Gene Forrester comes to learn that his war, the essential war, is fought on the battlefield within. Peace comes only when he faces up to this fact. The only escape, the price of peace, is self-awareness. One finds the resolution of Holden Caulfield's war, on the other hand, beyond him, in his relation to society. As Holden flees a corrupt world he is driven increasingly in upon himself, but towards collapse rather than awareness. Salinger presents the hope that is finally raised for him not in terms of self-knowledge but in the ability to move out of himself. It is not, then, awareness that is offered for him so much as a kind of accommodation; he must somehow learn to live, as Mr. Antolini tells him, with what is sickening and corrupt in human behavior. Although this implies facing up to what is corrupt in his own nature, this is not Salinger's emphasis. He seeks to focus the novel outside Holden rather than within him; and for this the conventional method of first-person narration with its tendency to narrow and intensify the story, eliminating the sense of distance vital for the narrator's self-understanding, is admirably suited. Knowles, using a similar but skillfully altered narrative method, develops a very different theme—that awareness, to put it baldly,

THE CHOCOLATE WAR AND ADOLESCENT DESPAIR

"If *The Chocolate War* ended not with Jerry's defeat but with the banishment of Brother Leon or The Vigils, or with an uprising that set things at least into a neutral or holding pattern, it would not end in despair. Instead, in the final pages of the novel Jerry wishes he could tell Goober 'don't try to disturb the universe. You can't.' Brother Leon, who, to serve himself, manipulates kids and other priests, remains in power. Hope vanishes. Despair remains. . . .

"Both Cormier's and Salinger's novels reflect the contemporary challenge to traditional institutions and conventions. Cormier's challenge is more severe; his world is pervasively evil, his characters are more seriously troubled. Neither author suggests that the repository of answers to the dilemmas which vex their characters is external to the efforts of human kind: the adolescents themselves, their parents, their adult role models, their professional helpers, representatives of their governments. Yet within this same secular, anti-theistic humanism, the answers which emerge in the novels are quite different. Holden finds that he is his own best hope for the phoniness of adult life. Cormier's characters come to no such faith. They are left without hope. The world grew darker between 1951 and 1974. Both writers skillfully create a realistic picture of the adolescent world, but unlike Salinger who offers discovery, Cormier offers only despair."

Rebecca Lukens

From "From Salinger to Cormier: Disillusionment to Despair in Thirty Years," in *Webs and Wardrobes: Humanist and Religious World Views in Children's Literature*, edited by Joseph O'Beirne Milner and Lucy Floyd Morcock Milner (Lanham, Md.: University Press of America, 1987), pp. 8, 11.

must precede accommodation, that to look without before having first searched within is tragically to confuse the human condition. To convey his theme Knowles modifies the first-person narrative to create for both narrator and reader an atmosphere of detachment that permits the novel to be focused within Gene, where, he shows, a basic truth of life is to be found.

By the early 1980s Joyce Carol Oates's short story "Where Are You Going, Where Have You Been?" was a mainstay of literary anthologies compiled for high-school and undergraduate students. Not surprisingly, critics turned their attention to this disturbing work. Much of this critical interest centered on Oates's style. Part Gothic nightmare, part allegorical horror story, "Where Are You Going, Where Have You Been?" possesses an eerie, beguiling atmosphere reminiscent of fairy tales and medieval legends. Most disturbing is the villain, Arnold Friend, who, despite his faux James Dean appearance, is often interpreted as a symbolic Satan figure. According to Tom Quirk, however, Oates based Friend on an actual murderer named Charles Schmid, who raped and killed three teenagers in Tuscon, Arizona, in the mid 1960s. As a source study—an analysis that examines the background materials inspiring a work—Quirk's essay explores how Oates recast details of the Schmid case to critique the rebel youth culture that enchants the protagonist of the story, Connie.

From Tom Quirk, "A Source for 'Where Are You Going, Where Have You Been?'" *Studies in Short Fiction*, 18 (Fall 1981): 413–420.

One of Joyce Carol Oates's most familiar and most disturbing short stories—"Where Are You Going, Where Have You Been?"—is so richly symbolic and her characters are so improbably dressed and motivated that one is tempted to see it exclusively as a play of primal forces rather than a fiction derived from and responsive to life itself. One critic, in fact, has argued that the story is an allegory. And, indeed, the characters in the story seem larger than life. Her villains (and there is no mistaking that they are villains) are actuated by raw emotions, or none at all, outfitted in the most unlikely and sinister ways, and possessed of an unaccountable knowledge of the victim and her family. The victim herself is a freshly washed, blond, blue-eyed picture of innocence. But however attractive a view it may be to imagine Ms. Oates conceiving of a modern "tale" in the tradition of Hawthorne and Poe which freely mingles the marvelous with the psychologically true, it is contrary to the overwhelming evidence that the author drew her inspiration for her story from a real event publicized in popular national magazines. This view also injures the story itself for it diverts our attention from the fact that the evil she portrays is all too real and renders ineffective the pointed criticism Oates makes of the American Dream, which is the larger purpose of her story. Rather, Oates modeled her story after real people and real events—though she did, as any gifted writer does, imaginatively transform the actual in a fiction of dramatic power. It is my purpose here, then, to identify the parallels between her story and the magazine reports of a real criminal and a real crime which seem to have had a germinal effect upon Oates's creative imagination and to suggest how her theme of the death of the American Dream may have been prompted by these magazines.

The source of and inspiration for Oates's friend, Arnold Friend, is not nearly as mysterious as the almost supernatural attributes of this character might suggest. Oates's character, as I shall demonstrate, was derived from the exploits, widely publicized by *Time, Life,* and *Newsweek* magazines during the winter of 1965–1966, of a real killer from Tucson, Arizona. Moreover, the publication of "Where Are You Going, Where Have You Been?" in *Epoch* (Fall 1966) suggests this influence, though the more accessible appearance of the story later in her collection of short stories, *The Wheel of Love* (1970), tends to obscure the implication that she probably wrote the story soon after her acquaintance with the grisly details of the three murders committed by a young man named Charles Howard Schmid and nicknamed by the author of the *Life* piece about him as the "Pied Piper of Tucson."[11]

Oddly enough, those very details which, by their peculiarity, tend to mark Arnold Friend as an inhuman, perhaps superhuman avatar of undiluted evil are derivative rather than invented. Charles Schmid, an extremely short and muscular man, was a mere five feet three inches tall but nevertheless had been a state champion in gymnastics during his high school years. After being suspended from high school for stealing tools from the auto shop, he continued to inhabit well beyond his teen years such high school haunts as drive-in restaurants, bowling alleys, and the public swimming pool. He was, in fact, twenty-three years old when he was arrested for the murders of Gretchen and Wendy Fritz, aged seventeen and thirteen, in the fall of 1965 and while an earlier third murder of Alleen Rowe, fifteen, was still being investigated. To compensate for his shortness and to disguise the fact that he was a good deal older than the teen-aged girls to whom he was attracted, Schmid went to bizarre and rather savage extremes. As all the national magazines pointed out, Schmid stuffed rags and folded tin cans into his black leather boots to appear a few inches taller. And he dyed his hair raven black, often wore pancake make-up, pale cream lipstick, and mascara. He sometimes darkened his face to a "tan" with make-up and painted a beauty mark on his cheek.

His behavior was as audacious as his appearance. He drove a gold colored car, in which he "cruised" Tuscon's Speedway Boulevard. And he was known to tell tall-tales about how he came into the money he habitually flourished—to his male admirers he suggested that he trafficked in drugs; to the females he bragged that he had been paid by women whom he had taught "a hundred ways to make love." He was also inclined to introduce himself by a number of aliases, his favorite being "Angel Rodriguez."

The parallels in "Where Are You Going?" to the reports of the Schmid case are too clear-cut to have been accidental. The young victim of Arnold Friend's attention, Connie, notices that he, like Schmid, is quite short: "He wasn't tall, only an inch or so taller than she would be if she came down to him."[12] But he, like the gymnast Schmid, is muscular as well. He wore a "belt that pulled his waist in and showed how lean he was, and a white pull-over shirt that was a little soiled and showed the hard, small muscles of his arms and shoulders. He looked as if he probably did hard work, lifting and carrying things. Even his neck looked muscular." And Arnold Friend totters and wobbles on his black leather boots and eventually almost loses his balance. This draws Connie's attention to his feet: "He had to bend and adjust his boots. Evidently his feet did not go all the way down; the boots must have been stuffed with something so that he would seem taller.". . .

Thus far our discussion of Oates's reaction to an actual incident has focused upon the particular ways she took suggestions from the documented reports of Schmid's violent crimes and dramatized them in her story. But, more significantly, she seems also to have taken her cues from these magazine reports in more general ways which may account for the related thematic elements of seductive rock and roll and violently extinguished innocence which permeate her story.

One cannot help but pause and ponder Oates's dedication of this story to Bob Dylan. However, it is a mistake to conclude with Marie Urbanski that the dedication is pejorative because Dylan made music "almost religious in dimension among youth."[13] Rather, it is honorific because the history and effect of Bob Dylan's music had been to draw youth away from the romantic promises and frantic strains of a brand of music sung by Buddy Holly, Chuck Berry, Elvis Presley and others. It was Bob Dylan, after all, who told us that the "times they are a changin'," and one of Oates's aims in her short story is to show that they have already changed. It is the gyrating, hip-grinding music of people like Elvis Presley, whom Schmid identified as his "idol," which emanates from Ellie's transistor radio, the "hard, fast, shrieking" songs played by the disk jockey "Bobby King" rather than the cryptic, atonal folk music of Bob Dylan.

Both Connie and Arnold Friend are enthusiastic about "Bobby King" and psychologically linked to one another by an appreciation of the rhythmic beat of the music he plays. Connie observes that Ellie's radio is tuned to the same station as her radio in the house, and when Arnold Friend says that King is "great," Connie concedes, "He's kind of great." Arnold counters: "Listen, that guy is *great*. He knows where the action is." Friend's statement of enthusiasm recalls the quotation that introduces the *Life* essay on Charles Schmid: "Hey, c'mon babe, follow me, / I'm the Pied Piper, follow me, / I'm the Pied Piper / And I'll show you where it's at." Arnold Friend does, indeed, show Connie "where it's at," and he draws her from the house with his alternating blandishments and threats much as a pied piper. Moreover, Connie's ultimate, mindless decision to go with Friend is meant to recall the beckoning tempo of rock and roll: "She cried out, she cried for her mother, she felt her breath start jerking back and forth in her lungs as if it were something Arnold Friend was stabbing her with again and again with no tenderness. A noisy, sorrowful wailing rose all about her and she was locked inside the way she was locked inside the house."

When Connie kicks the telephone away and opens the screen door to go with Friend, there can be little question where she is going nor where she has been. She is going to her death, and her fate is largely the result of a consciousness shaped by the frantic life of cruising in fast cars, sipping cokes out of sweating paper cups with anonymous boys, a consciousness epitomized by the frantic music she listens to.

Another alienated-youth novel that has garnered a great deal of critical attention is Sylvia Plath's *The Bell Jar*. Since it was published in America in 1971 (some eight years after it was first available in England, where it was published under the pseudonym Victoria Lucas), critics have described this novel as a "female *Catcher in the Rye*." The label is appropriate not just because Plath modeled her book on Salinger's. More broadly, *The Bell Jar* marks a feminist recasting of the coming-of-age plot, which has traditionally documented male maturation experiences. In "Plath's *The Bell Jar* as Female *Bildungsroman*" (1986)

Linda Wagner-Martin argues that the story of Esther Greenwood represents a new type of "novel of development," one more gender-conscious than its predecessors. In the first part of the essay Wagner-Martin draws from Jerome Hamilton Buckley's study *Season of Youth: The Bildungsroman from Dickens to Golding* (1974) to demonstrate the presence of standard bildungsroman elements in *The Bell Jar.* In the second part she explores the differences that distinguish Plath's novel from other exemplars of the genre to suggest the effect of gender on the development of the plot.

From Linda Wagner-Martin, "Plath's *The Bell Jar* as Female *Bildungsroman,*" *Women's Studies,* 12 (February 1986): 55–56, 66–68.

One of the most misunderstood of contemporary novels, Sylvia Plath's *The Bell Jar* is in structure and intent a highly conventional *Bildungsroman.* Concerned almost entirely with the education and maturation of Esther Greenwood, Plath's novel uses a chronological and necessarily episodic structure to keep Esther at the center of all action. Other characters are fragmentary, subordinate to Esther and her developing consciousness, and are shown only through their effects on her as central character. No incident is included which does not influence her maturation, and the most important formative incidents occur in the city, New York. As Jerome Buckley describes the *Bildungsroman* in his 1974 study *Season of Youth,* its principal elements are "a growing up and gradual self-discovery," "alienation," "provinciality, the larger society," "the conflict of generations," "ordeal by love" and "the search for a vocation and a working philosophy."[14]

Plath signals the important change of location at the opening of *The Bell Jar.* "It was a queer, sultry summer, the summer they electrocuted the Rosenbergs, and I didn't know what I was doing in New York. . . . New York was bad enough. By nine in the morning the fake, country-wet freshness that somehow seeped in overnight evaporated like the tail end of a sweet dream. Mirage-gray at the bottom of their granite canyons, the hot streets wavered in the sun, the car tops sizzled and glittered, and the dry, cindery dust blew into my eyes and down my throat."[15] Displaced, misled by the morning freshness, Greenwood describes a sterile, inimical setting for her descent into, and exploration of, a hell both personal and communal. Readers have often stressed the analogy between Greenwood and the Rosenbergs—and sometimes lamented the inappropriateness of Plath's comparing her personal angst with the actual electrocution—but in this opening description, the Rosenberg execution is just one of the threatening elements present in the New York context. It is symptomatic of the "foreign" country's hostility, shown in a myriad of ways throughout the novel.

In *The Bell Jar,* as in the traditional *Bildungsroman,* the character's escape to the city images the opportunity to find self as well as truths about life. Such characters as Pip, Paul Morel, and Jude Fawley idealize the city as a center of learning and experience, and think that once they have relocated themselves, their lives will change dramatically. As Buckley points out, however, the city is often ambivalent: "the city, which seems to promise infinite variety and newness, all too often brings a disenchantment more alarming and decisive than any dissatisfaction with the narrowness of provincial life."[16] For Esther Greenwood, quiet Smith student almost delirious with the opportunity to go to New York and work for *Ladies Day* for a month, the disappointment of her New York experience is cataclysmic. Rather than shape her life, it nearly ends it; and Plath structures the novel to show the process of disenchantment in rapid succession.

The novel opens in the midst of Greenwood's month in New York, although she tells the story in flashbacks; and for the first half of the book—nearly ten of its twenty chapters—attention remains there, or on past experiences that are germane to the New York experiences. Greenwood recounts living with the other eleven girls on the *Ladies Day* board at the Amazon Hotel, doing assignments for the tough fiction editor Jay Cee, going to lunches and dances, buying clothes, dating men very unlike the fellows she had known at college, and sorting through lifestyles like Doreen's which shock, bewilder, and fascinate her. Events as predictably mundane as these are hardly the stuff of exciting fiction but Plath has given them an unexpected drama because of the order in which they appear. *The Bell Jar* is plotted to establish two primary themes: that of Greenwood's developing identity, or lack of it; and that of her battle against submission to the authority of older people, and, more pertinently, of men. The second theme is sometimes absorbed by the first but Plath uses enough imagery of sexual conquest that it comes to have an almost equal importance. For a woman of the 1950s, finding an identity other than that of a sweetheart, girlfriend, and wife and mother was a major achievement. . . .

Inherent in the notion of *Bildungsroman* is the sense that such a novel will provide a blueprint for a successful education, however the word *successful* is defined. At times, as in *Jude the Obscure,* education comes too late to save the protagonist, but the issue is more the information to be conveyed than the factual ending of the character's saga. For Jerome Buckley, if the protagonist has the means to give life "some ultimate coherence," then education has been efficacious.[17] *The Bell Jar* gives the reader the sense that Esther has, at least momentarily, gained the ability to achieve that coherence. Because so few *Bildungsromane* deal with madness, however, exact comparisons between Plath's novel and those usually considered in such generic considerations are difficult; but because so many women's novels treat the subject of madness, *The Bell Jar* cannot be considered an anomaly. Its very representativeness is suggested in Patricia Spacks' comment that most female novels of adolescence "stress the world's threat more than its possibilities; their happy endings derive less from causal sequence than from fortunate accident."[18] The very titles of comparable novels indicate this difference. *The Bell Jar,* with its sinister implications of airlessness, imprisonment, and isolation, is a far remove from *Great Expectations;* and its most positive scenes cannot approach the ringing self-confidence of *A Portrait of the Artist as a Young Man,* although it is surely that novel writ female.

Among other differences between the conventional *Bildungsroman,* which usually deals with a young man's education, and the female novel of experience in adolescence would be the shift in role from father as crucial parent to mother. Much of the process of education is imitative, so that figures which serve as role models will also shift from male to female. A female *Bildungsroman* will thus seem to be peopled more heavily with women characters than with men, and although crucial patterns would keep men—economically, socially, and sexually—prominent. It may be because men must occur in female novels that they come to play the role of adversary or antagonist, whereas in the male *Bildungsroman* women can be simply omitted.

Educational experiences and choices leading to occupations will also differ, but none will be quite so persuasive as the female's need to choose between profession and domesticity. It is the inescapability of that choice that forces many a novel which would well be labeled *Bildungsroman* into the category of domestic novel. Underlying what would seem to be the choice of profession is the less obvious issue of sexuality, which again plays a very different role in female adolescence than in male. In the conventional *Bildungsroman*, sexual experience is but another step toward maturity. It suggests the eventual leaving one household to establish another. For a man, a move may mean only that he hangs his hat in a different closet. For a woman, however, the move means a complete change of status, from mistress to servant, personally responsible for housekeeping in ways she would never have been as the young daughter of a house. A parallel degradation occurs in most representations of the sex act. Biological necessity and physical size mean that the female is usually a more passive partner in intercourse. The accoutrements of a sexual relationship are therefore different for women than for men, and the relationship may loom central to the female *Bildungsroman*, while it may be almost peripheral to the male. Losing one's virginity unwisely seldom determines the eventual life of the male protagonist; it is the stuff of ostracism, madness, and suicide for the female, however. Plath's concern with Esther's sexual experience is relevant, certainly, for her choices will determine her life. Her aggression in finding Irwin so that she can be sexually experienced is a positive sign, but the characteristic irony—that she be the one in a million to hemorrhage after intercourse—mars the experience and tends to foreshadow the incipient bad luck which may follow cultural role reversal. As Plath knew only too well, society had its ways of punishing women who were too aggressive, too competent, and too masculine.

The apparent connections between Plath's experiences and Esther's are legitimate topics of discussion when *Bildungsromane* are involved because the strength of such novels usually depends on the author's emotional involvement in the themes. Buckley points out that a *Bildungsroman* is often an early novel, a first or second, and that much of the life—as well as the ambivalence—of the novel exists because the author is so involved in the process he or she is describing. In Plath's case, *The Bell Jar* was not only her first novel; it was also published under a pseudonym. Limited to British publication in the original 1963 printing, under the authorship of "Victoria Lucas," the novel was only a partially disguised statement of Plath's anger toward a culture, and a family, that had nourished her only conditionally— that would accept her only provided she did "acceptable" things. If one of the goals of writing such a book was self-discovery, then Plath's evident anger may have been as dismaying, for her in the early 1960s, as it was unexpected.

While critics such as Wagner-Martin are interested in how alienated-youth fiction incorporates the characteristics of traditional literary forms such as the bildungsroman, other commentators focus on how authors are influenced by popular-culture media, music in particular. In *Deliberate Speed: The Origins of a Cultural Style in the American 1950s* (1990), W. T. Lhamon Jr. shows how writers in the 1950s incorporated forms and themes from blues and jazz into their fiction. Aside from Lhamon's interest in how music influenced literature, his book merits attention because he draws parallels between two writers who, despite their prominence throughout the decade, are rarely linked together: Ralph Ellison and Kerouac. As Lhamon argues, both the structure and style of *Invisible Man* and *On the Road* reverberate with techniques associated with blues and jazz.

From W. T. Lhamon Jr., *Deliberate Speed: The Origins of a Cultural Style in the American 1950s* (Washington, D.C.: Smithsonian Institution Press, 1990), pp. 49–52, 70–72.

Recent critics have recognized *Invisible Man*'s connection to folklore, in general, and to the blues, in particular. Stanley Edgar Hyman and Albert Murray, two of Ellison's closest intellectual friends, have both written at some length about *Invisible Man* as a "blues novel" and a "literary extension of the blues . . . scored for full orchestra."[19] Ellison himself confronted this attention when he remarked in his introduction to the novel's Thirtieth Anniversary Edition that he began the book when its "ironic, down-home voice . . . as irreverent as a honky-tonk trumpet" and "persuasive with echoes of blues-toned laughter" disrupted another fiction he was composing. He started *Invisible Man* knowing he "would have to improvise upon [his] materials in the manner of a jazz musician putting a musical theme through a wild-star burst of metamorphosis."[20]

That metamorphosis is significant because the novel not only simulates and orchestrates blues tones but takes its transformational shape from the ethic behind the tones. The blues ethic is its grammar. The episodes of *Invisible Man* are disconnected, repetitious, and similar as the stanzas of a blues song, its themes as reiterative as the lines of a blues song. For all his eagerness to discover his authentic self, for all the existential overtones in this search, for all the rhetoric of individuality in the fifties, the formation in *Invisible Man* is not of a unique person but a socialized self. The youth hears his own heart when he acknowledges the specific shape of experience that his people developed living in America. The invisible youth's growth into the invisible man is his recognition of his blues self. What is truly unique about both the narrator and his author is the way both of them learn to manipulate and profit from their positions as members of a community.

The knowledge that *Invisible Man* teaches is the education of a blues song. Both proceed incrementally toward neither didacticism nor overwhelming revelation but toward understanding and engagement. Like the blues, *Invisible Man* offers its audience not the chance to transcend their condition but the capacity to cope with life's unconditional onslaught. Just as a blues song's opening stanza compactly conveys the singer's story and strategy, the first episode of *Invisible Man,* its often anthologized battle royal scene, projects the novel's themes and shape. Subsequent episodes elaborate that message, entertaining us more, emphatically repeating the world's evil. They indicate the same epistemology blues songs always express—the gradual dawning of a sufficient strategy for coping with, rather than evading or overcoming, the world.

By repetition of events in patterns as formulaic as those in blues songs, Ellison shows the invisible youth learning to see both the duplicity and the doubleness in things. Pieces of paper that purport to promote in fact deracinate him. The virgin statue at college is as covered as unveiled. Buttered yams are hot roots as well as Proustian madeleines. And men like Bledsoe, Trueblood, Rinehart, and Brother Jack are all many-faced. The youth comes to see these other aspects of his experience as he rethinks and reimagines it. He deconstructs what he originally experienced as the repetitions make him re-experience what he had naively felt.

But Ellison does not leave it there. Rather, he shows the youth reconstructing a new sense of the world and a new sense of identity. Like a singer gradually regaining control of embarrassing experience stanza by stanza while singing the blues, Ellison has the invisible youth regather and restate his story in the hole, putting it back before us as he felt it, by degrees. *Invisible Man* is a blues novel in structure, therefore, as well as theme. Those are important facts about the novel for itself, for its location in the history of black culture, and for its location in American culture, at the conception of the deliberately speeding epoch. *Invisible Man* is the novel that enacted the process of rebirth after the war, that showed people how to admit their differences from the shibboleths of high modernism. Ellison's blues novel enacted the process of rediscovering vernacular shape. It showed its characters and its readers how to assume responsible action. . . .

The connection between the blues ethic and its sympathetic outsiders passes directly and consciously through Jack Kerouac. When interviewers in 1968 asked [Allen] Ginsberg about William Shakespeare and Christopher Smart as sources for "Howl," he told them, "Lester Young, actually, is what I was thinking about," referring to the great jazz tenor saxophonist who came out of Kansas City with Count Basie and went on to name Billie Holiday "Lady Day," as she named him "The Pres." "'Howl' is all 'Lester Leaps In'" Ginsberg continued to claim. "And I got that," he said, "from Kerouac . . . he made me listen to it."[21] In fact, with the enthusiasm for black music in his novels, Kerouac made a lot of people listen to it. More significant than their enthusiasms, though, were Kerouac's and Ginsberg's reenactments of the blues ethic. Kerouac's improvisation, repetitions, stuttering starts and stops, insistence on coexisting with the world as it is, and love of late-night performance all came directly from the jazz worlds he entered on both coasts and both banks of the Mississippi River.

The first inkling of the blues ethic as it would crop up in *On the Road* and, much later, *Visions of Cody* appeared in 1955 under Kerouac's pseudonym "Jean-Louis," as "Jazz of the Beat Generation": "You can hear Lester blow and he is the greatness of America in a single Negro musician—he is just like the river, the river starts in near Butte, Montana, in frozen snow caps (Three Forks) and meanders on down across states and entire territorial areas of dim bleak land with hawthorn crackling in the sleet. . . . Lester blows all to Kansas City to ecstasy and now Americans from coast to coast go mad, and fall by, and everybody's picking up."[22] From such long sentences derived the long-lined ecstasies of "Howl," some of the impetus for Thomas Pynchon's catalogues in *V.* and *Gravity's Rainbow* and verification for many readers that there remained untapped resources in the energy of jazz. That is why he can end with "everybody's picking up." Indeed, everyone was cuing on the "muddy news from the land" that was the blues ethic.

Kerouac's extended simile links jazz to the tumble of muddy news that the Mississippi bears to New Orleans. His words imitated both that tumble and the syncopated beat of a Lester Young solo. This passage is striking first for its volubility gushing from Kerouac's typewriter as from the river's springs at Three Forks and from Young's horizontal horn. But also important is its precision. Abetting this precise gush is Kerouac's concision. Dropping articles and pronouns emphasizes his alliteration and speeds his logic. These conceits couple with the surprising rhythms to create a density that hinders the horizontal flow of the passage and also its linear time.

NOTES

1. Leslie A. Fiedler, *An End to Innocence: Essays on Culture and Politics* (Boston: Beacon, 1955), p. 209.

2. J. D. Salinger, "The Inverted Forest," *Cosmopolitan,* 123 (December 1947): 73.

3. Paul O'Neill, "The Only Rebellion Around," *Life,* 47 (30 November 1959): 130.

4. Ned Polsky, "The Village Beat Scene: Summer 1960," *Dissent,* 8 (Summer 1961): 339.

5. Dwight Macdonald, "A Caste, a Culture, a Market—I," *New Yorker,* 34 (22 November 1958): 67–68.

6. John Knowles, *A Separate Peace* (New York: Macmillan, 1960), p. 1.

7. Ibid., p. 2.

8. Ibid., p. 95.

9. Ibid., p. 31.

10. Ibid., p. 2.

11. Don Moser, "The Pied Piper of Tuscon: He Cruised in a Golden Car, Looking for the Action," in *"Where Are You Going, Where Have You Been?"* edited by Elaine Showalter (New Brunswick, N.J.: Rutgers University Press, 1994), pp. 51–66.

12. Joyce Carol Oates, "Where Are You Going, Where Have You Been?" in *Where Are You Going, Where Have You Been? Selected Early Stories* (Princeton, N.J.: Ontario Review Press, 1993), pp. 122–123.

13. Marie Mitchell Olesen Urbanski, "Existential Allegory: Joyce Carol Oates's 'Where Are You Going, Where Have You Been?'" in *"Where Are You Going, Where Have You Been?"* pp. 76–77.

14. Jerome Buckley, *Season of Youth: The Bildungsroman from Dickens to Golding* (Cambridge, Mass.: Harvard University Press, 1974), pp. vii, 18.

15. Sylvia Plath, *The Bell Jar* (New York: Harper & Row, 1971), p. 1.

16. Buckley, *Season of Youth,* p. 20.

17. Ibid., p. 282.

18. Patricia Meyer Spacks, *The Adolescent Idea: Myths of Youth and the Adult Imagination* (New York: Basic Books, 1981), p. 120.

19. See Stanley Edgar Hyman, "American Negro Literature and the Folk Tradition," *Partisan Review,* 25 (Spring 1958): 197–222; and Albert Murray, *The Omni-Americans: New Perspectives on Black Experience and American Culture* (New York: Outerbridge & Dienstfrey, 1970), p. 167.

20. Ralph Ellison, introduction to the thirtieth-anniversary edition of *Invisible Man,* in *Collected Essays of Ralph Ellison,* edited by John F. Callahan (New York: Modern Library, 1995), pp. 477–478.

21. Allen Ginsberg, *Composed on the Tongue,* edited by Donald Allen (Bolinas, Cal.: Grey Fox Press, 1980), p. 43.

22. Jack Kerouac (as Jean-Louis), "Jazz of the Beat Generation," *New World Writing,* 7 (1955): 14–15.

ALIENATED YOUTH IN OTHER FORMS OF POPULAR CULTURE

INTRODUCTION

A quick glance at the history of American popular culture since the 1950s reveals that the depiction of youthful alienation is not merely a literary phenomenon. From paperback fiction to movies and music, teenage tastes have reigned supreme in the cultural marketplace. Disturbed by the sudden onslaught of adolescent products in the mid 1950s, Dwight Macdonald complained in *The New Yorker* that "These days, merchants eye teenagers the way stockmen eye cattle."[1] This comment remains an aptly arch recognition of the frenzied competition within the culture industry for the $90 billion spent by young people each year. In the opinion of many critics, the result of this coveting of teen consumers is that American culture has come to reflect juvenile tastes. As youth-oriented styles have come to dominate the national landscape, control over mainstream tastes has passed from adults to adolescents. So complete has been this transformation that many consider *American culture* and *youth culture* interchangeable terms.

In general the representation of youthful alienation in other media parallels its depiction in literature. Like J. D. Salinger's *The Catcher in the Rye* and Jack Kerouac's *On the Road*, these works celebrate the disaffection of youth as a revolt against the stifling conformity of the adult world. Whether exuding Marlon Brando's defiant bravura, James Dean's brooding, or Elvis Presley's hip-shaking sensuality, the teenager in the 1950s came to symbolize the unrepentant individual seeking relief from the placid complacency of modern life. Images of adolescent alienation have changed little since the 1950s. Regardless of medium, young rebels continue to make compelling protagonists because their unwillingness to grow up conveys the plight of a society hesitant about its future.

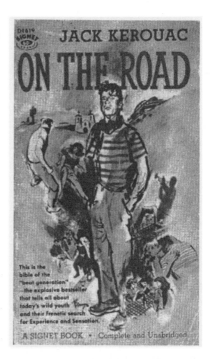

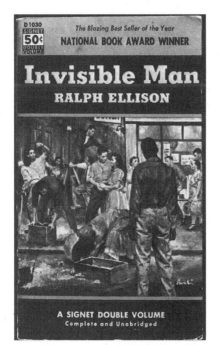

The cover art for alienated-youth fiction tended to be sensational, often to the authors' dismay.

YOUTH CULTURE AND THE PAPERBACK NOVEL

The most relevant popular-culture medium responsible for transforming the alienated adolescent into a cultural hero is the one through which *The Catcher in the Rye* and *On the Road* gained their fame: the paperback novel. As previously noted, the debut novels of Salinger and Kerouac—in addition to those of many other authors—achieved only middling success when initially published in hardback. These works did not achieve perpetual best-seller status until printed in inexpensive paperback editions that were not only more affordable but also more practical for adolescent audiences.

Contemporary readers are apt to think of hardbacks and paperbacks as two stages in the life of a novel. Once printed and bound, a hardback is promoted and reviewed in hopes of achieving sufficient sales for a publishing house to recoup its investment. Should a work achieve a modicum of hardcover success, the paperback version generally appears a year or so later under a publisher's imprint specializing in the softcover trade. (Owing to a trend toward consolidation in the publishing industry that began the 1970s, these paperback imprints are usually subsidiaries of the original publisher.) Although primitive paperbacks appeared in America as early as the 1840s, the form did not become a bona fide industry until the post–World War II era, when new imprints such as Pocket, Penguin, and Avon employed innovative marketing strategies to establish their products' popularity. Before the late 1940s a novel was considered a success if it sold more than twenty thousand copies. Paperbacks, in contrast, made the million-selling blockbuster a commonplace occurrence.

The sudden prominence of the paperback (initially priced at 25¢ and later at 50¢) shocked literary critics, who accorded the medium far less prestige than the hardback. With their clothbound covers and quality paper and print, hardbacks were granted the stature of objets d'art. They were deemed "highbrow" because they appealed to an elite, discriminating readership that valued fiction for its artistry rather than its entertainment value. Paperbacks, meanwhile, constituted a "lowbrow," mass-culture medium. They were accorded a lower status not only because of the lower-quality materials used in their manufacture. Softcover books were also directed at less affluent audiences, who, according to highbrow critics, craved diversion instead of edification. The distribution system for paperbacks further distinguished them from "literary" books. While hardcover novels were the province of refined bookstores that resembled libraries and appealed to an educated, urban readership, paperbacks could be found on magazine stands, in dime

THE JUVENILE-DELINQUENT NOVEL

"*The Amboy Dukes*, like many other novels of its type, plays upon the fantasy of an adult society visiting retribution on the nonconformist young, and it is direct rebellion against adults that provides most of the tension in the novel. The book is notable for its many instances of adult-adolescent interaction, most of which show gang members at first as formidable challenges to authority.... Nevertheless, in every case the authority of youth revolt is undermined by the fact of its systematic defeat. ... Time and time again in *The Amboy Dukes* juvenile delinquents are crushed by adult authority, physical strength, or greater wisdom, all of which reveal generational conflict and show youth subculture tarnished and weakened by adult intervention."

Thomas Newhouse

From *The Beat Generation and the Popular Novel in the United States, 1945–1970* (Jefferson, N.C.: McFarland, 2000), pp. 35–36.

stores and tobacco shops, and even in railway stations. In such venues a softcover text was a cultural commodity to be consumed and tossed aside rapidly. Thus, as paperback profits soared, critics viewed the form as one more worrisome sign that American culture was a mass culture, its quality and taste determined by marketeers' efforts to appeal to the lowest common denominator.

Of course, alienated-youth fiction is only one of the many genres that the paperback industry serviced, along with Westerns, science fiction, and crime and mystery thrillers. Despite this wide range of audience interests, softcover books were associated with youth culture for two reasons. First, as paperback firms scrambled for sensational content that they could package with lurid cover illustrations, they seized upon anxieties in the 1950s over juvenile delinquency. According to the historian Kenneth C. Davis, only Mickey Spillane's Mike Hammer detective novels outrivaled stories of wayward youth in notoriety: "After Spillane, perhaps the most infamous group of paperbacks was the surge of urban gang novels that emerged in the late forties and early fifties. The trend was visible in novels like Irving Shulman's *The Amboy Dukes* (Avon), which sold more than four million copies, Hal Ellson's *Duke* (Popular Library), *Tomboy* (Bantam), and *The Golden Spike* (simultaneous Ballantine hardcover/paperback)."[2]

Initially, Shulman's *The Amboy Dukes* was the best known of these titles, in part because the Select Committee on Current Pornographic Materials in the United States House of Representatives cited it in December 1952 as an example of the "filth and degeneracy" that paperbacks promulgated. The fame of Shulman's novel was soon supplanted by that of Evan Hunter's 1954 novel *The Blackboard Jungle*. As Davis writes, "One of the first books to be passed around by kids who 'indexed' the good pages, *The Blackboard Jungle* was especially well thumbed for two reasons: the scene in which a teacher is assaulted and an early appearance in paperback of the word *fuck* (until that time, it had been deleted, bowdlerized, or printed as 'f–k')."[3] Significantly, Salinger's use of that same profanity raised few eyebrows when *The Catcher in the Rye* was published in hardback. Not until the appearance of the paperback edition aimed at young readers did Holden's cursing lead to decades of debate over whether the novel should be taught in public schools.

Subject matter was not the only reason that critics viewed paperbacks as a reflection of the juvenile tastes of American culture. Softcover publishers marketed books in many genres (not just juvenile-delinquent fiction) to adolescent readers, recognizing that a growing high-school and undergraduate demographic was an ideal market for inexpensive books. The courting of teen audiences increased with the advent of the "trade" or "quality" paperback in the mid 1950s, which was designed to provide softcover editions of literary classics for classroom usage. (Because of its affiliation with education, the trade book was also known as the "egghead paperback.") For many commentators the selling of literature in softcover form was further proof that American culture pandered to young people. Leslie A. Fiedler attributed the popularity of paperbacks to marketeers' pursuit of the teenage dollar:

> We have been living through a revolution in taste, a radical transformation of the widest American audience from one in which women predominate to one in which adolescents make up the majority. Controlling the market (it is, for instance, largely to reach them that the more expensive paperbacks were invented and marketed in new ways by new generations of editors scarcely older than themselves), they control also the mode. And the mode demands, in lieu of the teenage novelists who somehow refuse to appear, Teenage Impersonators, among whom one might list, say, Norman Mailer, Jack Kerouac, even William Burroughs—certainly the Salinger who wrote *The Catcher in the Rye* and invented Holden Caulfield, a figure emulated by the young themselves.[4]

Only somewhat less condescending were critics who dubbed Salinger and Kerouac the "paperback literati," authors of literary fiction who built their reputation through paperback sales to teen audiences.

Attacks such as Fiedler's were rather unfair since novelists often had ambivalent feelings about their association with paperback culture. Salinger's dealings with softcover firms were particularly strained. Even before Little, Brown published the first edition of *The Catcher in the Rye* as a hardback in July 1951, the paperback rights had been purchased by New American Library (NAL), a firm that, despite deriving most of its profits from Spillane's crime novels, had a reputation for reprinting quality literary fiction (NAL also published a paperback edition of Ralph Ellison's *Invisible Man*). The firm's founder, Kurt Enoch, assigned cover-design duties to the illustrator James Avati, a recognized innovator in the field. Thomas L. Bonn describes Avati's technique: "Avati's unadorned realistic style, combined with his controlled shading of browns and grays, gave paperback cover art an honesty and emotional depth that the pulp-style and magazine-style illustrations lacked. His publisher called them 'Rembrandt-like.' Comprehensive in design, they offered a stage to the viewer on which the most dramatic scenes of the book were memorably portrayed."[5] For the cover of *The Catcher in the Rye* Avati painted a scene showing Holden, wearing a red hunting cap purchased on an earlier trip to New York and carrying a suitcase, walking in a Times Square neighborhood populated by prostitutes and pornography theaters. Although tame by paperback standards, the cover nevertheless implied a story of illicit sexual initiation, a suggestion underscored by a prominent blurb: "This unusual book may shock you, will make you laugh, and may break your heart—but you will never forget it." Salinger was outraged by the artwork, but he had no contractual say over the packaging of his book. When NAL's rights to *The Catcher in the Rye* expired several years later, he refused to continue his association with the firm and assigned the rights instead to NAL's chief rival, Bantam.

Despite Salinger's dislike for Avati's cover (the edition is now a collector's item), his frustration with NAL was nothing compared to his dismay when the British publisher Hamish Hamilton sold the paperback rights to *Nine Stories* to Ace Books in 1957. Ace was known for publishing books with titles such as *Jailbait* and *Jailbait Street*. Although Salinger was a best-selling author in the United States, Hamilton had reaped little success in England with either *The Catcher in the Rye* or *Nine Stories*. (He had even insisted on changing the title of *Nine Stories* to *For Esmé—With Love and Squalor, and Other Stories,* hoping to trick readers into thinking that the book was a novel, not a less-profitable short-story collection.) To recoup his investment in Salinger, Hamilton sold the rights to Ace for an edition of the story collection with a cover featuring a seductive blonde and a line of hyperbolic copy: "Explosive and Absorbing—A Painful and Pitiable Gallery of Men, Women, Adolescents, and Children." Salinger biographer Ian Hamilton describes the author's response: "Henceforth Salinger would insist on supervising the production of all his books, and he had special clauses written into contracts giving him the power to prohibit illustrated covers, biographical blurbs (except those written by himself), and quotations from reviews; his vigilance on these matters would extend even to the remotest foreign publication of his work. After their quarrel came to a head, he never spoke to Hamish Hamilton again."[6]

Kerouac's frustrations with paperback publishers had less to do with packaging than editorial and financial disputes. In the early 1950s he attempted to place *On the Road* with Ace after leading hardback publishers rejected it. One Ace editor, Carl Solomon—nephew of the firm's founder, A. A. Wyn—was a close friend of the Beat poet Allen Ginsberg, whom Solomon had met in 1949 when they were both patients in a psychiatric hospital. (Ginsberg's *Howl* was originally titled "Howl for Carl Solomon," and Solomon is mentioned by name throughout the poem.) Ace recognized that Beat Generation literature featured the requisite sex and drug scenes necessary for softcover success. Although desperate to see his book in print, Kerouac was leery of associating himself with the paperback world, fearing critics would never take his writing seriously if *On the Road* was a staple of magazine stands. Throughout 1952 he tried to convince Solomon to publish two versions of *On the Road,* one for the traditional literary marketplace and another for softcover audiences: "I have an idea we could publish ON THE ROAD regular hardcover *and* papercover, extracting 160-page stretch for 25¢ edition (the sexy narrative stretch, I'll designate it when I mail in full manuscript some time soon)." Kerouac even attempted to persuade Solomon that a hardback *On the Road* would boost Ace's credibility as well as his own: "Believe me, Carl, the full ROAD will make Wyn a first-rate reputation. —and t'would be foolish to sacrifice reputation for quick profit; and besides I wouldn't stand for it, *so let's do 2 editions.*"[7]

Although Kerouac knew the unlikelihood of Ace's agreeing to his plan, he was not prepared for Solomon's rejection of an experimental revision of *On the Road* on the grounds that it was incomprehensible. (This work was posthumously published in 1972 as *Visions of Cody,* in which Dean Moriarty is called Cody Pomeray.) In the span of a few months Solomon rejected two more submissions, the original Sal-and-Dean version of *On the Road* and *Maggie Cassidy* (eventually published in 1959), an autobiographical high-school love story. Kerouac was so infuriated that he fired off an angry letter to Solomon assuring him that, as a publisher of disposable books, Ace was undeserving of a writer of his merit: "All you will have succeeded in doing is putting another cookbook on your list to fill the gap I leave. You can spin a thousand neat epigrams to prove that any cookbook is better than the wild visions of Neal Pomeray and the Road. But not when the worms start digesting, brothers and sisters."[8]

Despite Kerouac's fear that paperback publishing was detrimental to the literary esteem he craved, he was not averse to the profits associated with softcover success. As *On the Road* climbed the best-seller lists in late 1957, publishers scrambled for the rights to his many unpublished works. Perhaps recognizing their inferior quality, Kerouac's agent, Sterling Lord, did not submit either *Maggie Cassidy* or *Tristessa* (1960), an account of Kerouac's affair with a Mexico City prostitute, to traditional hardback publishers. Instead Lord sold them to Avon Books, another major paperback firm, for a then-impressive advance of $7,500 each. With hyperbole typical of paperback publishers, Avon's promotional blurbs touted *Maggie Cassidy* as an exposé of adolescent lust: "Maggie Cassidy was no longer a girl. The vibrant, demanding, thrilling, woman body of her splashed over Jack's life like soft spring rain, warming him, coaxing him, pushing him into life. . . ." Similarly, the cover of *Tristessa* featured a nearly nude female figure bordered by a tantalizing plot summary: "A new and hauntingly different novel about a morphine-racked prostitute."[9] For critics who doubted Kerouac's claims to literary eminence, the packaging of these novels seemed further evidence that his books belonged in drugstores and bus stations, not in libraries.

YOUTH CULTURE AND THE "TEENPIC"

Like paperback publishers, the American motion-picture industry in the 1950s began regarding teenagers as a distinct target audience rather than a mere segment of the moviegoing public. Of course, young people were no strangers to Hollywood even before World War II. The clean-cut Andy Hardy, played by elfin actor Mickey Rooney from 1936 to 1946 in a series of Metro-Goldwyn-Mayer productions, was a cinematic version of the "amiable baby" (as one critic of the 1920s labeled the typical teen protagonist in the fiction of that time). The Hardy movies depicted the teenage years as a time of comic mishaps, with the naive Andy finding himself embroiled in misadventures requiring the assistance of his father, Judge Hardy. Other movies featured more troubled youth, including *The Devil is a Sissy* (1936) and *Dead End* (1937); the latter introduced an ensemble of urban juveniles known as the Dead End Kids. The presence of sarcastic, rough-hewn teens in these exposés of working-class life was always balanced by a strong adult role model, thus making it clear to audiences that Hollywood was not condoning hooliganism. (In 1930 the Motion Picture Producers and Distributors of America, popularly known as the Hays Office for its first president, Will Hays, instituted the Motion Picture Production Code, a series of regulations on the depiction of sex and violence ensuring that any production glamorizing delinquency would not have made it to theaters. Code restrictions relaxed in the early 1950s, paving the way for more-realistic depictions of juvenile delinquency.) By the early 1950s the demographic prominence of adolescents encouraged producers to develop projects that catered specifically to teen tastes without deferring to adults' moral authority. The result was dubbed the "teenpic," a genre that celebrated anti-authoritarianism as a coming-of-age rite.

Historians credit a trio of landmark movies of the 1950s with establishing the teenpic as a popular genre. The first, *The Wild One* (1954), was based on a 1947 incident in which a motorcycle gang terrorized the small town of Hollister, California. (It has since been determined that media reports of this event were wildly exaggerated.) The antihero, Johnny, played by Brando, created a new cinematic image of the juvenile delinquent, one far more antisocial than his predecessors. Johnny is contemptuous of pat sociological explanations for adolescent disaffection. In one classic scene a local girl in a diner spies the logo of his gang, the Black Rebels, on his leather jacket: "So what are you rebelling against?" she asks. "Whaddya got?" Johnny answers. The implication is that rebellion needs no explanation: for youth it is a form of recreation. Despite an opening disclaimer ("This is a shocking story. It could never take place in most American towns—but it did in this one. It is a public challenge not to let it happen again"), *The Wild One* never denounces the exhilaration that youth feel when they indulge in socially unacceptable behavior. As Johnny explains, defying convention is youth's lone respite from the dullness of everyday life: "A bunch of us get together after all week and it builds up. The idea is to have a ball. Now, if you're gonna stay cool, you've got to wail. You gotta put something down. You gotta make some jive."[10]

As Martha Bayles suggests, Brando's performance as Johnny owes a debt to the Beat Generation: "Among all the cliches one hears about *The Wild One,* the most accurate is that the main character—Johnny, the softhearted nihilist portrayed by Brando—is the first embodiment, in popular culture, of the beat sensibility. The true model for Johnny is Neal Cassady, the magnetic, bisexual beat who never wrote a page but managed to get written about, to the point of obsession, by all others, from John Clellon Holmes to Kerouac to Ginsberg."[11] (Although *On the Road* was still unpublished when *The Wild One* debuted on screens, the Beat Generation was already a phenomenon thanks to the popularity of Holmes's novel *Go.*) By infusing the juvenile delinquent with the Beat spirit of restlessness, Brando made Johnny a sympathetic misfit rather than an anarchic threat to society. His only real crime is that, unlike the residents of the ironically named Wrightsville (the fictional version of Hollister), where the Black Rebels park their bikes, he cannot abide the drudgery of adulthood.

The Beat spirit is absent from Richard Brooks's movie *Blackboard Jungle* (1955), which may explain why it proved a far more controversial

Marlon Brando created a persona in *The Wild One* (1954) that fused the juvenile delinquent with the restless Beat Generation youth.

representation of alienated adolescence than *The Wild One*. The uproar caused by this cinematic adaptation of Hunter's novel *The Blackboard Jungle* may now seem incomprehensible because of its happy ending, in which teacher Richard Dadier (Glenn Ford) and his unruly class, led by Gregory Miller (Sidney Poitier), unite against the chief delinquent, Artie West (Vic Morrow), to uphold law and order. Despite this upbeat resolution, organizations as diverse as the Communist Party and the Girl Scouts denounced the movie, their response no doubt spurred by reports of sporadic teen riots during its theatrical run. The negative reaction to *Blackboard Jungle* climaxed when the American ambassador to Italy, Claire Booth Luce, forced the distributor, Metro-Goldwyn-Mayer, to remove it from the 1955 Venice Film Festival. Not surprisingly, this move only increased the box-office receipts for the picture. Thomas Doherty suggests why the movie troubled adults: "Throughout *Blackboard Jungle* there is a real sense that the terms of the social contract between young and old have changed. On film at least, the relationship had never been so frightening, ambivalent, or antagonistic. In the end teacher Glenn Ford reasserts adult authority in the classroom only through superior force of arms. Unlike so many of his predecessors in the 1930s and '40s, Morrow's young punk never acknowledges the moral superiority of the social order. He's just beaten down."[12]

Youth's antagonism toward adults is best conveyed in the most notorious scene in *Blackboard Jungle,* in which Artie and his gang destroy a teacher's prized phonograph collection. Mark Thomas McGee and R. J. Robertson describe the melee that occurs when the teacher, an effete math instructor portrayed by Richard Kiley, attempts to entertain his class with the music of his favorite jazz artist, Bix Beiderbecke: "His students don't want to hear Bix Beiderbecke. While the soundtrack throbs to a new sound, rock-and-roll, the kids make quick work of Kiley's music, leaving him alone to search through the pieces of the broken 78s, shattered memories of a once popular culture."[13] The music that accompanies the rampage is actually Beiderbecke's jazz, not rock and roll, and the delinquents identify Frank Sinatra, not Elvis Presley (who had yet to appear on the cultural scene), as their hero. Nevertheless, McGee and Robertson rightly note the symbolism of the shattered records. By smashing their teacher's records, the teenage hoods not only display their disdain for authority but also demonstrate their anarchic intent to reduce mainstream adult culture to rubble.

Only a few months after *Blackboard Jungle* reached theaters, Warner Bros. released the quintessential 1950s teenpic, Nicholas Ray's *Rebel Without a Cause*. In many ways, the depiction of adolescence in this movie parallels that in *The Catcher in the Rye*. Both works depict teenage disaffection as a suburban, middle-class phenomenon rather than a problem exclusive to the urban underclass. Like Holden, Jim Stark (James Dean) finds little in the adult world worthy of respect. His father is a weak, ineffectual figure who prances about in an apron while cooking his shrewish wife's dinner. Mr. Stark's symbolic emasculation typifies the resentful attitude the movie adopts toward parents and adults. From the opening scenes of police hauling a drunken Jim to juvenile hall, *Rebel Without a Cause* places the blame for adolescent alienation on elders who have created a world rife with uncertainty. Jim expresses his anguished confusion when his parents bicker over the causes of his discontent: "You're tearing me apart! You say one thing, he says another, and everyone changes back again!"[14] The other adolescent protagonists, Judy (Natalie Wood) and Plato (Sal Mineo), are likewise bedeviled by familial dysfunction. Judy's blossoming sexuality embarrasses her uptight father, who believes expressing affection to his daughter would be inappropriate. (When Judy kisses his cheek, he slaps her.) Plato, meanwhile, resents his biological father, who has abandoned him to the care of a black caretaker. In case moviegoers missed the point, advertisements for *Rebel Without a Cause* explicitly indicted mothers and fathers for failing their children. As one promotional blurb read, "JIM STARK. A KID IN THE YEAR 1955. WHAT MAKES HIM TICK LIKE A TIME BOMB? MAYBE THE POLICE SHOULD HAVE ARRESTED HIS PARENTS INSTEAD."[15]

Rebel Without a Cause further resembles *The Catcher in the Rye* in that Jim, like Holden, strains to uphold values irrelevant in the modern world. Judy and Plato are drawn to him in part because of his sincerity. Unlike the hoodlums who haze him during his first day at a new high school and draw him into a switchblade fight, Jim never pretends to be tough or nihilistic. When gang leader Buzz Gunderson (Corey Allen) challenges him to a type of drag race called a "chickie run," Jim consents only because his honor has been besmirched. "Why do we do

Richard Dadier (Glenn Ford) confronts delinquent Artie West (Vic Morrow) in *Blackboard Jungle* (1955).

---

this?" he asks Buzz as they prepare to race a pair of stolen automobiles toward a cliff edge to test who will jump first from his car. "Well, you gotta do something now, don't you?" Buzz responds, undaunted by the senselessness of the ritual. When Buzz subsequently goes over the cliff because his leather jacket is caught in the door handle of his car, Jim faces a new crisis of conscience. He wants to confess his participation in the illegal pastime, but his parents discourage him from aiding the police investigation, insisting that he will destroy his future. "Mom, just once I want to do something right!" Jim exclaims in despair. (This adult obliviousness to the pain of growing up ultimately turns tragic when delinquent-fearing police gun down Plato.) At once sensitive and sensual, vulnerable yet strong and persevering, Jim exudes a quality rare in cinematic treatments of alienated youth, whether in the 1950s or the present: complexity of character.

It is impossible to separate the influence of *Rebel Without a Cause* on 1950s youth culture from the cult of celebrity surrounding the star. On 30 September 1955, just weeks before the movie was to arrive in theaters, Dean died in a California car wreck at the premature age of twenty-four. For adolescent audiences the tragic demise of the hitherto little-known actor—*Rebel Without a Cause* was only his second major role—enhanced the aura of edgy fatalism in his moody, anguished screen presence. Striking wounded, solemn poses, Dean conveyed both sensitiv-

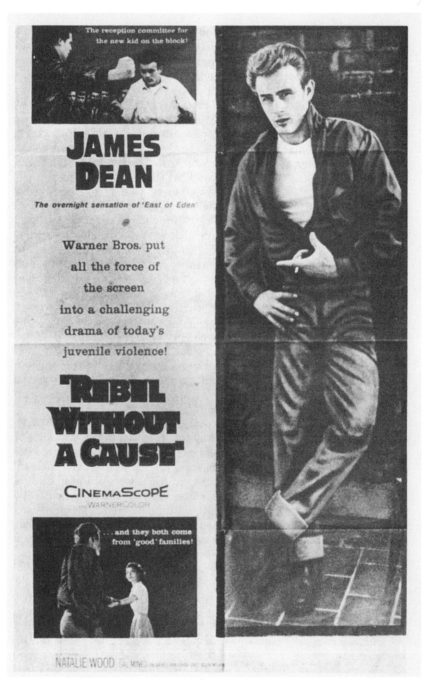

As Jim Stark in *Rebel Without a Cause* (1955), James Dean made youthful alienation cool.

JAMES DEAN: A CELLULOID CATCHER IN THE RYE

"James Dean, who was worshiped by his fans with a religious love that has been accorded to no one since Valentino, based his film appeal on a kind of childishness. In his relationships with both Judy (Natalie Wood) and Plato (Sal Mineo) in *Rebel Without a Cause,* the sexual aspect was strongly underplayed. He was seen not as a lover but a close, childhood friend. In Rebel the three teenagers, Jim, Judy, and Plato, make up a family that, during their brief idyll in the deserted house, provides them with a security and happiness lacking in their real home lives. 'Playing at families' they find the game infinitely preferable to the real thing. Jim, like 'the catcher,' is a big brother and protector. In his mannerisms—the disconnected, hesitating speech, his slouching walk and unexpected, whimsical gestures—he expresses a childish uncertainty and confusion similar to that suggested by Holden through language."

David Leitch

From "The Salinger Myth," *Twentieth Century,* 167 (November 1960): 428-435.

ity and intensity. As one commentator has suggested, "One part of the youth of the world recognized itself as though in a mirror in the face of that young hero. By his death James Dean became the full hero: death had authenticated his *fureur de vivre,* and the adolescent's challenge to life, which is always a challenge to death."[16] No sooner was *Rebel Without a Cause* enjoying brisk box-office business than teenagers began copying Dean's mannerisms and style of dress. For $22.95, they could even purchase a red "windcheater" jacket like the one Jim wears during the chickie run. So influential was Dean in shaping the look of adolescence in the 1950s that one pundit suggested a new name for young people—"dean-agers."

YOUTH CULTURE AND ROCK AND ROLL

Stories of teenagers rioting during the theatrical run of *Blackboard Jungle* were a common if not always substantiated news item in the mid 1950s. According to newspaper reports, the cause of this unrest was neither the script nor the actors' performances but the song that accompanied the title sequence: "Rock Around the Clock," performed by Bill Haley and His Comets. This was the earliest use of rock-and-roll music in a Hollywood movie. A raucous blend of black rhythm and blues and white western swing, the tune moved to a beat far more aggressive than that heard in the mainstream pop music of the time. Although by no means the first rock-and-roll song, "Rock Around the Clock" was the first rock-and-roll hit single, selling three million copies by late 1955. Significantly, most of these records were purchased by white, middle-class adolescents who claimed this new musical form as the exclusive province of youth. Rock and roll offended adults because its roots in African American rhythm and blues allowed it to cross racial boundaries and thus defy the nation's segregationist sensibilities. Equally important, the music encouraged a rebellious attitude. In the context of *Blackboard Jungle*, "Rock Around the Clock" sounded like anti-authoritarianism incarnate, and critics were quick to label the new music the preferred listening choice of juvenile delinquents. Strengthening the association between rock and roll and deviance were scattered outbreaks of adolescent mischief that the media were quick to publicize. In one event that made national news, a disc jockey in Buffalo, New York, exhorted his young audience to honk their car horns if they wanted to hear "Rock Around the Clock." The result was a cacophonous traffic jam that temporarily shut down local roadways.[17]

Although they enjoyed several hit songs after "Rock Around the Clock," Bill Haley and His Comets lacked one ingredient necessary to establish themselves as teenage-rebel icons: they looked nothing like juvenile delinquents. Rock and roll did not produce a performer with the charisma of Brando and Dean until Presley came to national attention in 1956. Bayles describes how Presley surpassed Haley's popularity by tapping into the rebel style: "The long sideburns and the 'DA' [ducktail] haircut, the flashy clothes, the curled lip, the uninhibited body language— these visual cues opened a chasm between the stardom of Haley and the supernovadom of Presley. His image was that of the mythical creature sired by social scientists, gestated among beats, and midwifed by Hollywood: the beat JD [juvenile delinquent]. One TV producer thought Presley fit this description so perfectly that he dubbed him 'a guitar-playing Marlon Brando.'"[18] Presley's look was by no means an accident. As he informed one interviewer during the height of his early fame, "I've made a study of Marlon Brando. I've made a study of poor Jimmy Dean. I've made a study of myself, and I know why girls, at least the young 'uns, go for us. We're sullen, we're broodin', we're something of a menace. I don't understand it exactly, but that's what the girls like in men. You can't be a rebel if you grin."[19]

Presley's rebel allure almost single-handedly established rock and roll as the recording industry's most profitable sector. In 1956 alone the singer sold ten million records, 15 percent of the total music-industry revenues that year. Even more important, Presley transformed the rebellious youth into a mass-marketing phenomenon. No sooner had he topped the charts than "Elvis" merchandise flooded store shelves with a much wider array of goods than even the Dean cult had inspired. In addition to music, fans could purchase shirts, hats, blue jeans, mittens, charm bracelets, and several other accessories bearing Presley's image. Young women adorned themselves in Presley-inspired lipsticks with colors such as "Tutti Frutti Red," while young men sported Elvis cologne and wristwatches. In 1956 Presley's licensing agreements generated $22 million in profits. The successful

By modeling himself after Brando and Dean, Elvis Presley gave rock and roll a rebellious look. Beat Generation writers such as Kerouac claimed Presley as their descendant after his popularity skyrocketed in 1956.

merchandising of the "King of Rock and Roll" ensured that future rebels without a cause were to find themselves in a paradoxical position—condemned as an outrage to adult society on the one hand but courted by a culture industry eager to cash in on adolescent crazes on the other. As the marketplace proved, teenage alienation and rebellion might foretell worrisome social problems, but they were also hot commodities.

Authors such as Salinger and Ellison were too predisposed to dismiss rock and roll to appreciate how it channeled the same frustrations as their alienated-youth fiction did. Only Beat Generation writers understood that Presley was an indirect descendant of their subculture. Kerouac was among the millions of Americans who tuned into Presley's famous September 1956 performance on *The Ed Sullivan Show,* during which censors prevented the singer from being filmed below the waist so as to spare the nation the sight of his gyrating hips. In the essay "Aftermath: The Philosophy of the Beat Generation" (1958) the King of the Beats claims that the King of Rock and Roll owed his rebellious look to the Beat fashion that Kerouac and Cassady originated: "The clothes style of the beat hipsters carried over to the new rock 'n' roll youth via Montgomery Clift (leather jacket), Marlon Brando (T-shirt), and Elvis Presley (long sideburns), and the Beat Generation, though dead, was resurrected and justified."[20] According to Kerouac biographer Gerald Nicosia, the Beats realized that rock and roll and Presley in particular represented an irresistible undermining of 1950s repression: "Although many connoisseurs of the blues didn't cotton to their slick debasement of Elvis's gold records, Jack and his friends applauded the giant crack the singer was making in the wall of fifties' sexual and social hypocrisy. Respectable matrons who lightened their work listening to 'Hound Dog' or 'Blue Suede Shoes' or 'Jailhouse Rock' would find it a little harder to pretend that 'sinners' didn't have fun and feelings too."[21]

THE 1960S AND BEYOND

By the early 1960s the fusion of the Beat hipster and the juvenile delinquent that Brando, Dean, and Presley represented gave way to other rebel youth subcultures. Leather jackets and blue jeans were replaced by longer hair (for boys) and shorter skirts (for girls), fashion statements that undermined middle-class notions of propriety from within rather than by identification across class lines. Despite changing visual styles, Salinger and Kerouac remained defining influences on the baby-boom generation, the legacy of their rebelliousness readily apparent in such trendsetting 1960s figures as Bob Dylan and the Beatles. (According to legend, the Beatles took their name from the Beats, while Dylan—at one point rumored to be starring in movie versions of both *On the Road* and *The Catcher in the Rye*—patterned his lyrics on Beat poetry.) Strains of Holden Caulfield and Sal Paradise still resonate in contemporary popular culture. As one critic recently argues, youth-oriented television programming often employs a Holdenesque voice, replete with rambling sentences punctuated by outbursts of sarcasm.[22] Similarly, Beat-styled narratives of youth seeking relief from conformity by indulging in drugs and sexual experimentation are still prevalent, whether in fiction, movies, or music. The omnipresence of the alienated adolescent suggests that, after decades of obsessing over the coming-of-age process, American culture has hardly begun to exhaust its fascination with the teenager.

NOTES

1. Dwight Macdonald, "A Caste, a Culture, a Market—I," *New Yorker,* 34 (22 November 1958): 70.

2. Kenneth C. Davis, *Two-Bit Culture: The Paperbacking of America* (Boston: Houghton Mifflin, 1984), pp. 185–186.

3. Ibid., p. 186.

4. Leslie A. Fiedler, "Up from Adolescence," *Partisan Review,* 29 (Winter 1962): 127.

5. Thomas L. Bonn, *Under Cover: An Illustrated History of American Mass-market Paperbacks* (New York: Penguin, 1982), p. 102.

6. Ian Hamilton, *In Search of J. D. Salinger* (New York: Random House, 1988), p. 160.

7. Jack Kerouac to Carl Solomon, 7 April 1952, in *Jack Kerouac: Selected Letters, 1940–1956,* edited by Ann Charters (New York: Viking, 1995), pp. 342–343.

8. Kerouac to Solomon, 5 August 1952, in *Jack Kerouac: Selected Letters, 1940–1956,* p. 377.

9. Quoted in *Jack Kerouac: Selected Letters, 1957–1969,* edited by Charters (New York: Viking, 1999), pp. 205, 259.

10. *The Wild One,* Columbia Pictures, 1954.

11. Martha Bayles, *Hole in Our Soul: The Loss of Beauty and Meaning in American Popular Music* (New York: Free Press, 1994), p. 119.

12. Thomas Doherty, *Teenagers and Teenpics: The Juvenilization of American Movies in the 1950s* (Boston: Unwin Hyman, 1988), p. 76.

13. Mark Thomas McGee and R. J. Robertson, *The J.D. Films: Juvenile Delinquency in the Movies* (Jefferson, N.C.: McFarland, 1982), p. 25.

14. *Rebel Without a Cause,* Warner Bros., 1955.

15. Quoted in David M. Considine, "The Cinema of Adolescence," *Journal of Popular Film and Television,* 9 (Fall 1981): 130.

16. Edgar Morin, quoted in John Howlett, *James Dean: A Biography* (London: Plexus, 1997), p. 149.

17. See William Graebner, *Coming of Age in Buffalo: Youth and Authority in the Postwar Era* (Philadelphia: Temple University Press, 1990), p. 5.

18. Bayles, *Hole in Our Soul,* p. 120.

19. Elvis Presley, quoted in Peter Guralnick, *Last Train to Memphis: The Rise of Elvis Presley* (New York: Little, Brown, 1994), pp. 323–324.

20. Kerouac, "Aftermath: The Philosophy of the Beat Generation," in *Good Blonde and Others,* edited by Donald Allen (San Francisco: Grey Fox Press, 1993), pp. 48–49.

21. Gerald Nicosia, *Memory Babe: A Critical Biography of Jack Kerouac* (New York: Grove, 1983), p. 530.

22. See Barbara Bell, "'Holden Caulfield in Doc Martens': *The Catcher in the Rye* and *My So-Called Life,*" *Studies in Popular Culture,* 19 (October 1996): 47–57.

REPRESENTATIVE DEPICTIONS OF YOUTHFUL ALIENATION

I n a study of adolescent culture Jason Cohen and Michael Krugman call attention to a trend in the promotional copy for several novels from the late twentieth century. A prominent book-cover blurb declares Jay McInerney's *Bright Lights, Big City* a "*Catcher in the Rye* for the M.B.A. set." The jacket copy for Bret Easton Ellis's *Less Than Zero* labels that tale of troubled youth "an updated *Catcher in the Rye*." A blurb for Douglas Coupland's *Shampoo Planet* (1992), taken from a *Cosmopolitan* review, features an even odder reference to Holden Caulfield's story: "Having called Coupland's first book [*Generation X*] a *Catcher in the Rye* for our time, I hereby repeat myself." Such comparisons to J. D. Salinger are hardly a recent phenomenon. A 1960 paperback edition of *A Separate Peace* deems John Knowles "the successor to Salinger." William Wharton's *Birdy* is called "*Catcher in the Rye* plus *Wind in the Willows*." Jamaica Kincaid's *Annie John* (1985) is praised as a "Calypso *Catcher in the Rye*." As Cohen and Krugman rightly assert, "Comparisons to Salinger confirm that the story of Holden Caulfield is the yardstick against which all other alienated-youth fiction is measured."[1]

Blurbs that describe a character as a "Southern Holden Caulfield" or new novel as a "*Catcher in the Rye* for the Grunge generation" also suggest the range of settings, subcultures, and generational histories found in alienated-youth fiction. A representative sampling of texts illustrates the variety of these coming-of-age experiences. Whatever their differences, these works share at least one similarity: they glorify youth as the most exciting time of life. At once exhilarating and confounding, adolescence is fraught with the joys of experimentation and the pitfalls of excess, with freedom and confinement. However the protagonists respond to the challenges of growing up, these novels and stories imply that, upon reaching adulthood, these heroes and heroines will never again experience life with such intensity or mystery.

The dust-jacket author photo for Truman Capote's *Other Voices, Other Rooms* (1948) was nearly as notorious as the novel. Striking a pose at once tortured and tantalizing, the twenty-three-year-old Capote conveyed an image of decadent youth.

Algren, Nelson. *A Walk on the Wild Side*. New York: Farrar, Straus & Cudahy, 1956.

A Walk on the Wild Side is a picaresque novel in which the young hero, Dove Linkhorn, lives a vagabond existence on the outskirts of society. Among the many misfortunes Dove suffers is being blinded by a legless man, whose lover Dove has stolen. Dove's handicap turns out to be a blessing, for it garners him compassion for the outcasts with whom he is now identified.

Anonymous. *Go Ask Alice*. New York: Simon & Schuster, 1971.

Rivaled only by Sylvia Plath's *The Bell Jar* and Joanne Greenberg's *I Never Promised You a Rose Garden* in popularity, *Go Ask Alice* remains one of the best-selling youth-oriented paperbacks of the late twentieth century. The appeal of the book stems from its supposed factuality; as an opening editor's note states, "*Go Ask Alice* is based on the actual diary of a fifteen-year-old drug user. It is not a definitive statement on the middle-class, teenage drug world. It does not offer any solutions. It is, however, a highly personal chronicle. As such, we hope it will provide insights into the increasingly complicated world in which we live."[2] These complications include commonplace adolescent crises (parental conflict, weight and appearance anxieties, and peer pressure to become sexually active), which lead to the heroine's addiction to marijuana and LSD. The young woman runs away from home, is forced to trade sexual favors for drugs, and is institutionalized in a sanatorium similar to those in *The Bell Jar* and *I Never Promised You a Rose Garden*. A stark epilogue renders the protagonist's tentative rehabilitation poignant: "The subject of this book died three weeks after her decision not to keep another diary. Her parents came home from a movie and found her dead. Was it an accidental overdose? A premeditated overdose? No one knows, and in some ways that question isn't important. What must be of concern is that she died, and that she was only one of thousands of drug deaths that year."[3]

Baldwin, James. *Go Tell It on the Mountain*. Garden City, N.Y.: Doubleday, 1953.

Not unlike Ralph Ellison's *Invisible Man*, Baldwin's debut novel offers an important portrait of growing up black in America. Yet,

THE AMBIGUOUS ORIGINS OF *GO ASK ALICE*

In "The House that Alice Built" (1979) Alleen Pace Nilsen sets out to determine the degree to which a former drug counselor, Beatrice Sparks, fictionalized the supposedly anonymous diary published as *Go Ask Alice* (1971). Sparks's name was first associated with the book in 1978, when a blurb on the cover of her young-adult book *Voices* described her as "the author who brought you *Go Ask Alice*." According to Nilsen, Sparks based the book on journals given to her by a teenage drug abuser she met after speaking at a youth convention in the late 1960s.

"The question of how much of *Go Ask Alice* was written by the real Alice and how much by Beatrice Sparks can only be conjectured. The two diaries which Alice wrote are locked away at Prentice-Hall, but even with these it would be an impossible question because as Sparks deciphered the notes from pieces of brown paper bags and other scrap paper, she says she thoughtlessly dropped these parts of the diaries into her wastebasket. Also, in seeking a release from Alice's parents, which she knew would be hard to obtain, Sparks asked for the right to use the diaries as the basis to which she would add other incidents and thoughts gleaned from similar case studies. This was Sparks's compromise between her conscience and Alice's request that her parents never see the diaries."

Alleen Pace Nilsen

From "The House that Alice Built: An Interview with the Author Who Brought You *Go Ask Alice*," *School Library Journal*, 26 (October 1979): 111.

whereas *Invisible Man* is a story about politics, *Go Tell It on the Mountain* is steeped in religion. Throughout the book, protagonist John Grimes struggles to balance his spirituality with his awakening sexual desires, including a homosexual attraction to his friend Elisha. John's uncertainties put him at odds with his stepfather, the preacher Gabriel Grimes, whose wrathful denunciations of sin obscure his long history of infidelity. Yearning for an heir who will follow him into the ministry, Gabriel projects his anguish over his son Roy's profligacy onto John. Even when John undergoes a religious vision at the climax of the novel, Gabriel doubts the sincerity of the experience, leaving John to realize that he must resolve his spiritual confusion without the support of his family.

Bellow, Saul. *The Adventures of Augie March.* New York: Viking, 1953.

Bellow's story of a young Jewish man's coming of age from the Depression through World War II is a comic picaresque narrative in the mode of eighteenth-century novels such as the British author Henry Fielding's *Joseph Andrews* (1742) and *Tom Jones* (1749). A born daydreamer, Augie rejects his family's settled ideas of success and adulthood, drifting instead through a series of relationships, odd jobs, and pilgrimages throughout the American Midwest, Mexico, and Europe, all in an effort to avoid leading "a disappointed life."[4] In the end the sole lesson Augie draws from his travels is not to regret the thirst for discovery that drives his vagabond soul: "I am a sort of Columbus of those near-at-hand and believe you can come to them in this immediate *terra incognita* that spreads out in every gaze. I may well flop at this line of endeavor. Columbus too thought he was a flop, probably, when they sent him back in chains. Which didn't prove there was no America."[5] As such passages suggest, Bellow celebrates Augie's restlessness as an embodiment of the national spirit of adventure.

Capote, Truman. *Other Voices, Other Rooms.* New York: Random House, 1948.

The publication of this debut novel catapulted twenty-three year-old Capote to literary celebrity on the strength of the eccentric characters and bizarre plot. The thirteen-year-old protagonist, Joel Knox, leaves New Orleans for a rural Louisiana parish to reacquaint himself with his errant father, Ed Sansom. Upon arrival Joel is introduced to his father's wife, Miss Amy; a local black girl named Zoo; and his "cousin" Randolph. Over the course of the narrative Joel discovers that Randolph has shot and paralyzed Sansom. He also learns another striking secret: Randolph dresses as a woman when he is in his room. Amid the sexual confusion of adolescence, Joel finds himself attracted to Randolph. In the final passage he prepares to join the young man in a homosexual encounter.

Cisneros, Sandra. *The House on Mango Street*. New York: Vintage, 1989.

Often described as a "Chicana *Catcher in the Rye*," *The House on Mango Street* chronicles the adolescent confusion of a young Mexican American girl named Esperanza Cordero. As one of six children in a family dominated by a stern, distant father, Esperanza comes to resent the passivity expected of women in her culture and begins to rebel against the restrictions imposed on girls her age. Perhaps her most rebellious act is to become an artist. Following the example of her friend Minerva, she begins writing to discover her identity. Unlike most male protagonists of novels in the bildungsroman form, Esperanza learns that she need not abandon her family to discover who she is. Indeed, she learns that the community will need her to help guide younger women who can benefit from her experience during their own journeys of self-discovery. As Esperanza's aunt tells her, "When you leave you must remember always to come back . . . for the others. A circle, you understand? You will always be Esperanza. You will always be Mango Street. . . . You can't forget who you are."[6]

Coupland, Douglas. *Generation X*. New York: St. Martin's Press, 1991.

More than any other novel of the Reagan-Bush era, *Generation X* influenced media perceptions of the post–baby-boom generation. As Coupland's characters suggest, youth in the early 1990s suffered from paralyzing uncertainty when making both professional and personal choices. Having weathered parental divorces, post-Vietnam cynicism, and the "yuppie" materialism of the 1980s, the main protagonists—Andy, Claire, and Dag—retreat into a detachment that prevents them from committing to any action associated with adulthood. Lacking both plot and character development, the narrative consists of disturbing vignettes detailing the protagonists' ennui. *Generation X* also garnered attention for Coupland's innovative use of marginalia, in which he offers statistics, generational dictionaries, and illustrations to support his view of this age group.

Fariña, Richard. *Been Down So Long It Looks Like Up to Me*. New York: Random House, 1966.

A cult favorite of the baby-boom generation, Fariña's novel about the campus unrest of the 1960s is notable for the author's satiric view of the various youth subcultures that populated American universities at that time. When Gnossos Pappadopoulis returns to Athené (a fictional version of Cornell University), he is entangled in a conspiracy to control student behavior involving Machiavellian administrators, drug-addled beatniks, dormitory revolutionaries, and a seductive sorority sister with a taste for treachery. Gnossos is an avatar of free love, hallucinogenic wisdom, and anti-authoritarian irreverence. His freewheeling ways pose such a threat to academic order that "the System" must set in motion a far-reaching plot to halt his hedonistic influence, including the ultimate 1960s symbol of adult tyranny, the draft notice. Despite its sometimes juvenile humor, *Been Down So Long It Looks Like Up to Me* coveys the era's surreal, paranoid vision of young people as victims of adult machinations.

Gibbons, Kaye. *Ellen Foster*. Chapel Hill, N.C.: Algonquin, 1987.

Gibbons specializes in Southern coming-of-age novels. *Ellen Foster,* her debut work, is often described as a female *Adventures of Huckleberry Finn*. When her mother dies, nine-year-old Ellen must escape her drunkard father and domineering grandmother. In her effort to find a caring home, she becomes the ward of a local couple, Julia and Roy. Despite her tumultuous childhood, Ellen learns not to feel sorry for herself. Through her friendship with an African American girl named Starletta, she understands that others face even more obstacles. At the conclusion Starletta joins Ellen for a sleepover in Ellen's new foster home: "I came a long way to get here but when you think about it old Starletta came even farther. . . . And all this time I thought I had the hardest road to hoe. That will always amaze me."[7]

Hinton, S. E. *Rumble Fish*. New York: Delacorte, 1975.

The last and darkest novel in Hinton's *Outsiders* trilogy (the first two are *The Outsiders* and *That Was Then, This Is Now*), *Rumble Fish* tells the story of Rusty-James, a would-be gang member whose misfortune (in his eyes) is to come of age at a time when gangs no longer rule his neighborhood. Instead, Rusty-James is left to idolize his older brother, Motorcycle Boy, a former gang leader now also adrift in life. As Rusty-James attempts to establish a sense of identity and direction, he drifts through a series of violent incidents but is saved in each case by his protective older brother. When Motorcycle Boy is shot and killed while breaking into a local pet store, Rusty realizes he must face the future alone.

Hinton. *That Was Then, This is Now*. New York: Viking, 1971.

In the second novel of the *Outsiders* trilogy Hinton explores the end of an adolescent friendship against the backdrop of concerns about drugs and Vietnam during the late 1960s. Two sixteen-year-olds, Bryon and Mark, find their mutual loyalty tested through a series of violent incidents, including the death of one friend and the drug addiction of another. Ultimately, the major theme of the book—change—is reflected in Bryon's realization that he and Mark have little in common as adolescents. When Bryon suspects Mark of pushing drugs, he reports him to the police, thereby ending their relationship.

Holmes, John Clellon. *Go*. New York: Scribners, 1952.

Published five years before Jack Kerouac's *On the Road,* Holmes's *Go* holds the distinction of being the first Beat Generation novel—a fact that Kerouac so resented that he accused Holmes of plagiarism. The book is a roman à clef featuring Gene Pasternak (Kerouac), Hart Kennedy (Neal Cassady), and David Stofsky (Allen Ginsberg). The autobiographical protagonist, Paul Hobbes, is introduced to the Beat scene of the late 1940s. As Hobbes details the endless parties, jazz, and romantic entanglements, he and his wife, Marion, come to realize that they do not share the group's bohemian values, although Marion does succumb to a brief romantic infatuation with Pasternak. To publicize his novel, Holmes wrote an essay, "This is the Beat Generation," that was published in *The New York Times* in November 1952, shortly after *Go* appeared. It became the first widely read Beat manifesto.

Kerouac, Jack. *The Dharma Bums*. New York: Viking, 1958.

Kerouac's second-most-popular novel after *On the Road* tells the story of Ray Smith (Kerouac) and Japhy Ryder (the poet Gary Snyder), two free-spirited Beats who journey across America on a religious quest to reconcile the flesh and spirit. As with all of Kerouac's fiction, *The Dharma Bums* is a roman à clef; the story is based on Kerouac's California adventures in October 1955. In addition to Kerouac and Snyder, the book includes portraits of Ginsberg (as Alvah Goldbook) and Cassady (as Cody Pomeray). The book is best remembered for the opening scenes, which recount the legendary debut reading of Ginsberg's epic poem *Howl* (called *Wail* in the novel) at the Gallery Six in San Francisco. *The Dharma Bums* also represents Kerouac's most in-depth exploration of Zen Buddhism, with Ryder acting as the guru who teaches Smith to cater to his spirit instead of his physical appetites.

Kerouac. *The Subterraneans*. New York: Grove, 1958.

Another Beat novel published following the success of *On the Road,* Kerouac's *The Subterraneans* was written over three nights in October 1953 in the aftermath of the author's affair with Alene Lee, one of the few African American women associated with the Greenwich Village Beat coterie. In the novel Leo Percepied (Kerouac) meets Mardou (Lee), a young black drifter, and immediately becomes infatuated with her, believing she embodies a spirit of noble suffering. Aside from the taboo subject matter of interracial romance, *The Subterraneans* is notable for two characteristics. The writing style is championed as Kerouac's most sustained use of his spontaneous-prose method after *On the Road.* The novel also reveals his early ambivalence toward the Beat subculture to which his name was irrevocably tied. At the conclusion Percepied allows another Beat writer, Yuri Gligoric (based on the poet Gregory Corso), to steal Mardou so he might have an excuse to abandon the lifestyle associated with his bohemian friends. As Percepied declares, he lets Mardou go "so as to get back to more comfortable modes of life, like say, stay at home all week and write and work on the three novels to make a lot of money."[8]

Kincaid, Jamaica. *Annie John*. New York: Farrar, Straus & Giroux, 1985.

Kincaid's autobiographical first novel involves a young Antiguan girl's conflicts with her domineering mother. As Annie John undergoes the normal initiation experiences associated with female adolescence (menstruation, awakening sexuality), her mother attempts to prevent her maturing, fearing the girl will suffer the same humiliations that she has endured. The result is mutual ambivalence: "My mother and I each grew two faces: one for my father and the rest of the world, and one for us when we found ourselves alone with each other."[9] After Annie John recovers from a serious illness, she decides to leave her family and Antigua. Parting from her mother, the girl remains confused by mixed feelings: "We looked at each other for a long time with smiles on our faces, but I know the opposite of that was in my heart. As if responding to some invisible cue, we both said, at the very same moment, 'Well.'"[10]

Kincaid. *Lucy*. New York: Farrar, Straus & Giroux, 1990.

Kincaid's second novel is the story of nineteen-year-old Lucy, an Antiguan who immigrates to America to work as an au pair for an affluent couple, Lewis and Mariah. While taking care of the family's four daughters, Lucy begins to perceive the couple's marital dissatisfaction. In one scene she notes how Lewis and Mariah are incapable of discussing their problems: "I thought, In the history of civilization, they notice everything; even the water glass shattered on the floor—something is said about that—but there is not one word on the misery to be found at a dining room table."[11] The family's slow dissolution teaches Lucy that she would rather pursue a career than become a wife. After Lewis and Mariah separate, Lucy establishes her independence by taking a job as a secretary.

Dust jacket for Jamaica Kincaid's first novel, published in 1985, about an Antiguan girl who has a stormy relationship with her mother

Marshall, Paule. *Brown Girl, Brownstones*. New York: Random House, 1959.

Set among a community of Barbadian immigrants in Depression-era Brooklyn, *Brown Girl, Brownstones* chronicles the Boyce family's struggle for middle-class respect, symbolized by their desire to own their own home. As seen through the eyes of daughter Selina, the narrative focuses on the domestic discord between Deighton and Silla, the girl's parents, as the family becomes acculturated to life in Amer-

HOLDEN CAULFIELD AND ANNIE JOHN

"In Salinger's book [*The Catcher in the Rye*] a well-honed sense of hypocrisy, the 'phoniness' so apparent to Holden, allows adults to hold in safe solution the yearnings and perceptions of the individual spirit and the compromises one must make to pursue success and status. The hypocritical maturity is commended by all—parents, teachers, even young friends—and is there for Holden to embrace if and when he is willing to do so. Holden has the luxury of choosing to reject the adult world. . . .

"In Annie's world, however, as defined by her all-powerful mother, there is no viable maturity. Furthermore, the girl's involuntary onset of maturation is treated by the mother as a crime for which she must be punished. While Holden resists the readily apparent route of successful maturation by flunking out of one school after another, Annie tries to find a way to mature acceptably, hoping to win back her mother's affection by excelling in her studies. Yet, for Annie, unlike Holden, there appears to be no route to successful maturation; indeed, there can be no such thing, for order in her mother's kingdom—and, by reflection, in colonial Antigua—requires more than a willingness to submerge the individual point of view in the societal soup."

Diane Simmons

From *Jamaica Kincaid* (New York: Twayne, 1994), pp. 101-102.

ica. While Silla is adamant that the Boyces will reap the rewards of prosperity, Deighton longs to return to his native land. When he abandons the family to join a religious community, Silla reports him to immigration officials, and his wounded pride drives him to suicide. Realizing that the American pursuit of prosperity has rent her family apart, Selina resolves to return to Barbados to discover her cultural roots.

Mason, Bobbie Ann. *In Country*. New York: Harper & Row, 1986.

Set in Hopewell, Kentucky, during the Reagan era, Mason's first novel explores the struggle of the generation born in the 1960s to emerge from the shadow of that tumultuous decade. The summer after graduating from high school, Sam Hughes investigates her family history, which has been affected by the Vietnam War. Sam's father, Dwayne, died in the conflict shortly before her birth, and her uncle Emmett has never quite been normal since his stint "in country" (American soldiers' term for serving a tour of duty in Vietnam). No one in the family cares to discuss the past, however, leaving Sam feeling isolated in her small hometown. For consolation she immerses herself in the popular culture of the 1960s, becoming an aficionado of the Beatles and other musical groups. Her obsession with Vietnam leads her to camp in the woods to understand what her father experienced as an army grunt under enemy fire. The family finally agrees to discuss their memories of that era, leading them to journey to the Vietnam Veterans Memorial in Washington, D.C., where Sam discovers her father's name etched on the wall.

McCorkle, Jill. *The Cheer Leader.* Chapel Hill, N.C.: Algonquin, 1984.

Southern writer McCorkle's first novel tells the story of Jo Spencer, who was a perfectionist in high school but suffers an identity crisis during her first year of college. For reasons she cannot quite understand, Jo finds her classes uninspiring; although she was one of the most popular girls in her high school, she has trouble making friends. In one Holdenesque moment, a professor attempts to motivate her by quizzing her on interests that might spark her ambition: "'What are you good in?' 'Swimming,' she says and laughs. For some reason this man makes her feel very honest. 'Dogs. I know almost all of the tunes to the old T.V. shows.' 'And out of all that, you can't find a career?' He laughs."[13] In the end Jo learns to appreciate education as an opportunity for personal growth rather than for career training.

McCullers, Carson. *The Heart is a Lonely Hunter.* Boston: Houghton Mifflin, 1940.

Georgia-born McCullers specialized in portraits of Southern grotesques, characters whose emotional and physical disabilities render them as odd and freakish as circus performers. Her debut novel, published when she was twenty-three, explores the fascination of a quartet of characters with a deaf-mute, John Singer, who provides a measure of companionship to these lonely, alienated people. Among the group is thirteen-year-old Mick Kelly, a frustrated musician whose ambitions are hampered by her family's rural poverty. Like the three adults drawn to Singer, Mick believes that he understands her problems, and she spends long hours talking to (as opposed to with) him. While Mick sneaks away for a sexual liaison with a shy neighbor, Singer commits suicide, mourning the loss of his friend and fellow deaf-mute Spiros Antonapoulos, who has died in a mental institution. Singer's self-destruction shocks Mick, forcing her to realize that her friendship with this strange man was a one-sided affair that gave him none of the comfort it gave her.

McCullers. *The Member of the Wedding.* Boston: Houghton Mifflin, 1946.

McCullers's third novel explores the heroine's anguish over awakening sexuality. On the verge of turning thirteen, tomboy Frankie Addams is bewildered by pubescence—or, rather, by how her newfound femininity disturbs her family and community. After years of sleeping (innocently) in her widower father's bed, she is banished to her own room. A drunken sol-

Dust jacket for Carson McCullers's first novel, published in 1940

dier tries to seduce Frankie, forcing her to realize that she has lost her childhood naiveté. Longing to run away, her only hope of escaping her sleepy Georgia home is to join her brother, Jarvis, and his prospective bride, Janice, after their wedding ceremony. At the climactic moment in the novel, Frankie attempts to depart with the couple: "*You are the we of me,* her heart was saying, but she could only say aloud: 'Take me!' And they pleaded and begged with her, but she was already in the car. At the last she clung to the steering wheel until her father and somebody else dragged her from the car, and even then she could only cry in the dust of the empty road: 'Take me! Take me!'"[14] McCullers successfully adapted the novel for the Broadway stage; the play opened in January 1950, with Julie Harris appearing as Frankie. *The Member of the Wedding* was also adapted as a motion picture in 1952. Like the play, the movie, in which Harris reprised her role, was a popular success.

McMurtry, Larry. *Horseman, Pass By.* New York: Simon & Schuster, 1961.

This debut novel by the prolific McMurtry is best remembered as the inspiration for the Academy Award–winning film *Hud* (1963), starring Paul Newman. Set in 1954 among the cattle ranches of Thalia, Texas, the novel explores the growing awareness of the protagonist, Lonnie, that the values of his grandfather Homer are becoming obsolete. Embodying the materialism of the modern era is the brash cattle hand Hud, Homer's stepson, who openly schemes to take over his stepfather's land. When Homer is wounded in a fall from a horse, Hud shoots him dead, leaving Lonnie to wonder whether the stepson's actions were a gesture of mercy or greed.

McMurtry. *The Last Picture Show.* New York: Dial, 1966.

Two local boys in Thalia, Sonny and Duane, stave off boredom by indulging in various sexual escapades. While Sonny begins an affair with the wife of his basketball coach, Duane lusts after Jacy Farrow, the town's flirtatious heartbreaker. When Sonny courts Jacy, a fight ensues between the friends that leaves Sonny half-blind. He and Jacy elope, only to have her parents rescue her before the marriage can be consummated. The two boys renew their friendship, but Sonny realizes that he has lost his innocence—a loss symbolized by the closing of the movie theater in the title of the novel. At the conclusion Duane departs for the Korean War, leaving Sonny stranded in Thalia and uncertain of his future. Just as McMurtry's *Horseman, Pass By* inspired the motion picture *Hud, The Last Picture Show* was made into an award-winning movie in 1971, directed by Peter Bogdanovich.

Oneal, Zibby. *The Language of Goldfish.* New York: Viking, 1980.

Like McCullers's *The Member of the Wedding,* Oneal's *The Language of Goldfish* is about a young girl who resists entering adolescence for fear of losing her childhood innocence. In order to maintain that innocence, Carrie—who attempted suicide a year before the narrative opens—retreats to an island of rocks in her family's backyard goldfish pond, where she and her sister pretend to invent a language with which to speak to the fish. Only through the help of her therapist and art teacher, Mrs. Ramsay, can Carrie overcome her dread of growing up. Paralleling her development is her artistic growth. At first, under Mrs. Ramsey's tutelage, Carrie only sketches shadows, but gradually she is able to draw objects, her blossoming talent indicative of her ability to cope with life's complexities.

Purdy, James. *Malcolm.* New York: Farrar, Straus & Cudahy, 1959.

For a brief period in the early 1960s critics regarded this picaresque novel as a comic alternative to depictions of adolescent disaffection in the manner of *The Catcher in the Rye.* In a farcical series of vignettes, fifteen-year-old Malcolm encounters several eccentric adults, including an astrologer, an undertaker, a midget painter and his Amazonian wife, and a nymphomaniacal chanteuse. All of these characters adopt and educate the young man, but their lessons expose him to various social foibles, including infidelity, alcoholism, and greed. These encounters sap Malcolm's innate innocence, leading to his death from drinking and sex. This loss of innocence underscores Purdy's thematic affinities with Salinger. Despite its overwrought black comedy, *Malcolm,* like *The Catcher in the Rye,* portrays Eisenhower-era America as spiritually and morally bankrupt. Upon Malcolm's death, his adult friends wipe his memory from their minds, his good-natured innocence leaving nary a ripple of redemption or enlightenment in their corrupt world.

Salinger, J. D. "Zooey." In his *Franny and Zooey*. Boston: Little, Brown, 1961.

First published in *The New Yorker* in 1957, "Zooey" is Salinger's sequel to "Franny," his story about a young coed, Franny Glass, whose spiritual anxieties lead to a breakdown in a campus restaurant. In the aftermath of her emotional crisis Franny retreats to the sofa of her family's Manhattan home, where she is tended by her mother, Bessie, and her brother Zachary ("Zooey"). The story has no plot per se but involves instead a series of dialogues between family members over the meaning of spirituality. The Glasses are haunted by the suicide of the oldest son in the family, Seymour (an incident recounted in Salinger's 1948 story "A Perfect Day for Bananafish"). Franny has taken to studying Seymour's favorite prayer book for clues not only to his death but also to her own inability to function in the crass, modern world. In the end, Zooey reveals to Franny his key to survival, which he learned from Seymour. As children, the Glass siblings had been contestants on a radio quiz show. When Zooey complained that they were being exploited, Seymour urged him to perform for an ideal audience whom he dubbed "the Fat Lady": "There isn't anyone *anywhere* that isn't Seymour's Fat Lady. Don't you know that? Don't you know that goddam secret yet? And don't you know—listen to me, now—*don't you know who that Fat Lady really is?* . . . Ah, buddy. Ah, buddy. It's Christ Himself. Christ Himself, buddy."[15] The parable of the Fat Lady comforts Franny because it teaches her that all people—even those who seem most self-absorbed and egotistical—possess the potential for spiritual growth and that she must engage the world rather than withdraw from it.

Shulman, Irving. *The Amboy Dukes*. Garden City, N.Y.: Doubleday, 1947.

An early juvenile-delinquent novel, *The Amboy Dukes* was also one of the first works to demonstrate the popularity of paperback books, selling four million copies by the early 1950s. The plot centers around sixteen-year-old Frank Goldfarb, a Brooklyn Jew trapped in a violent, working-class world. The only outlet for exhilaration in this world is a local gang, the Amboy Dukes, to which Frank is drawn, despite the protests of his girlfriend and the one adult concerned about his future, his coach at the local community center. Frank's involvement with the Dukes leads to the accidental killing of his high-school shop teacher, an event that in turn leads to Frank's own death at the hands of a fellow gang member. Although *The Amboy Dukes* was marketed as an exploitation novel, it advanced an influential sociological critique of gang violence, blaming it on poverty and familial breakdown in urban America.

Tartt, Donna. *The Secret History.* New York: Knopf, 1992.

Recalling Ellis's *Less Than Zero,* this best-selling debut novel revolves around a student murder at Hampden College, a fictional campus based on Tartt's alma mater, Bennington College in Vermont. When nineteen-year-old Richard Papen arrives at the elite New England institution, he meets a group of outcast scholars who re-create the violent, orgiastic bacchanals described in their beloved Greek literature. When the students accidentally kill a farmer during one ritual reenactment, they plot to cover up their crime, even murdering a member of their own clique to elude culpability. Guilt over the deaths results in a lengthy descent into debauchery, including drugs, suicide, and even incest. Although Richard's part in the killings is never uncovered, he confesses at the end of the novel that his conscience continues to punish him.

Updike, John. "A&P." In his *Pigeon Feathers and Other Stories.* New York: Knopf, 1962.

As the title suggests, Updike's most anthologized short story is set in a supermarket in which the nineteen-year-old narrator, Sammy, is a checkout clerk who spends his dreary days ridiculing the "houseslaves in pin curlers" who idle up and down the aisles like "scared pigs in a chute."[16] One summer day, three girls in bikinis wander into the store. Sammy is smitten both by their beauty and their utter lack of self-consciousness, a symbol of their innocence. Other patrons are shocked, however, and the pious store manager lectures the girls on the importance of public decency. Annoyed, Sammy impulsively quits his job. "You'll feel this for the rest of your life," the manager declares, but Sammy cannot stomach the older man's insistence that bikinis offend community tastes. As he rushes outside to catch up with the girls, Sammy acknowledges the futility of his protest, for the young women whose virtue he has defended have disappeared, oblivious of his sacrifice. Alone in the parking lot, he is struck by a sudden awareness of "how hard the world was going to be to me hereafter."[17]

Webb, Charles. *The Graduate.* New York: New American Library, 1963.

Upon graduating from college, Benjamin Braddock returns to his wealthy parents' California residence to ponder his future. His uncertainty is compounded when Mrs. Robinson, the wife of his father's law partner, seduces him. Benjamin finds their lovemaking humiliating, but he is powerless to stop the affair. Although Mrs. Robinson forbids him to date Elaine, her daughter, he falls in love with Elaine and realizes that he must confess the affair with her mother in order to make amends. Mrs. Robinson retaliates by claiming Benjamin raped her. When Elaine discovers the truth, she forgives him, but not before her parents pressure her into an engagement with an unassuming suitor. As the couple prepares to exchange their wedding vows, Benjamin storms the church and rescues Elaine, much to the dismay of her parents. The novel ends with the reunited pair riding a city bus; they are unclear about where the bus is headed, much less about where their own lives will lead them.

NOTES

1. Jason Cohen and Michael Krugman, *Generation Ecch!* (New York: Simon & Schuster, 1994), p. 97.

2. Editor's note to *Go Ask Alice* (New York: Simon & Schuster, 1971).

3. Ibid., p. 185.

4. Saul Bellow, *The Adventures of Augie March* (New York: Viking, 1953), p. 2.

5. Ibid., p. 536.

6. Sandra Cisneros, *The House on Mango Street* (New York: Vintage, 1989), p. 123.

7. Kaye Gibbons, *Ellen Foster* (Chapel Hill, N.C.: Algonquin, 1987), p. 126.

8. Jack Kerouac, *The Subterraneans* (New York: Grove, 1958), p. 81.

9. Jamaica Kincaid, *Annie John* (New York: Farrar, Straus & Giroux, 1985), p. 87.

10. Ibid., p. 147.

11. Kincaid, *Lucy* (New York: Farrar, Straus & Giroux, 1990), p. 75.

12. Norman Mailer, *Why Are We in Vietnam?* (New York: Putnam, 1967), pp. 202–203.

13. Jill McCorkle, *The Cheer Leader* (Chapel Hill, N.C.: Algonquin, 1984), p. 252.

14. Carson McCullers, *The Member of the Wedding* (Boston: Houghton Mifflin, 1946), p. 138.

15. J. D. Salinger, "Zooey," in his *Franny and Zooey* (Boston: Little, Brown, 1961), pp. 201–202.

16. John Updike, "A&P," in his *Pigeon Feathers and Other Stories* (New York: Knopf, 1962), p. 132.

17. Ibid., p. 136.

RESOURCES FOR STUDY OF
ALIENATED-YOUTH FICTION

STUDY QUESTIONS

1. Read J. D. Salinger's *The Catcher in the Rye* and two selections from his *Nine Stories* ("A Perfect Day for Bananafish" and "For Esmé—with Love and Squalor," for instance). What do children symbolize for Salinger? Does he suggest in these works that innocence can be preserved, or does he insist that youth inevitably succumbs to experience?

2. Discuss Salinger's depiction of youthful alienation in *The Catcher in the Rye*. Does the novel condone or lament teenage disaffection? Does Salinger offer any remedy for young people's discontent with the phoniness of modern American culture?

3. Write a new final chapter to *The Catcher in the Rye*. Imagine Holden Caulfield at age twenty-one, five years after the events recounted in the novel. How would he change after his treatment at the California psychiatric clinic in the final episode? Would he take Mr. Antolini's advice and apply himself in school, or would he remain a discontented dropout?

4. Compare and contrast *The Catcher in the Rye* with Sylvia Plath's *The Bell Jar*. In what ways are Holden and Esther Greenwood similar? How are they dissimilar? How does the gender of the two protagonists affect their alienation?

5. Apply the exercise in the third question to *The Bell Jar*. What experiences would Esther undergo during the five years subsequent to the events in the novel? How would her relationship with her mother differ in her mid twenties?

6. Compare and contrast *The Catcher in the Rye* to Jack Kerouac's *On the Road*. How does Holden differ from Sal Paradise? Is Holden similar to Sal's friend Dean Moriarty in any significant way? How may the themes of the novels be compared?

7. What does Dean symbolize for Sal in *On the Road?* In what ways does Dean embody such American archetypes as the cowboy and the hobo? In what ways is Dean depicted as a saint?

8. Analyze the significance of jazz in *On the Road.* How do Dean and Sal imagine the music as embodying their idea of "IT"? Compare and contrast Kerouac's use of jazz to Ralph Ellison's use of jazz and blues in *Invisible Man.* How do African American musical forms have a different meaning for Ellison's black characters than for Kerouac's white outcasts?

9. Compare and contrast *The Catcher in the Rye* with John Knowles's *A Separate Peace.* How are Holden's characteristics reflected in Knowles's portrayal of his two main characters, Gene and Phineas? In what ways do they differ from Holden?

10. Analyze the antiwar theme of *A Separate Peace.* How does Gene's understanding of why he bounced Phineas from the tree branch reflect his attitude toward World War II? Why does Gene come to believe that Phineas is too good-natured to serve as a soldier?

11. Read the excerpt from Ronald Weber's "Narrative Method in *A Separate Peace*" in the fifth chapter. Support Weber's thesis that Gene achieves greater understanding of his dilemmas than does Holden by analyzing specific examples from both *The Catcher in the Rye* and *A Separate Peace.* Do any scenes or episodes in either book counter Weber's argument?

12. Discuss the character Arnold Friend in Joyce Carol Oates's "Where Are You Going, Where Have You Been?" In what ways does Oates depict Friend as manipulating teenagers' desire to rebel? How does the motif of music in the story contribute to this theme?

13. Choose three novels with journey plots (*The Catcher in the Rye, On the Road,* and *Invisible Man,* for example) and apply the definition of the quest narrative cited in the third chapter to each novel. Which works should be classified as quests? In which ones do the characters merely seem to be attempting to escape from their problems?

14. Discuss the form of *Invisible Man* according to the genre definitions of the picaresque tale and the bildungsroman given in the third chapter. What elements of each form does the novel include? How does Ellison's use of these elements distinguish his novel from *The Catcher in the Rye* and *On the Road?*

15. Compare and contrast *The Bell Jar* with Joanne Greenberg's *I Never Promised You a Rose Garden.* How do these rehabilitation narratives

portray teenage life in a sanatorium? In what ways do their depictions of female maladjustment differ?

16. Compare and contrast *The Catcher in the Rye* with Charles Webb's *The Graduate*. In what ways does Holden's discontent parallel that of Benjamin Braddock? Which of Salinger's adults most resembles Mrs. Robinson, the Braddock family friend who seduces Benjamin?

17. Choose two adult villains from different novels (Dr. Gordon in *The Bell Jar* and Dr. Bledsoe in *Invisible Man*, for instance) and contrast them with two positive role models (Dr. Fried in *I Never Promised You a Rose Garden* and Richard Dadier in *The Blackboard Jungle*, for example). Based on the contrasts between such villains and positive role models, discuss what attitudes toward youth an adult should possess to merit an adolescent character's respect.

18. Choose two lost young people from different works (Joan Gilling in *The Bell Jar* and Brinker Hadley in *A Separate Peace*, for instance). How do the dilemmas of these doppelgänger figures double those of the main characters?

19. Compare the function that Dean and Phineas serve for Sal and Gene in *On the Road* and *A Separate Peace*, respectively. How does friendship with these "mad," saintly figures transform the protagonist in each novel?

20. Analyze the ambiguous endings of *The Catcher in the Rye, On the Road*, and *The Bell Jar*. Do the main characters resolve their problems? If so, how? If not, why would the authors end these novels without depicting some definitive character growth?

21. Analyze the epilogue to *Invisible Man*. What accounts for the narrator's insistence that he must return to the outside world after holing himself up for so long in his abandoned basement? How does his growth distinguish him from the main characters of other works of alienated-youth fiction?

22. Compare and contrast William Wharton's *Birdy* with *A Separate Peace*. How does each novel depict war as an initiation experience? In what ways are Birdy and Phineas similar? How do their dilemmas affect their friends Al and Gene?

23. Analyze the flight motif in *The Catcher in the Rye, On the Road*, and *Birdy*. What does the protagonists' desire to "light out for the Territory" (in the words of Mark Twain's Huckleberry Finn) say about the authors' positions on the passage from innocence to experience?

24. Analyze the motif of the fall in *The Catcher in the Rye, A Separate Peace,* and *Invisible Man.* Which of these works argue for the idea of *felix culpa,* the fortunate fault? In other words, how does the fall from innocence benefit each protagonist?

25. Choose two novels (*The Catcher in the Rye* and *I Never Promised You a Rose Garden,* for example) and discuss how each addresses adult readers. How does each novel appeal to elders sensitive to the plight of adolescents?

GLOSSARY OF TERMS

Allegory. An allegory is a narrative in which the characters, plot, and setting evoke a secondary, metaphorical significance in addition to the literal or realistic meaning. Joyce Carol Oates's "Where Are You Going, Where Have You Been?" is often interpreted as allegorical because the principal characters, Connie and Arnold Friend, may be said to represent good and evil, respectively.

Allusion. An allusion is a reference to a literary work, character, or setting used to suggest unexpressed significance that a reader may or may not perceive. An allusion may be explicit, as when Holden Caulfield refers to the protagonist of Charles Dickens's *David Copperfield* in the opening sentence of J. D. Salinger's *The Catcher in the Rye:* "If you really want to hear about it, the first thing you'll probably want to know is where I was born, and what my lousy childhood was like, and how my parents were occupied and all before they had me, and all that David Copperfield kind of crap, but I don't feel like going into it, if you want to know the truth" (3). An allusion may also be implicit or understated.

Ambiguity. Ambiguity refers to meaning that is unclear or unspecific. In everyday conversation, the vagueness that makes language ambiguous can be detrimental to communication. In literature, however, ambiguity may be considered an artistic quality, for it creates a sense of complexity that makes interpretation more challenging than commonplace discourse. The conclusion of both *The Catcher in the Rye* and Sylvia Plath's *The Bell Jar* are ambiguous. Although Holden and Esther Greenwood achieve significant insight into the causes of their alienation, they fail to resolve their problems fully, leaving readers wondering how each will cope with growing up after the novel ends.

Antihero. An antihero is a protagonist who lacks the qualities that inspire readers' admiration. While heroes possess strength, courage, and moral certainty, antiheroes are either deeply flawed, conflicted people or outright villains. Critics in the 1950s deemed Holden an antihero because his sarcasm conveyed disrespect for adult authority. Contemporary critics, however, argue that Holden merits too much sympathy to qualify as a true antihero; a more likely candidate is Clay, the detached narrator of Bret Easton Ellis's *Less Than Zero,* who proves indifferent to his friend Julian's drug addiction.

Archetype. An archetype is a character, theme, image, or event common to a broad array of cultures and social groups. The passage from innocence to experience, for example, can be considered archetypal because ritual initiations into adulthood are found in many societies. In most works of alienated-youth fiction, initiation is portrayed as a fall from purity into imperfection through allusions to the Christian story of Adam and Eve's expulsion from the Garden of Eden.

Beat Generation. A term coined by Jack Kerouac in 1948 to describe the values of a subculture of writers that included Kerouac himself, Allen Ginsberg, William S. Burroughs, John Clellon Holmes, Gregory Corso, and Gary Snyder. Beat Generation works such as Kerouac's *On the Road* are autobiographical in content and experimental in style and form. Beat writing also tends to celebrate jazz, open sexuality, cross-country driving, and Zen Buddhism as modes of ecstasy that liberate the individual self from the conformity of modern American culture.

Bildungsroman. A German term translated as "novel of development" or "novel of formation," *bildungsroman* denotes a narrative genre in which a young protagonist, typically from a rural environment, travels to the city to undergo a variety of initiation experiences that contribute to his or her maturity. Unlike other traditional genres from which alienated-youth fiction borrows, the bildungsroman concludes with the main character's relinquishing youth to assume adult status. German criticism distinguishes several subtypes of the bildungsroman, including the *Erziehungsroman* (the novel of education) and the *Küntslerroman* (the artist novel). Most American critics eschew these secondary distinctions, preferring to speak in general of the bildungsroman.

Culture Industry. A term associated with a group of Marxist critics who made up what is known as the Frankfurt School, *culture industry* describes the post–World War II social condition, in which culture is manufactured and distributed across a national expanse rather than developed in local, regional centers.

Doppelgänger. A German term meaning "double," a doppelgänger is a literary device by which the characteristics of a protagonist are emphasized through the presence of another figure whose dilemmas parallel those of the main character. Joan Gilling is Esther's doppelgänger in *The Bell Jar*, while James Castle is Holden Caulfield's in *The Catcher in the Rye.*

Dramatis Personae. In Latin, "persons of the drama." A term denoting the cast of characters in a play. By extension, it applies to characters in any form of fiction.

Epiphany. Literally, *epiphany* means "manifestation" or "showing forth." In Christian theology it refers to any revelation of God's presence on earth. In a literary context, an epiphany denotes any sudden insight or awareness on the part of a character. In many works of alienated-youth fiction an epiphany marks the climax of the plot; it is the point at which the protagonist gains an unexpected understanding of his or her dilemma.

Felix Culpa. In Latin, "fortunate fault." According to some versions of Christian theology, Adam and Eve's expulsion from the Garden of Eden was beneficial to mankind. In exposing humanity to the burden of sin, the Fall not only blessed people with Christ's grace but invested them with the power of free will.

Genre. *Genre* is a French term used to denote categories of literature. Genres may be organized according to form (the novel or short story) as well as content (alienated-youth fiction). These broad designations can be further divided into subtypes. Thus, one can identify at least three kinds of troubled-teen narratives: the initiation story, the rehabilitation story, and the youth-at-risk narrative.

Image. An image is a mental picture of a scene or event conveyed through words that appeal to readers' senses. The rhetorical tools employed to create an image range from figurative language (such as metaphors and similes) to literal or concrete description.

Initiation Story. An initiation story is a narrative in which the protagonist undergoes a significant experience that irrevocably changes his or her worldview. Critics adopted the idea of initiation from anthropology, where it describes the rituals or rites of passage by which an individual passes from adolescence to adulthood.

Leitmotif. See **Motif.**

Liminality. Another term associated with anthropology, *liminality* refers to the state of being on some kind of threshold. As used in the anthropological studies of Victor Turner, the term describes the state of individuals caught between social categories. Adolescence is a liminal experience, for instance, because it is an intermediary stage between childhood and adulthood. While adolescents enjoy greater freedom and independence than children, they lack the complete autonomy of adults and thus suffer from residual dependency on their elders.

Metaphor. A figure of speech in which a word or phrase connotes the qualities of another object or emotion than the thing or concept that it literally denotes. A metaphor differs from a simile in that the latter makes an explicit comparison between two things, whereas in a metaphor the relationship between the two terms is implied. Thus, "love is a rose" is a metaphor, while "love is like a rose" is a simile.

Motif. A motif is a symbol, image, or incident that recurs throughout a work to help convey the theme. Motifs may be found either within single works or among many different texts. In the first case, their repetition creates a sense of internal coherence; thus, images of falling constitute a motif in *The Catcher in the Rye* because they foreground Salinger's theme of the sad inevitability of losing one's innocence. In the second case, motifs shared by different works enable critics to group these texts into a genre. Two motifs abound in alienated-youth fiction: flight, which dramatizes the attempt to elude initiation; and the fall, which marks the passage from adolescence into adult knowledge. (Critics use the term *leitmotif*, or "guiding motif," interchangeably with *motif*.)

Naturalism. A literary style in which individuals are depicted as powerless over the environmental forces conspiring against them. In naturalistic works, characters generally lack humanistic qualities (soul, imagination) and are portrayed instead as quasi animals struggling against the hostility of nature. Influenced by the Darwinian theory of evolution, literary naturalism first came into vogue in the late nineteenth century through the fiction of the French writer Emile Zola, the English novelist Thomas Hardy, and American authors such as Frank Norris, Stephen Crane, and Upton Sinclair. Although naturalism fell out of favor by the 1920s, many contemporary authors continue to draw inspiration from this short-lived tradition. Oates's 1969 novel *them* is often described as a naturalistic novel, although the author herself has insisted that her intent was to highlight the shortcomings of the style by creating characters with greater psychological complexity than those found in the works of Zola, Norris, and Crane.

The *New Yorker* School. A term used by critics in the 1940s and 1950s to describe the type of fiction associated with the prestigious magazine *The New Yorker*. A typical *New Yorker* story of the period employed an episodic form, flat characterization, and an ironic, surprise ending to convey the disorienting alienation of modern life. Critics often cited Salinger's stories "A Perfect Day for Bananafish" and "Franny" as quintessential *New Yorker* stories. With their urban sensibility and aura of angst, such stories feature protagonists dissatisfied with the spiritual apathy of postwar America but powerless to articulate more-invigorating alternatives.

Picaresque story. A fictional form in which a roguish protagonist sets off on a series of adventures that expose the moral corruption of his or her society. First appearing in sixteenth-century Spain as a satire of the aristocratic society associated with the quest narrative, the picaresque story is episodic in form because its hero generally achieves little growth or insight into society's foibles. Among works of alienated-youth fiction, Kerouac's *On the Road* most clearly manifests the influence of the picaresque story. Many American picaresque novels can be identified as such by their titles: Mark Twain's *Adventures of Huckleberry Finn* and Saul Bellow's *The Adventures of Augie March,* for example.

Postmodernism. A period of literary history dating from the end of World War II to the early 1990s. The dominant tone of postmodern works is absurdity, deemed by many critics the only logical response to the bizarreness of a world ravaged by Nazism, the Cold War, and the threat of nuclear annihilation. Postmodernism is also notable for rejecting the complexity of modernist literature in favor of simpler styles that emphasize the detachment and transitoriness of postwar life. Finally, the mode is known for rejecting the idea that literature is an art form associated with "high culture," insisting instead that it is a popular medium of mass culture akin to jazz and movies.

Postlapsarian. Latin for "after the fall," the term refers to humanity's condition after Adam and Eve's expulsion from the Garden of Eden.

Prelapsarian. The opposite of *postlapsarian, prelapsarian* is Latin for "before the fall," denoting the innocence and purity of humanity before Adam and Eve tasted the forbidden fruit from the tree of knowledge.

Quest. At once a plot type and a motif prevalent throughout the history of Western literature, the quest narrative involves a young protagonist who sets out from home in search of a lost artifact, person, or ideal. Quest stories written before the twentieth century usually involve the pursuit of an item of religious importance that is vital to redeeming the hero's fallen culture (hence, the motif in medieval literature of the quest for the holy grail). In a modern quest, the journey more likely involves personal discovery as the main character attempts to establish his or her identity against the dictates of society.

Roman à clef. Literally, this French phrase means "novel with a key." The term refers to narratives in which fictional characters are modeled on real-life people whom readers are meant to recognize. *On the Road* is a roman à clef because Kerouac based Sal Paradise on himself and other characters on his Beat Generation peers. (For instance, Dean Moriarty is based on Neal Cassady, Carlo Marx on Ginsberg, and Old Bull Lee on Burroughs.) Kerouac's fictional works make up an extended roman à clef, with the members of his literary coterie appearing as different characters from novel to novel.

Romanticism. In literature, a period dating roughly from 1775 to 1848 that emphasized the innate innocence of childhood. For Romantic authors, youth represented the stage of life during which one was most attuned to one's spirituality and to the creative power of the imagination. Romantic writers also celebrated individuality over conformity, emotion over reason, rural life over urban, and creative innovation over strict adherence to traditional literary forms and genres. Among the Romantic authors intrigued with the child as a symbol of innocence were Johann Wolfgang von Goethe (1749–1832), Jean-Jacques Rousseau (1712–

1778), and William Wordsworth (1770–1850).

Symbol. A symbol is an object or action that stands for an idea. Thus, in *The Bell Jar* the restrictions that Esther feels impede her growth are symbolized by the glass container denoted by the title. Similarly, critics often interpret the tree from which Gene and Phineas leap in John Knowles's *A Separate Peace* as a symbol representing the biblical tree of knowledge.

Theme. A theme is the overall point or message of a narrative. In most modern fiction, the theme is implicit; that is, authors decline to declare their purpose overtly, leaving it to readers instead to determine the significance of a work.

Voice. In literary criticism, voice is most often a metaphor for style. Thus, when an author is said to have a recognizable voice, commentators are saying that he or she has developed idiosyncratic rhetorical devices and mannerisms that express a particular attitude or point of view toward the subject matter. Additionally, a fictional work is often celebrated when the characters speak in a distinct style. Thus, for *The Catcher in the Rye* Salinger fashioned what in 1951 was considered a peculiar but realistic mode of expression for Holden, whose slang and sarcasm were intended to convey the teenage point of view.

BIBLIOGRAPHY

PRIMARY SOURCES

Blackboard Jungle. 1955. Metro-Goldwyn-Mayer.

Cormier, Robert. *The Chocolate War.* New York: Pantheon, 1974.

Ellis, Bret Easton. *Less Than Zero.* New York: Simon & Schuster, 1985.

Ellison, Ralph. *The Collected Essays of Ralph Ellison,* edited by John F. Callahan. New York: Modern Library, 1995.

Ellison. *Flying Home and Other Stories,* edited by Callahan. New York: Random House, 1996.

Ellison. *Invisible Man.* New York: Random House, 1952.

Fitzgerald, F. Scott. "The Author's Apology." In *F. Scott Fitzgerald on Authorship,* edited by Matthew J. Bruccoli with Judith S. Baughman. Columbia: University of South Carolina Press, 1996.

Fitzgerald. *The Basil and Josephine Stories,* edited by Jackson R. Bryer and John Kuehl. New York: Scribners, 1973.

Fitzgerald. *The Beautiful and Damned.* New York: Scribners, 1922.

Fitzgerald. *This Side of Paradise.* New York: Scribners, 1920.

Fitzgerald. "Winter Dreams." In *The Short Stories of F. Scott Fitzgerald: A New Collection,* edited by Bruccoli. New York: Scribners, 1989.

Ginsberg, Allen. *Composed on the Tongue,* edited by Donald Allen. Bolinas, Cal.: Grey Fox Press, 1980.

Greenberg, Joanne (as Hannah Green). *I Never Promised You a Rose Garden.* New York: Holt, Rinehart & Winston, 1964.

Hemingway, Ernest. *The Complete Short Stories of Ernest Hemingway.* New York: Scribners, 1987.

Hemingway. *Green Hills of Africa.* New York: Scribners, 1935.

Hemingway. *The Sun Also Rises.* New York: Scribners, 1926.

Hinton, S. E. *The Outsiders.* New York: Viking, 1967.

Hinton. "Teen-agers Are for Real." *New York Times Book Review,* 27 August 1967, pp. 26–29.

Hunter, Evan. *The Blackboard Jungle.* New York: Simon & Schuster, 1954.

Kerouac, Jack. *Good Blonde and Others,* edited by Allen. San Francisco: Grey Fox Press, 1993.

Kerouac. *Jack Kerouac: Selected Letters, 1940–1956,* edited by Ann Charters. New York: Viking, 1995.

Kerouac. *Jack Kerouac: Selected Letters, 1957–1969,* edited by Charters. New York: Viking, 1999.

Kerouac (as Jean-Louis). "Jazz of the Beat Generation." *New World Writing,* 7 (1955): 7–16.

Kerouac. *On the Road.* New York: Viking, 1957.

Knowles, John. *Phineas: Six Stories.* New York: Random House, 1968.

Knowles. *A Separate Peace.* New York: Macmillan, 1960.

Oates, Joyce Carol. *them.* New York: Vanguard, 1969.

Oates. "Where Are You Going, Where Have You Been?" In *Where Are You Going, Where Have You Been? Selected Early Stories.* Princeton, N. J.: Ontario Review Press, 1993.

Plath, Sylvia (as Victoria Lucas). *The Bell Jar.* London: Heinemann, 1963. As Plath. New York: Harper & Row, 1971.

Plath. *Collected Poems of Sylvia Plath,* edited by Ted Hughes. New York: Knopf, 1982.

Plath. *Johnny Panic and the Bible of Dreams and Other Prose Writings.* London & Boston: Faber & Faber, 1977. Republished as *Johnny Panic and the Bible of Dreams: Short Stories, Prose, and Diary Excerpts.* New York: Harper & Row, 1979.

Plath. *Letters Home: Correspondence, 1950–1963,* edited by Aurelia Schober Plath. New York: Harper & Row, 1975.

Plath. *The Unabridged Journals of Sylvia Plath,* edited by Karen V. Kukil. New York: Anchor, 2000.

Rebel Without a Cause. 1955. Warner Bros.

Salinger, J. D. *The Catcher in the Rye.* Boston: Little, Brown, 1951.

Salinger. *Franny and Zooey.* Boston: Little, Brown, 1961.

Salinger. "I'm Crazy." *Collier's,* 116 (22 December 1945): 36, 48, 51.

Salinger. "The Inverted Forest." *Cosmopolitan,* 123 (December 1947): 73–80, 85–86, 88, 90, 92, 95–96, 98, 100, 102, 107, 109.

Salinger. *Nine Stories.* Boston: Little, Brown, 1953.

Salinger. "Slight Rebellion Off Madison." *New Yorker,* 22 (21 December 1946): 82–86.

Twain, Mark. *Adventures of Huckleberry Finn.* New York: Webster, 1885.

Twain. *The Adventures of Tom Sawyer.* Hartford, Conn.: American Publishing, 1876.

Twain. *Mark Twain–Howells Letters: The Correspondence of Samuel L. Clemens and William D. Howells, 1872–1910,* edited by Henry Nash Smith and William M. Gibson. 2 volumes. Cambridge, Mass.: Harvard University Press, 1960.

Twain. "The Story of the Good Little Boy Who Did Not Prosper." In *Collected Tales, Sketches, Speeches, & Essays,* edited by Louis J. Budd. Volume 1. New York: Library of America, 1992.

Wharton, William. *Birdy.* New York: Knopf, 1979.

The Wild One. 1954. Columbia Pictures.

Wordsworth, William. "Ode: Intimations of Immortality." In *Selected Poems,* edited by John O. Hayden. New York: Penguin, 1994.

Zindel, Paul. *The Pigman.* New York: Harper & Row, 1968.

SECONDARY SOURCES

BOOKS

Acland, Charles. *Youth, Murder, Spectacle: The Cultural Politics of "Youth in Crisis."* Boulder, Colo.: Westview Press, 1995.

Alexander, Paul. *Salinger: A Biography.* Los Angeles: Renaissance, 1999.

Bailey, Beth L. *From Front Porch to Back Seat: Courtship in Twentieth-Century America.* Baltimore: Johns Hopkins University Press, 1988.

Bawer, Bruce. *Diminishing Fictions: Essays on the Modern Novel and Its Critics.* St. Paul, Minn.: Gray Wolf Press, 1988.

Bayles, Martha. *Hole in Our Soul: The Loss of Beauty and Meaning in American Popular Music.* New York: Free Press, 1994.

Beidler, Philip D. *Scriptures for a Generation: What We Were Reading in the '60s.* Athens: University of Georgia Press, 1994.

Bonn, Thomas L. *Under Cover: An Illustrated History of American Mass-Market Paperbacks.* New York: Penguin, 1982.

Brooks, Van Wyck. *The Writer in America.* New York: Dutton, 1953.

Buckley, Jerome Hamilton. *Season of Youth: The Bildungsroman from Dickens to Golding.* Cambridge, Mass.: Harvard University Press, 1974.

Carter, Betty. *Best Books for Young Adults: The Selections, the History, the Romance.* Chicago: American Library Association, 1994.

Cart, Michael. *From Romance to Realism: 50 Years of Growth and Change in Young Adult Literature.* New York: HarperCollins, 1996.

Charters, Ann. *A Bibliography of Works by Jack Kerouac, 1939–1975.* Revised edition. New York: Phoenix Book Shop, 1975.

Charters. *Kerouac: A Biography.* San Francisco: Straight Arrow, 1973. Republished, New York: St. Martin's Press, 1994.

Cowley, Malcolm. *Exile's Return: A Narrative of Ideas.* New York: Norton, 1934. Revised and enlarged as *Exile's Return: A Literary Odyssey of the 1920s.* New York: Viking, 1951.

Davis, Kenneth C. *Two-Bit Culture: The Paperbacking of America.* Boston: Houghton Mifflin, 1984.

Doherty, Thomas. *Teenagers and Teenpics: The Juvenilization of American Movies in the 1950s.* Boston: Unwin Hyman, 1988.

Erikson, Erik H. *Childhood and Society.* New York: Norton, 1950. Revised and enlarged, 1963.

Erikson. *Young Man Luther: A Study in Psychoanalysis and History.* New York: Norton, 1962.

Fiedler, Leslie A. *An End to Innocence.* Boston: Beacon, 1955.

Fiedler. *Love and Death in the American Novel.* New York: Stein & Day, 1960. Revised, 1966.

French, Warren. *J. D. Salinger, Revisited.* Boston: Twayne, 1988.

Geismar, Maxwell. *American Moderns: From Rebellion to Conformity.* New York: Hill & Wang, 1958.

Goodman, Paul. *Growing Up Absurd: Problems of Youth in the Organized System.* New York: Random House, 1960.

Graebner, William. *Coming of Age in Buffalo: Youth and Authority in the Postwar Era.* Philadelphia: Temple University Press, 1990.

Guralnick, Peter. *Last Train to Memphis: The Rise of Elvis Presley.* New York: Little, Brown, 1994.

Hall, G. Stanley. *Adolescence; Its Psychology and Its Relations to Physiology, Anthropology, Sociology, Sex, Crime, Religion and Education.* 2 volumes. New York: Appleton, 1904.

Hamilton, Ian. *In Search of J. D. Salinger.* New York: Random House, 1988.

Hassan, Ihab. *Radical Innocence: The Contemporary American Novel.* Princeton: Princeton University Press, 1961.

Hebdige, Dick. *Hiding in the Light: On Images and Things.* New York: Comedia, 1988.

Hoffman, Frederick. *The Twenties: American Writing in the Postwar Decade.* New York: Viking, 1955.

Howlett, John. *James Dean: A Biography.* London: Plexus, 1997.

Hunt, Tim. *Kerouac's Crooked Road: Development of a Fiction.* Hamden, Conn.: Archon, 1981. Revised, Berkeley: University of California Press, 1996.

Johnson, Greg. *Invisible Writer: A Biography of Joyce Carol Oates.* New York: Dutton, 1998.

Jones, Jack. *Let Me Take You Down: Inside the Mind of Mark David Chapman, the Man Who Killed John Lennon.* New York: Villard, 1992.

Kiell, Norman. *The Adolescent through Fiction: A Psychological Approach.* New York: International Universities Press, 1959.

LeSeur, Greta. *Ten is the Age of Darkness: The Black Bildungsroman.* Columbia: University of Missouri Press, 1995.

Lewis, R.W.B. *The American Adam: Innocence, Tragedy, and Tradition in the Nineteenth Century.* Chicago: University of Chicago Press, 1955.

Lhamon, W. T., Jr. *Deliberate Speed: The Origins of a Cultural Style in the American 1950s.* Washington, D.C.: Smithsonian Institution Press, 1990.

Mailloux, Steven. *Rhetorical Power.* Ithaca, N.Y.: Cornell University Press, 1989.

McGee, Mark Thomas, and R. J. Robertson. *The J. D. Films: Juvenile Delinquency in the Movies.* Jefferson, N. C.: McFarland, 1982.

Mumford, Lewis. *The City in History: Its Origins, Its Transformations, and Its Prospects.* New York: Harcourt, Brace & World, 1961.

Murray, Albert. *The Omni-Americans: New Perspectives on Black Experience and American Culture.* New York: Outerbridge & Dienstfrey, 1970.

Nicosia, Gerald. *Memory Babe: A Critical Biography of Jack Kerouac.* New York: Grove, 1983.

Palladino, Grace. *Teenagers: An American History.* New York: BasicBooks, 1996.

Peck, David. *Novels of Initiation: A Guidebook for Teaching Literature to Adolescents.* New York: Teachers College Press, 1989.

Pinsker, Sanford, and Ann Pinsker. *Understanding The Catcher in the Rye: A Student Casebook to Issues, Sources, and Historical Documents.* Westport, Conn.: Greenwood Press, 1999.

Reich, Charles A. *The Greening of America: How the Youth Revolution Is Trying to Make America Livable.* New York: Random House, 1970.

Showalter, Elaine, ed. *"Where Are You Going, Where Have You Been?"* New Brunswick, N.J.: Rutgers University Press, 1994.

Spacks, Patricia Meyer. *The Adolescent Idea: Myths of Youth and the Adult Imagination.* New York: Basic Books, 1981.

Steinle, Pamela Hunt. *In Cold Fear: The Catcher in the Rye Censorship Controversies and Postwar American Character.* Columbus: Ohio State University Press, 2000.

Stout, Janis P. *The Journey Narrative in American Literature: Patterns and Departures.* Westport, Conn.: Greenwood Press, 1983.

Turner, Victor. *Dramas, Fields, and Metaphors: Symbolic Action in Human Society.* Ithaca, N.Y.: Cornell University Press, 1974.

Wagner-Martin, Linda. *Sylvia Plath: A Biography.* New York: St. Martin's Press, 1987.

Wallach, Glenn. *Obedient Sons: The Discourse of Youth and Generations in American Culture, 1630–1860.* Amherst: University of Massachusetts Press, 1997.

Westervelt, Linda A. *Beyond Innocence; or, The Altersroman in Modern Fiction.* Columbia: University of Missouri Press, 1997.

Witham, W. Tasker. *The Adolescent in the American Novel, 1920–1960.* New York: Ungar, 1964.

ESSAYS

Baumbach, Jonathan. "The Young Man as Saint: A Reappraisal of *The Catcher in the Rye*." *Modern Language Quarterly,* 25 (December 1964): 461–472.

Bell, Barbara. "'Holden Caulfield in Doc Martens': *The Catcher in the Rye* and *My So-Called Life*." *Studies in Popular Culture,* 19 (October 1996): 47–57.

Considine, David M. "The Cinema of Adolescence." *Journal of Popular Film and Television,* 9 (1981): 123–136.

Dillistone, Frederick W. "The Fall: Christian Truth and Literary Symbol." In *Comparative Literature: Matter and Method,* edited by A. Owen Aldridge. Urbana: University of Illinois Press, 1969.

Epstein, Joseph. "Grow Up, Why Dontcha?" In his *Narcissus Leaves the Pool: Familiar Essays.* Boston: Houghton Mifflin, 1999.

Erikson, Erik H. "Youth: Fidelity and Diversity." In *The Challenge of Youth,* edited by Erikson. Garden City, N.Y.: Doubleday, 1965.

Fiedler, Leslie A. "Boys Will Be Boys!" *New Leader,* 41 (28 April 1958): 23–26.

Fiedler. "From Redemption to Initiation." *New Leader,* 41 (26 May 1958): 20–23.

Fiedler. "The Profanation of the Child." *New Leader,* 41 (23 June 1958): 26–29.

Fiedler. "Up from Adolescence." *Partisan Review,* 29 (Winter 1962): 127–131.

Friedberg, Barton C. "The Cult of Adolescence in American Fiction." *Nassau Review,* 1 (Spring 1964): 26–35.

Friedman, Ellen G. "Joyce Carol Oates." In *Modern American Women Writers.* New York: Scribners, 1991.

Frum, David. "It's Not the Parents Who Are the Aggressors Against Freedom: Teachers Shouldn't Be Allowed to Abuse the Ideals of Literature and Learning." *Toronto Financial Post,* 15 February 1997, p. 28.

Grenz, Dagmar. "Literature for Young People and the Novel of Adolescence." In *Aspects and Issues in the History of Children's Literature,* edited by Maria Nikolajeva. Westport, Conn.: Greenwood Press, 1995.

Hill, Hamlin. "The Composition and Structure of *Tom Sawyer.*" *American Literature,* 32 (January 1961): 379–392.

Howe, Irving. "More Reflections on the Glass Menagerie." *New York Times Book Review,* 7 April 1963, pp. 4–5, 34.

Howells, William Dean. "My Mark Twain." In *A Selected Edition of W. D. Howells,* volume 32: *Literary Friends and Acquaintance: A Personal Retrospective of American Authorship,* edited by David F. Hiatt and Edwin H. Cady. Bloomington: Indiana University Press, 1968.

Hyman, Stanley Edgar. "American Negro Literature and the Folk Tradition." *Partisan Review,* 25 (Spring 1958): 197–222.

Jameson, Fredric. "Postmodernism and Consumer Society," in *The Anti-Aesthetic,* edited by Hal Foster. Port Townsend, Wash.: Bay Press, 1983.

Marcus, Mordecai. "What is an Initiation Story?" *Journal of Aesthetics and Art Criticism,* 19 (Winter 1960): 221–228.

Macdonald, Dwight. "A Caste, a Culture, a Market—I." *New Yorker,* 34 (22 November 1958): 57–102.

McMillan, Priscilla Johnson. "An Assassin's Portrait." *New Republic,* 185 (12 July 1982): 16–18.

Mertz, Maia Pank, and David A. England. "The Legitimacy of American Adolescent Fiction." *School Library Journal,* 30 (October 1983): 119–123.

Ohmann, Richard. "The Shaping of a Canon, 1960–1975." *Critical Inquiry* 10 (September 1983): 199–223.

O'Neill, Paul. "The Only Rebellion Around." *Life,* 47 (30 November 1959): 127–137.

Podhoretz, Norman. "The Know-Nothing Bohemians." *Partisan Review,* 25 (Spring 1958): 305–318.

Polsky, Ned. "The Village Beat Scene: Summer 1960." *Dissent,* 8 (Summer 1961): 339.

Quirk, Tom. "A Source for 'Where Are You Going, Where Have You Been?'" *Studies in Short Fiction,* 18 (Fall 1981): 413–420.

Rascoe, Burton. "A Youth in the Saddle," In *F. Scott Fitzgerald: The Critical Reception,* edited by Jackson R. Bryer. New York: Franklin, 1978.

Roosevelt, Eleanor. "Restlessness of Youth: An Asset of Free Societies." *Department of State Bulletin* (21 January 1952): 94–96.

Scott, James F. "Beat Literature and the American Teen Cult." *American Quarterly,* 14 (Summer 1962): 150–160.

Seelye, John. "Holden in the Museum." In *New Essays on J. D. Salinger's The Catcher in the Rye,* edited by Jack Salzman. Cambridge: Cambridge University Press, 1991.

Wagner-Martin, Linda. "Plath's *The Bell Jar* as Female *Bildungsroman*." *Women's Studies* 12 (February 1986): 55–68.

Weber, Ronald. "Narrative Method in *A Separate Peace*." *Studies in Short Fiction,* 3 (Fall 1965): 63–72.

FOR FURTHER READING

Alsen, Eberhard. *Salinger's Glass Stories as a Composite Novel.* Troy, N.Y.: Whitston, 1983. A thorough overview of the themes of innocence versus experience and spiritual questing in Salinger's works after *The Catcher in the Rye.*

Bloom, Harold, ed. *Holden Caulfield.* New York: Chelsea House, 1990. Essays analyzing various aspects of Holden's character.

Bryant, Hallman Bell. *A Separate Peace: The War Within.* Boston: Twayne, 1990. An informative introduction to Knowles's *A Separate Peace,* with special emphasis on the theme of the fortunate fall.

DeMarr, Mary Jean, and Jane S. Bakerman. *The Adolescent in the American Novel Since 1960.* New York: Ungar, 1986. A comprehensive update of W. Tasker Witham's *The Adolescent in the American Novel, 1920–1960.*

Engel, Steven, ed. *Readings on The Catcher in the Rye.* San Diego: Greenhaven Press, 1998. Includes essays on various themes and issues in the novel.

Gregory, Thomas West. *Juvenile Delinquency in Literature.* New York: Longman, 1980. Examines representations of adolescent rebellion from the nineteenth to the twentieth century.

Hipkiss, Robert A. *Jack Kerouac, Prophet of the New Romanticism: A Critical Study of the Published Works of Kerouac and a Comparison of Them to Those of J. D. Salinger, James Purdy, John Knowles, and Ken Kesey.* Lawrence: Regents Press of Kansas, 1976.

Karson, Jill, ed. *Readings on A Separate Peace.* San Diego: Greenhaven Press, 1999. Selected criticism on Knowles's novel.

Macpherson, Pat. *Reflecting on The Bell Jar.* New York: Routledge, 1991. An important study of themes and symbols in *The Bell Jar.*

Marsden, Malcom M., ed. *If You Really Want to Know: A Catcher Casebook.* Chicago: Scott, Foresman, 1963. A collection of the most influential essays on Salinger written before 1963.

Medovoi, Leerom. "Democracy, Capitalism, and American Literature: The Cold War Construction of J. D. Salinger's Paperback Hero." In *The Other Fifties: Interrogating Midcentury American Icons*, edited by Joel Foreman. Urbana: University of Illinois Press, 1997. A discussion of Salinger's reputation as a paperback hero to youth in the 1950s.

Newhouse, Thomas. *The Beat Generation and the Popular Novel in the United States, 1945–1970*. Jefferson, N.C.: McFarland, 2000. Explores the connections between Beat Generation fiction and popular paperbacks of the postwar era, with an important analysis of the juvenile-delinquent novel.

Rollin, Lucy. *Twentieth-Century Teen Culture by the Decades: A Reference Guide*. Westport, Conn.: Greenwood Press, 1999. An excellent overview of youth subcultures from the 1920s to the 1990s.

Rose, Jacqueline. *The Haunting of Sylvia Plath*. London: Virago, 1991. A psychoanalytical study of Plath, including an analysis of *The Bell Jar.*

Salzman, Jack, ed. *New Essays on The Catcher in the Rye*. Cambridge: Cambridge University Press, 1991. Important essays on Salinger's cultural influence, with particular emphasis on the ways in which the novel reflects postwar American culture.

Swartz, Omar. *The View from On the Road: The Rhetorical Vision of Jack Kerouac.* Carbondale: University of Southern Illinois Press, 1999. Examines how Kerouac's theory of spontaneous prose affected his writing style, with special emphasis on the influence of jazz.

Trites, Roberta Seelinger. *Disturbing the Universe: Power and Repression in Adolescent Literature*. Iowa City: University of Iowa Press, 2000. A complex study of authority issues in young-adult fiction.

Wagner-Martin, Linda. *The Bell Jar: A Novel of the Fifties*. Boston: Twayne, 1992. An introduction to Plath's novel, with emphasis on its affinities with the bildungsroman tradition.

Watson, Steven. *Birth of the Beat Generation: Visionaries, Rebels, and Hipsters, 1944–1960*. New York: Pantheon, 1995. An illustrated history of the Beat movement, with a detailed chronology and several previously unpublished photographs.

White, Barbara A. *Growing Up Female: Adolescent Girlhood in American Fiction*. Westport, Conn.: Greenwood Press, 1985. Examines the representation of female initiation in twentieth-century novels.

Whitfield, Stephen. "Cherished and Cursed: Towards a Social History of *The Catcher in the Rye*." *New England Quarterly*, 70, no. 4 (1997): 567–700. An examination of the role of *The Catcher in the Rye* in American popular culture, with particular emphasis on censorship cases involving the novel.

INDEX